新・阪大英文学会叢書2

英語学の深まり・英語学からの広がり

南 佑亮　本田 隆裕　田中 英理　編著

英宝社

はしがき

　阪大英文学会叢書は 2004 年から 2008 年までの第 1 期に 1 巻から 5 巻、2011 年から 2015 年までの第 2 期に 6 巻から 8 巻を刊行し、一度区切りがつけられていましたが、この度、阪大英文学会から援助を受け、若手を中心とした論文集である「新」阪大英文学会叢書を 2 巻刊行する運びとなりました。その第 2 巻の本書は、英語学編であり、大阪大学英語学研究室（通称「阪大英語学研究室」）の出身者による 19 本の論文が掲載されています。

　阪大英語学研究室の大きな特徴は、研究分野・理論的立場の多様性にあります。生成文法理論、形式意味論、認知・機能主義言語学、関連性理論など様々な理論的スタンスで研究を進める大学院生たちが同じ教室で授業を受け、同じ研究室を利用し、ときに勉強会（読書会）も開きながら互いに切磋琢磨する、という稀有な環境があります。ですからこの研究室の出身者が例外なく「自分の研究は言語研究全体の中でどのような位置にあるのか」という視点を持ちながら研究を進める能力を身につけていることは決して偶然ではありません。阪大英語学研究室の出身者に関して、さらに特筆すべきなのは、英語の研究を継続し、さらに深めていく人も数多くいる一方で、英語の研究で得た知見とスキルを他言語の分析にまで幅広く応用していく人々も同じくらいいる、という事実です。

　本書には、阪大英語学研究室のこのような 2 つの特徴が凝縮されています。『英語学の深まり・英語学からの広がり』という本書のタイトルどおりの二部構成となっていますが、以下のように、どちらも理論的立場・研究手法の面で実に多様なものから構成されています。

　第 I 部「英語学の深まり」は、英語を研究対象とする 9 編の論文から成ります。前川貴文氏の論文は、英語の an hour's delay のような単数名詞の度量属格における冠詞の特異な振る舞いについて HPSG による名詞句の

分析が有効であることを論じています。田中英理の論文は、英語の by を
ともなった度量表現の分布を観察し、尺度論から説明を与えようとしてい
ます。山口麻衣子氏の論文は統語論の研究であり、英語における叙実の島
（factive island）の特性に関して、主要部移動による分析を提案していま
す。

　次の 2 編は関連性理論（Relevance Theory）の論文です。岩橋一樹氏の
論文は、英語の具体名詞が複合語において修飾語として用いられた際に生
じるメタファー的意味の理解過程についての考察です。黒川尚彦氏の論文
は、the other way (a)round という副詞句が明示的に伝達する 2 種類の意味
内容が生じる解釈プロセスについて明らかにしています。

　続く 4 編は、認知・機能主義的な立場からの研究です。水谷謙太氏の
論文は、形容詞の後置修飾を可能にする条件に関する先行研究の分析の問
題を指摘し、直示的視点システムを援用した代案を提示しています。南佑
亮の論文は、前置詞句を伴う have 構文のうち、抽象的な属性を表す名詞
を目的語にとるタイプのもの（例：His voice had an edge to it.）の特徴を
明らかにし、その分析方法について議論しています。米倉よう子氏の論文
では、二重目的語構文の 2 種類の受動態のうち Recipient 項に主格を与え
るタイプの受動態の発達について初期近代英語期の分布を調査し新たな事
実が実証されています。岡田禎之氏の論文は、特定のレジスターにおいて
因果関係を表す副詞句 because of N/NP の of が脱落し N/NP の範疇が拡大
している現象に着目し、その発生原因について、他の類似表現の調査も踏
まえながら考察しています。

　第 II 部「英語学からの広がり」は、英語学の関連領域、および英語以
外の言語に研究対象を広げた研究に関わる以下の 10 編の論文が含まれま
す。

　吉本圭佑氏の論文は、英語話者コーパスで散見される非標準的な用法の
like について、日本人学習者コーパスにおける使用頻度を調査することで、
口語表現の中間言語分析を試みています。

　次の 4 編は形式意味論の立場による研究論文です。平山裕人氏は、英
語・日本語の証拠性表現（evidentials）を取り上げ、それらが否定や認識
的法副詞よりも必ず広いスコープをとるという現象について、証拠性表現

が証拠命題に課す制約から説明しようとしています。嶋村貢志氏は、日本語のスクランブリングを扱っています。格助詞の意味論を新ディヴィドソン流の事象意味論で記述し、そのスクランブリング現象への帰結を検討しています。田中秀治氏の論文は、格をもつ名詞句に加えて生じる日本語の「も」を修飾語として扱う分析に反論する論考です。西口純代氏の論文は、英語、日本語、タガログ語における dog after dog のような畳語（reduplication）について、英語やタガログ語では全称量化であるのに対して、日本語は英語などの不定名詞に対応すると分析しています。

　続く 4 編は統語論の研究論文です。山口真史氏は、英語には存在するが日本語では観察されないタイプの結果構文を分析し、日英語の結果構文が異なる構造から派生されている可能性を指摘しています。今西祐介氏の論文では、琉球諸語の一つである喜界語（喜界島方言）のデータに基づき、名詞句の省略現象と属格標識との関係を議論しています。本田隆裕の論文は、日本語の格助詞と英語の前置詞がどちらも音形を持たない空要素と共起不可能な点に着目することで、日本語格助詞と英語前置詞の共通性を探っています。

　最後の 2 編は、認知・機能主義的な立場からの研究成果です。森英樹氏の論文は、日本語に見られる過去命令文という現象が英語では実現しない理由について、視点移動という観点からの説明を試みたものです。町田章氏は、間主観性の類型（対峙型・同化型）を提案し、これにより、話し手主語のゼロ化の可否、冠詞の有無、ゼロ代名詞の有無、という日英語の差異が顕在化する 3 つの現象が統一的に説明されることを論じています。

　以上 19 本の論文は著者それぞれの理論的立場からの最新の研究成果ですから、いかなるタイプの読者の方にとっても、何かしらの関心を引き、また考察・研究のヒントになることが見つけられる一冊になっているのではないかと期待しております。

　昨今は、「多様性」を尊重することの重要性が様々な局面で話題になりますが、もしかすると言語の研究についても同じことがあてはまるのかもしれません。研究の方法論や研究対象の画定に関しては、伝統を確実に踏襲しながらも、常に新しい可能性を探る視点を持つことがこれからますます重要になってくると思われます。新しい発見や創造は、往々にして、同

じところをじっと見続けているときよりもむしろまったく別のところを見ているときに起こりがちなものであることは、科学研究の歴史に刻まれている数々の有名なエピソードが教えてくれています。もし本書が、同じ学術的コミュニティの中に―場合によっては一人の研究者の中にさえ―多様な理論的志向・関心が同居していることの重要性をあらためて認識していただく一助となれば、これに勝る喜びはありません。

　令和2年2月

南　佑亮

本田隆裕

田中英理

目　次

II 英語学からの広がり

英語学の深まり・英語学からの広がり

I　英語学の深まり

度量属格を通して見る英語名詞句の統語構造 *

前川 貴史

キーワード：度量属格，単数形可算名詞，限定詞，Head-Driven Phrase
Structure Grammar (HPSG)

1. はじめに

　本論は、英語の単数形可算名詞と「度量属格 (Genitive of Measure,
Measure Genitive)」と呼ばれる構造との関係を観察することを通じて、英
語名詞句の統語構造のあるべき姿について論じる。

　まず、Carter and McCarthy (2006: 336) からの例文 (1) における単数形
可算名詞の振る舞いを見てみよう。

(1)　Would you pass *(the) teapot please?

(1) の単数形可算名詞 teapot のように、英語では通常、単数形可算名詞は
限定詞がないと文中に生起できない。[1] これを (2) のように一般化してみ
よう。

(2)　英語の単数形可算名詞は限定詞が義務的である。

　度量属格は、属格（所有格）の数多い用法のうちのひとつで、(3) のイ
タリック体部分が典型的な例である。

(3)　a. *an hour's* discussion, *a minute's* hesitation, *two hours'* sleep
　　　b. *arm's* length, *a stone's* throw
　　　c. *fifty pounds'* worth, *two dollars'* worth　　　(Biber et al. (1999: 296))

(3a) は「期間」、(3b) は「距離」や「長さ」、(3c) は「価値」を表す度量属

格である。

　単数形可算名詞が度量属格として用いられるとき、あるいは度量属格と同じ名詞句の中に現れるとき、その単数形可算名詞が一般化 (2) に従わない例が存在する。本論では、Head-Driven Phrase Structure Grammar（以下 HPSG; Pollard and Sag (1994)）の枠組みにおいては、これらのデータについて一般性を損なうことのない説明が可能であることを示す。

2. 度量属格の性質

　本節では、先行研究に基づいて度量属格の意味的・統語的性質を観察する。[2,3] 属格の最も典型的な用法である Paul's dog 等のような所有の属格と対比しながら論を進める。

　まず、所有の属格は意味的に定性 (definiteness) をもつことが、(4a) を (4b) へと書き換えることで明らかとなる (Huddleston and Pullum (2002:470))。

(4)　a. a friend's dog　　　　　b. the dog of a friend

(4b) のように限定詞 the が付いた表現に書き換え可能であるという事実は、(4a) の a friend's には the のような定性があるということを示している。

　一方、度量属格をもつ (5a) を同じように書き換えると (5b) のように the のない表現となる (Huddleston and Pullum (2002:470))。限定詞 the を持つ (5c) とは同じ意味にはならない (Willemse (2007: 551))。

(5)　a. an hour's delay　　　　c. the delay of an hour
　　　b. delay of an hour

このように、度量属格は所有属格のような定性を持たないと言える。

　次に、所有の属格は限定詞とは共起しない。

(6)　(*a/*the) *Paul's* dog

所有の属格が限定詞とは共起できないのは、所有の属格自体が限定詞の役割を果たしているからである。現代英語においては名詞句中に 2 つ以上の限定詞が現れてはならない。

(7)　a. *this the dog　　　　　b. *the this dog

それに対して、度量属格は (8) のように限定詞と共起できる。

(8)　a *ten days'* absence　　　　　　　(Quirk et al. (1985: 1333))

限定詞と共起できるということは、度量属格は限定詞ではない。
　それでは、度量属格は名詞句中でどのような機能を持つのであろうか。(8) を見ると、度量属格 ten day's は限定詞 a の後にある。これは (9) の long のように、修飾語が典型的に表れる位置である。

(9)　a *long* absence　　　　　　　　　(BNC[4]: ADM 1530)

また、度量属格は左側に修飾語を置くことができる。

(10)　a. a <u>second</u> *one hour's* delay　　(Huddleston and Pullum (2002: 470))
　　　b. a <u>second</u> *five-year* term　　　　　　　(BNC: HL0 424)

(10a) では、one hour's という度量属格の左側に second という修飾語が置かれている。これは (10b) の five-year のような通常の修飾語の左側に修飾語を重ねることができるのと同様である。つまり、Huddleston and Pullum (2002:470) がすでに指摘しているように、度量属格は一種の修飾語であると考えることができる。
　一方、所有の属格は左側に修飾語を置くことができない。修飾語を置くとするならば (11b) のように所有の属格と主要部名詞の間でなければならない。

(11)　a. *second *Paul's* dog　　　　　　b. *Paul's* second dog

左側に修飾語を置けないのは、所有の属格が限定詞だからである。

　以上この節では、所有の属格が限定詞であるのに対して、度量属格は修飾語として機能することを確認した。

3. 度量属格と単数形可算名詞

　本節では、単数形可算名詞と度量属格との関わり合いから浮かび上がってくる興味深い問題点を明らかにする。そのためにまず、度量属格を持つ以下の名詞句の構成素構造を考えてみる。

(12)　a. an hour's delay
　　　　b. one week's holiday　　　　　　　(Huddleston and Pullum (2002: 470))

(12) の 2 つの名詞句はそれぞれ「1 時間の遅れ」、「1 週間の休暇」という意味を持つので、限定詞の an と one はそれぞれ hour's と week's を限定している。つまり構成素構造は (13) になる。

(13)　a. [an hour's] delay　　　　　b. [one week's] holiday

また上の (5) で、an hour's delay は delay of an hour に書き換えられると述べた。an hour をひとまとめにして後置できるということは、(13a) のような構成素を成していることのさらなる証拠となる。

　以上の構成素構造の観点から (14a) と (14b) を観察してみると、非常に興味深い事実が明らかになる。

(14)　a. a week's conference　　　　　　　　　　(Desagulier (2008))
　　　　b. this hour's delay　　　(Huddleston and Pullum (2002: 470))

まず (14a) について見てみる。ここでは、限定詞 a は (13a) の an hour's の場合と同様に week's を限定している。(15) に (14a) の構造を示す。

(15)

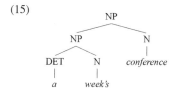

(15) の構造において、a week's は既述のように修飾語であり、限定詞ではない。そうすると、単数形可算名詞 conference には、必要なはずの限定詞が存在しない。これは、単数形可算名詞には限定詞が義務的であるという一般化 (2) に反している。

　次に (14b) this hour's delay を見てみる。(14b) は (16) のように書き換えることができる。

(16)　this delay of an hour

この書き換えが可能であるということは、(14b) で限定詞 this は hour's ではなく delay を限定している。よって (14b) の構成素構造は (17) のようになる。

(17)

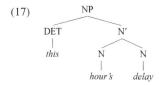

この名詞句の中で唯一の限定詞である this が delay を限定するものであるということは、単数形可算名詞 hour's が義務的に必要とする限定詞はここには存在しないということを意味している。これは一般化 (2) への反例であると言える。

　また、(14b) についてもうひとつ注目したいのは (18) である。

(18)　*(this) hour's delay

　これは、(14b) の this hour's delay において、限定詞 this が義務的であるということを表している。delay を不可算名詞と解釈すると限定詞は必要ではない。そうすると、(18) に限定詞が義務的であるのは、単数形可算名詞 hour's からの要請であると考えざるを得ない。

　つまり、this はあくまでも delay を限定するのであるが、this と hour's との間にも何らかの統語的関係を保証する必要があるのである。

　以上本節では、単数形可算名詞と度量属格との関わり合いを観察することにより、(14a) や (14b) のような例において、単数形可算名詞が一般化 (2) に反する振る舞いをしていることを明らかにした。

　以下ではこれらの例について HPSG (Pollard and Sag (1994)) の枠組みで説明を行う。次節ではまず、そのための理論的前提を述べる。

4. HPSG における名詞句の構造

　英語の単数形可算名詞と限定詞はそれぞれ以下のように表示される (Van Eynde (2006))。

(19)　a.　$\begin{bmatrix} \text{HEAD} & noun \\ \text{MRK} & incomplete \end{bmatrix}$　　b.　$\begin{bmatrix} \text{HEAD} & determiner \\ \text{MRK} & marked \\ \text{SELECT} & [\text{MRK} \quad \neg marked] \end{bmatrix}$

HPSG では、全ての言語表現の持つ情報は素性（スモールキャピタルで表示）とその値（イタリック体で表示）のペアで表現される。HEAD 素性の値は、品詞情報を表示する。MARKING（略して MRK）素性の値は、その語句が限定詞を持っているかどうか、あるいは限定詞を必要とするかどうかを表示する。(19a) の MRK の値が incomplete であるのは、この語が限定詞を必要とし、限定詞がなければ文中に生起できないことを示している。つまりこの枠組みでは、単数可算名詞の MRK の値を incomplete と規定することによって一般化 (2) を捉えるのである。

　(19b) は限定詞の語彙情報である。ここでの MRK 素性は marked という値を持っている。これは、当該の語句がすでに限定詞を持っているか、それ自体が限定詞であることを表す。SELECT 素性の値は、その語句が他の

どのような語句を選択するかを示す。(19b) SELECT が表すのは、限定詞は MRK の値が *marked* ではない語句を選択するということである。つまり、限定詞はすでに限定詞を持つ要素を選択できないということであり、上記 (6) や (7) のような例の非文法性を捉える。

次に、限定詞と単数形可算名詞が組み合わさって名詞句が形成される様子を見てみよう（Van Eynde (2006) 等参照）。

(20)

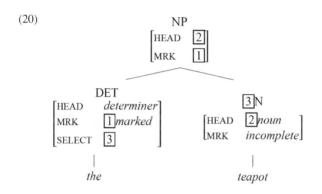

HEAD の値は主要部から句レベルに継承される (Pollard and Sag (1994))。ゆえに主要部 teapot の HEAD 素性は the teapot という句の HEAD 素性と値を共有している。HPSG では、値が共有されていることを ②などのタグを用いて表示する。

単数可算名詞 teapot と限定詞との組み合わせは、the の SELECT 素性の値によって保証される。the が teapot を選択していることが ③によって示されている。(19b) で見たように限定詞は MRK の値が *marked* でないものを選択するが、*incomplete* は *marked* ではないので、teapot は the の SELECT の規定に合致している。

最後に、MRK 素性の値は非主要部から句レベルに継承される (Van Eynde (2006))。それによって、the teapot の MRK 素性の値は非主要部の the から継承されて *marked* となる。この値の継承は ①で示されている。このように、主要部の単数形可算名詞の MRK の値は *incomplete* であるが、限定詞と組み合わさることによって句レベルでは *marked* となり、名詞句

として文中に生起できるようになるのである。

　以上、本節では単数形可算名詞と限定詞の表示と、それらが組み合わせられてできる名詞句の構造を概観した。

5. 度量属格を持つ名詞句の構造

　前節で導入した名詞句の構造に基づくと、度量属格を持つ名詞句 an hour's delay の統語構造は以下のように表示できる[5]。

(21)

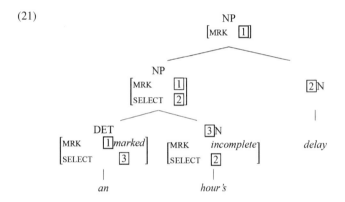

度量属格 hour's は単数形可算名詞であるので、MRK の値は *incomplete* である。不定冠詞 an が SELECT の値によって hour's を選択し（[3]で表示）、両者が組み合わせられる。前述のように MRK の値は非主要部から句レベルへ継承されるため、an の MRK の値 *marked* が an hour's へ継承される（[1]で表示）。

　次に an hour's は delay と組み合わせられる。この組み合わせには度量属格 hour's の持つ SELECT の情報が役割を果たす。普通名詞は通常、形容詞や副詞のように他の語句を選択することはないが、(22)のように、属格名詞の多くは他の語句を選択する機能を持つ。

(22)　a. *Mrs Johnson's* passport　　c. *the family's* support
　　　 b. *the boy's* application　　　　(Quirk et al. (1985: 321–322))

度量属格もこの属格一般の性質を引き継いでいるとしよう。

SELECT の値は主要部から句レベルに継承されるとする (Van Eynde (2006))。よって hour's の持つ SELECT の値が an hour's に継承され、delay との組み合わせが保証される（2で表示）。an hour's delay の MRK の値は、非主要部 an hour's から継承されて *marked* となる。

2 節で確認したように、an hour's delay において an は hour's だけを限定しているので、名詞句全体の中では限定詞としての機能はない。しかし、その MRK の値が上位レベルに順次継承されることによって、an hour's delay 全体の MRK の値を *marked* にするのである。

このことによって、以下の構造の非文法性を捉えることができる。

(23)　*this *an hour's* delay　　　　　(Huddleston and Pullum (2002: 470))

2 節で確認したように an hour's delay において an hour's は delay の修飾語であり、限定詞ではない。そうすると、この名詞句の構造は (24) と同じく、修飾語と主要部のみから成り立っていると言える。

(24)　*unavoidable* delay　　　　　　　(BNC: J79 1086)

(24) は限定詞を持たないので、(25) のように左側に限定詞を置くことできる。

(25)　<u>this</u> *unavoidable* delay　　　　　(BNC: CLX 1517)

そうすると、なぜ an hour's delay の場合には (23) が示すように左に限定詞を置くことができないのだろうか。(19b) において、限定詞は MRK の値が *marked* ではないものを選択すると規定した。しかし上で議論したように an hour's delay は *marked* である。よって限定詞はこれを選択することができず、(23) は非文法的となるのである。

6. 問題となる構造の分析

　この節では、3 節において一般化 (2) に反する振る舞いが見られると述べた (14a) と (14b) の構造を分析する。

　まず (14a) は、(26) のような統語構造を持つと提案する。

(26)

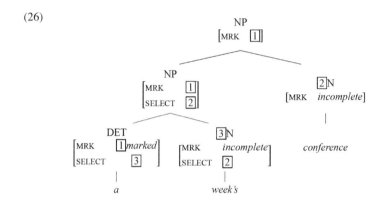

　限定詞 a が単数形可算名詞 week's と組み合わせられることで、a の MRK の値である *marked* が a week's に継承される。単数可算名詞 conference は MRK の値が *incomplete* であるが、MRK の値は非主要部から継承されるので、a week's からの継承によって、a week's conference の MRK の値は *marked* となる。

　このように (26) では、a は week's の限定詞であると同時に、a week's conference という句全体の MRK の値を *marked* にする役割も果たす。そのため、conference が限定詞を持たず、一般化 (2) に反しているとしても、非文法的になることはないのである。

　次に (14b) は以下のような統語構造を持つと提案する。

(27)

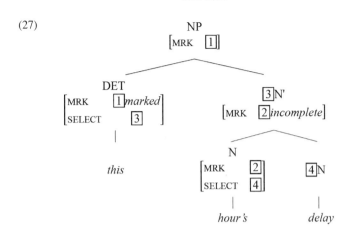

(27) の hour's は単数可算名詞であるので MRK の値は *incomplete* である。hour's delay という句の MRK の値は hour's から継承されて *incomplete* となる（2で表示）となる。しかし NP レベルの this hour's delay の MRK の値は限定詞 this から継承されて *marked* となる（1で表示）。

このように、単数形可算名詞 hour's に限定詞がなく、一般化 (2) に反しているとしても、this が句全体の MRK の値を *marked* にするので、this hour's delay という名詞句は問題なく文中に生起できるのである。

7. おわりに

度量属格が用いられた名詞句の中には、(14a) a week's conference の conference や (14b) this hour's delay の hour's などのように、一般化 (2) では捉えられない単数形可算名詞の用法が観察される。本論は、HPSG 流の名詞句構造を仮定すると、一般的な名詞句と全く同じ道具立てによる説明を (14) に対して行うことができることを示した。

言語現象というものは、一般性の高いものから特殊なものまでの連続体であり、言語理論はその連続性を捉えるものでなければならない。本論はそのような観点から一般的な名詞句と (14) の名詞句の連続性を把握し、その両方に自然な説明を与えるものである。

注

* 本論は、日本言語学会第 155 回大会 (2017 年 11 月 25 日、於：立命館大学) における口頭発表に加筆修正したものである。また、その基となったバージョンを第 2 回龍谷言語学研究会 (2017 年 11 月 1 日、於：龍谷大学) で発表した。なお、本研究は JSPS 科研費 17K02829 の助成を受けている。

[1] 下例における hospital や bicycle のように単数形可算名詞が無冠詞で使用されることがある。この場合、これらの語は本来の指示対象を持たず、一種の不可算名詞として使用されていると考えられる (Huddleston and Pullum (2002:409))。

    (i) Ed is in *hospital*.   (ii) We went by *bicycle*.

[2] Biber et al. (1999: 296)、Curme (1931: 83–84)、Desagulier (2008)、Huddleston and Pullum (2002: 470)、Poutsma (1914: 63ff)、Quirk et al. (1985: 322) などを参照。

[3] 度量属格についての理論的研究はほとんどなく、Taylor (1996) や Barker (1996) にも度量属格についての体系的な議論は見られない。

[4] British National Corpus (BNC) の検索は BNC*web* を用いて行った (http://bncweb.lancs.ac.uk)。

[5] 以下では議論に直接関係しない HEAD 素性などの情報は省略する。

参考文献

Barker, Chris (1996) *Possessive Descriptions*, Dissertations in Linguistics, CSLI Publications, Stanford.

Biber, Douglas, Stig Johansson, Geoffrey Leech, Susan Conrad and Edward Finegan (1999) *The Longman Grammar of Spoken and Written English*, Longman, London.

Carter, Ronald and Michael McCarthy (2006) *Cambridge Grammar of English*, Cambridge University Press, Cambridge.

Curme, George O. (1931) *Syntax*, D.C. Heath and Company, Boston.

Desagulier, Guillaume (2008) "Cognitive Arguments for a Fuzzy Construction Grammar," *From Gram to Mind: Grammar as Cognition*, ed. by Jean-Rémi Lapaire, Guillaume Desagulier and Jean-Baptiste Guignard, 125–150, Presses Universitaires de Bordeaux. <https://halshs.archives-ouvertes.fr/halshs-00627702>

Huddleston, Rodney and Geoffrey K. Pullum (2002) *The Cambridge Grammar of the*

English Language, Cambridge University Press, Cambridge.

Pollard, Carl J. and Ivan A. Sag (1994) *Head-Driven Phrase Structure Grammar*, University of Chicago Press, Chicago.

Poutsma, Hendrik (1914) *A Grammar of Late Modern English, Part II: The Parts of Speech. Section I, A, Nouns, Adjectives and Articles*, P. Noordhoff, Groningen.

Quirk, Randolph, Sydney Greenbaum, Geoffrey Leech and Jan Svartvik (1985) *A Comprehensive Grammar of the English Language*, Longman, London.

Taylor, John R. (1996) *Possessives in English: An Exploration in Cognitive Grammar*, Clarendon Press, Oxford.

Van Eynde, Frank (2006) "NP-internal Agreement and the Structure of the Noun Phrase," *Journal of Linguistics* 42, 139–186.

Willemse, Peter (2007) "Indefinite Possessive NPs and the Distinction between Determining and Nondetermining Genitives in English," *English Language and Linguistics* 11, 537–68.

二種類の Measure Phrases と尺度理論 *

田中 英理

キーワード：裸の MPs, *by*-MPs, 尺度水準

1. はじめに

本稿は、以下のような二種類の測量句（Measure Phrases, 以下 MPs とする）の分布について扱う。

(1) a. Galileo dropped the ball (*by) 55 meters.
　　 b. The temperature dropped (by) 5 degrees.
　　 c. John missed the target *(by) just several inches.

by-MPs と裸の MPs は (1b) のような場合にはほとんど意味の差がなく使えるが、(1a) や (1c) のような事実を見る限り、全くの同義と考えることはできないであろう。管見の限り、この二つの MPs の違いに明確に言及しているのは、Huddleston and Pullum (2002: 690-692) である。そこでは、これらの違いを動詞が表す内容が空間移動か何らかのスケール上の変化を表すかに帰している。これにしたがうと、(1a) は、ボールの空間的な移動を表し、(1b) は気温の温度というスケール上の変化を表しており、*by*-MPs は後者でのみ許されるということになる。なお、Huddleston and Pullum (2002) では、(1c) のタイプについての言及はない。

しかし、この空間移動 vs. スケール上の変化という対立だけではこれらの分布の違いを説明できない（田中 (2014)）。

(2) a. His jaw dropped (by) 2 cm.
　　 b. He swivels right (by) ninety.

(2) で記述されているのは、空間移動である。しかし、この場合には、*by*-MPs も裸の MPs も両方とも可能である。さらに、(1c) のように、*by* を必ず要求する場合については、空間 vs. スケールの区別からは何も予測することができない。そこで、本稿は、(1) の MPs の分布全般を捉えることができるような MPs の意味論を提案することを目標とする。

　本稿の構成は以下の通りである。2 節でデータの整理を行う。3 節で数学における尺度理論と尺度水準について概観し、これに基づいた Sassoon (2010) の MPs の理論を紹介する。4 節はこれに基づいて、Sassoon (2010) の理論を拡張し、*by*-MPs がある種の尺度水準に基づかないことを明示するマーカーである、と主張する。5 節は結論である。

2. データの整理

　本節では、動詞と裸の MPs と *by*-MPs との共起関係についてまとめる。[1] Huddleston and Pullum (2002) に従って、(1a-b) の MPs は動詞が表す空間移動やスケール上の変化の全体範囲 (overall extent) を修飾し、MPs の役割はこれらの範囲がどれくらいであるかを測ることであると考える。例えば、(3a) では、ジョンが歩いた空間移動の全体範囲を *5 km* で計っている。MPs がどの次元を測量するかは動詞の語彙的な意味に一部依存している。*widen* は長さであるし、*swivel* であれば、角度ということになるだろう。一方、*drop, arise, rise, soar,* …などの動詞は、主語や目的語の性質によって空間的な長さでも温度などでもよい。

(3)　a. John walked five kilometers.
　　b. Galileo dropped the ball 55 meters.
　　c. The gap widened 5 cm.
　　d. The temperature has dropped 5 degrees.
　　e. ….and put a toe down to pivot as she swiveled her bike 180 degrees.

(COCA)

　1 節で見たように、(3) のように裸の MPs を許すもののうち、*by*-MPs も許すのは、(3c-e) である。(3b) と (3d) では、同じ *drop* という動詞であ

るが、距離を測るのか温度変化を測るのかによって *by*-MPs の許容度が変わる。この現象は、上記の drop 類の動詞に共通する性質である。

(4) a. *John walked by five kilometers.
 b. *Galileo dropped the ball by 55 meters.
 c. The gap widened by 5 cm.
 d. The temperature has dropped by 5 degrees.
 e. With the soles of his feet pressing against the floor and his arms pressing against the armrests of the leather chair, <u>he swivels right by ninety to a hundred degrees</u> in order to have a look at said window shade.

((4e) は平沢 (2013)，下線は筆者)

(1c) に挙げたような *by*-MPs しか許さない動詞は、(1a-b) の動詞群と MPs が修飾するのが全体範囲ではないという点で異なる。これらの動詞はある二つの事柄（点数や年齢など）に違いがあることを明示し、*by*-MP はその差の大きさを指定している。

(5) a. It's [=an asteroid's, ET] supposed to miss us *(by) a cosmic inch, just 17,000 miles.　　　（ABC News の例に基づく）
 b. Japan beat the US *(by) two goals in soccer.
 c. The incident came at an awkward time, preceding ?(by) a few days a visit by the Chief Rabbi.　　　（BNC の例に基づく）
 d. John overestimated his income ?(by) 100 dollars.
 e. She outlived her husband ??(by) twenty years.

(1a-b)/(3)-(4) の動詞群は、いずれもその動詞で表される事象が大きく（つまり長く）なればなるほど、全体範囲も大きくなる。また逆にある事象の一部の持つ全体範囲は、それを含む事象の全体範囲より必ず小さなものとなる。一方、(1c)/(5) のタイプの動詞は、このような関係にない。例えば、「的を外す (missing the target)」事象は、その事象がより大きくなればなるほど的から外れる距離が長くなるわけではない。また、その事象の一部はそもそも missing the target と言える事象ではない。裸の MPs はこうした

動詞群とは共起することはできない。

　以上をまとめると、表 1 のようになる。

動詞の種類		MPs	by-MPs	例
Walk 類	全体範囲	OK	*	*walk, run, cycle, push something,* …
Drop 類	全体範囲	OK	空間移動 *	*drop, rise, raise, slide, soar*…
			それ以外 OK	
Increase 類	全体範囲	OK	OK	*increase, decrease, expand, reduce, cut, grow, boost, decline, improve, plunge, plummet,* …
Rotate 類	全体範囲	OK	OK	*move, rotate, revolve, tilt, swivel, incline, turn,* …
形容詞 +en	全体範囲	OK	OK	*lengthen, heighten, widen, shorten, thin, warm, cool,* …
Miss 類	全体範囲 ではない	*	OK	*miss, beat, win, precede, exceed,*…
Out-/over-V	全体範囲 ではない	??	OK	*outlive, outnumber, overrun, overstate, overestimate,* …

表 1 *by*-MP と裸 MP と動詞の共起関係（田中 (2014) を一部改変）

3. 尺度論 (Measurement Theory)

3.1. 尺度論と MPs の意味論

　MPs の意味論は、段階性形容詞の意味論と密接に関連して研究されてきている。段階性形容詞とは、程度副詞（*very, extremely, completely, slightly* 等）で修飾でき、比較構文を許すような形容詞群（例：*tall, short, wide, bent, straight,* …）である（e.g., Bierwish (1989), Kennedy (1999)）。これらの形容詞は非段階性形容詞（例：国籍を表す *Japanese* など）と異

なり、その語彙的な意味として、程度 (degrees) の集合であるスケールと個体を関連づける機能をもつ。[2]

　段階性形容詞は、(6) のように MPs と共起しうるが、*tall-short* のように反意語をなしているペアのうち、無標の方とのみ共起する。[3] 無標となる形容詞は、あるスケール上で「より大きな値がよりその性質を増す」ことに対応する意味を持つ方であるのが通常である。背が高い (*tall*) ということは背の高さのスケール上で他より大きな値を持っているということだが、背が低い (*short*) ということは、他よりも小さな値を持っていることに対応する。したがって、*tall-short* の場合は、*tall* が無標の形容詞で、MPs と共起する。(6b) に示すように、この差は比較文にすると解消する。

(6)　a. John is 5 feet {tall/*short}.
　　　b. John is 2 inches taller/shorter than Bill.

　Sassoon (2010) は、(6a-b) の違いをスケールの尺度水準に求めることを提案している。ある対象に与えられた測定値や変数に対して可能な数学的な操作は、その測定の尺度水準に依存する。尺度水準は、名称尺度、順序尺度、間隔尺度、比率尺度の 4 つのレベルに分けられる。[4]

　名称尺度は、単に物を分類することができるのみである。ヒトを性別で男と女に分ける時の「男」や「女」はそのグループの名称であって、その変数に対しては同値関係のみが定義できる。

　順序尺度は、順番に意味がある尺度である。コンテストにおける 1 位と 2 位は、前者と後者に大小関係がある。しかしこの数値の差を取ることに意味はない。

　間隔尺度と比率尺度は順序尺度の性質を維持し、演算が関わることのできるレベルである。間隔尺度は、二つの数の間の間隔に意味がある。今日摂氏 25 度で、昨日摂氏 30 度であったならば、その差が 5 度である、ということには意味がある。しかし剰余には意味がない。30 度が 25 度の 1.2 倍である、ということには意味がない。一方、比率尺度は剰余にも意味がある。10km は 5km の 2 倍であるということには意味があるので、距離は比率尺度である。ただし、間隔尺度に基づく場合でも、差の比率には意味がある。

間隔尺度と比率尺度の最も大きな違いは、絶対的なゼロがあるかどうかである。摂氏・華氏での温度を測定する場合、0は任意の値（摂氏の場合は、１気圧で水が氷になる温度）であるが、絶対温度（ケルビン）では、物質の運動が完全に静止している点を0とする。したがって、摂氏や華氏では、マイナスの値がありうるが、0ケルビンより下の値はありえない。以上を表2に簡単にまとめる。

	a=b	a > b	a - b	a/b	例
名称尺度	OK	--	--	--	グループ分け
順序尺度	OK	OK	--	--	順位
間隔尺度	OK	OK	OK	--	摂氏・華氏温度
比率尺度	OK	OK	OK	OK	絶対温度、距離

表2 尺度水準と可能な演算

Sassoon (2010) は、この尺度水準をMPsが生じる環境に直接適用できると主張している。より具体的には、段階性形容詞が比率尺度であるようなスケールを表す場合にのみMPsが許される、ということになる。比率尺度では、ある物体の測定値はどのような度量単位であろうとも比率が保持される。例えば、「高さ」は以下のような性質を持つ（Dは全ての個体の集合、Cはコンテクストの集合とする）。

(7) Context invariant ratios (height)
$\forall x \in D. \forall c \in C.$ entities with n times x's height are mapped to n × height(x) in c. （Sassoon 2010: 158, 改変）

Sassoon (2010) は、*foot* や *meter* といった単位を表す名詞は、その１単位を表し、数は、その単位をあるスケール上でn倍することを表すとする（=(8)）。

(8) ⟦*foot*⟧= $\lambda G_{(e,d)}. \lambda n. \lambda x.$ *x is n times as G as a foot unit, where G is a measure function.*
(9) ⟦*tall*⟧= $\lambda x.height (x)$ （タイプ <e,d>）

(10)　⟦*John is 5 feet tall*⟧= *1 iff in any context c, height(j) = 5 × r_foot in c, where r_foot denotes a foot unit*

(8) のように、*tall* の語彙的な意味を、個体をとってその語彙が指定するスケール上での値を返すような測量関数 (measure function, タイプ <e,d>) とする（注 2 参照）。(6a) の *tall* の例文は、「どのコンテクストにおいてもジョンの背の高さは 1 フット単位の 5 倍である」という意味を持つ（= (10)）。

　一方で、反意語の *short* は、意味を背の高さのスケール上の任意の値 n から個体が持っている値への差として規定する（=(11)）。n はコンテクストによって変化しうるものである。つまり、*short* は *tall* と異なって絶対的な 0 を持たない間隔尺度を表すのである。(6a) の *short* の例文は、「どのコンテクストにおいても任意の n とジョンの背の高さの差は 1 フット単位の 5 倍である」という意味を持つ。しかし、この真理条件が満たされることはない。これが (6a) の *short* の例文の奇妙さの原因である。

(11)　⟦*short*⟧= *λx.n-height(x),where n is some real number.*

(12)　⟦**John is 5 feet short*⟧=*1 iff in any context c, n- height(j) = 5 × r_foot in c.*

　比較構文の場合に一転して MPs が許されるようになるのは、差同士の比率は考えることができるからである。

(13)　⟦John is 2 inches shorter than Bill.⟧=1,iff in any context c,(n-height(j))-(n-height(b))=2 × r_inch in c.

Kennedy (1999) や Schwarzschild (2005) では、(6a) の *tall-short* の違いは、MPs が「限定された範囲」を修飾するかどうかに帰されている。つまり、*short* は、「ある事物の背の高さが持っていない値」を指しており、その範囲を指定することはできないのに対して、*tall* はスケールの 0 点から「ある事物が持っている値（の最大値）」を指し、この範囲の大きさを MPs が修飾できるのだと考える。Sassoon (2010) では、この効果は単位の持つ意味とスケールの性質のみから導出することが可能となっている。あ

る１単位の乗法は限定された数量になるからである。

4. 動詞への拡張

4.1 Rotate 類について

　本節では、1 節、2 節で観察した動詞と MPs の共起関係のうち、全体範囲を表すものについてまず考えよう。これらの動詞群では、by-MPs は MPs より分布が限定されている。したがって、比率尺度であるスケールであることに加えてさらに by-MPs のみが満たす条件があることが予測される。

　そこで、これらの動詞が表す空間移動や変化がどのようなスケールに基づいているかを考えてみよう。形容詞の場合と異なるのは、動詞の表す事象の時間経過とともにこれらのスケール上の値を増やしていく点である。まず、walk 類と形容詞派生動詞を対比して考えると、前者は、移動の始まりが経路の距離の 0 と合致する。一方、widen のような形容詞派生動詞は、基体形容詞の wide が指定する幅（長さ）のスケールと関連づけられるとすると（Kennedy and Levin 2008）、これらの動詞の表す事象の始まりが必ずしもスケール上の 0 と合致するわけではない。むしろ、長さのスケール上の任意の値を事象の始まりとして、そこから事象の終了時点での値との差が widen の全体範囲であることになる（図 1 参照）。

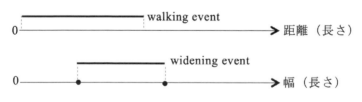

図 1 walking と widening に関わるスケール

このように考えると、walk 類と形容詞派生動詞では、関連するスケールが同じ（この場合は長さ）であったとしても、事象の始まりがスケールの 0 にならざるを得ないかそうでないかに違いがあることになる。これらの事象における全体範囲の計測に関する大きな違いは、widening の場合に

は、事象の始発点と終了点の差をとって初めてその長さがわかるということである。この違いは、drop 類の二種類の意味にもそのまま当てはめることができる。[5]

　次に、walk 類と同様に空間的な移動を表す rotate 類について考えてみよう。Rotate 類は、その動作の前提に「位置移動していない状態」があると考えられる。その状態を 0 として、そこから移動が行われる。rotate 類はこの点で形容詞派生動詞や drop 類の非空間移動解釈と共通している。

　このような違いは、述語否定がどのような含意を生みやすいかに現れている。Walk 類や drop 類の空間移動の否定では、その対比として別の動作が含意されやすい。一方、rotate 類や drop 類の非空間移動解釈では初めの状態を保持していることが対比として含意される。

(14)　a. John didn't walk. (He ran.)
　　　b. John didn't rotate the picture. (It stays at the same position before.)
(15)　a. John didn't drop the ball. (He threw it.)
　　　b. The temperature didn't drop. (It stays the same.)

　これらの考察に基づいて、walk 類、rotate 類の意味を以下のように提案する。まず、段階性形容詞と異なり、動詞には語彙的にスケールを設定する必然性がない。そこで、音形のない測量関数 μ を導入し、これが事象を何らかの次元で計測すると考える。例えば、*John walked three hours.* では、この次元は時間軸となるし、*John walked three kilometers.* では空間的な距離となる。(16) の μ は事象をこうした次元上の値に返すような関数である。[6]

(16)　$\llbracket \mu \rrbracket = \lambda P_{<st>}.\lambda d.\lambda e.\ P(e)\ \&\ \mu(e) \geq d$
(17)　walk 類（drop 類の空間移動解釈を含む）
　　　a. $\llbracket \text{walk} \rrbracket = \lambda e.\ \text{walk}\ (e)$
　　　b. $\llbracket \mu\ \text{walk} \rrbracket = \lambda d\lambda e.\ \text{walk}\ (e)\ \&\ \mu(e) \geq d$
(18)　rotate 類（drop 類の非空間移動解釈を含む）
　　　a. $\llbracket \text{rotate} \rrbracket = \lambda e.\exists e'.\ \text{rotate}\ (e)\ \&\ \text{INI}(e) = \text{END}(e')\ \&\ \neg\text{rotated}\ (e')$
　　　b. $\llbracket \mu\ \text{rotate} \rrbracket = \lambda d\lambda e.\exists e'.\ \text{rotate}\ (e)\ \&\ e' \leq e\ \&\ \text{INI}(e) = \text{END}(e')\ \&$ $\neg\text{rotated}(e')\ \&\ \mu(e) \geq d$, where INI is a function that maps events into its

initial component and END is a function that maps events into its final component.

(17) の walk 類と (18) の rotate 類の違いは、rotate 類が rotate に先行する事象（状態も含む）の最終部分が rotate の初めの部分と合致するという条件が加わっている点である。μ(e) は、walk 類も rotate 類も事象の始まりから終わりまでの量となるので、全体範囲を計測することは同じである。しかし、rotate 類の初めの値は、先行する事象に依存するので、結果として、(18b) における μ(e) の値は、rotate 事象の初めの値と終わりの値の差である。一方、walk 類は、常に 0 からの計測ということになる。つまり、rotate 類は、その全体範囲を測るのに必ず差をとるのに対し、walk 類はその必要がないということである。

　これらの考察から、by-MPs の分布について、以下の一般化を立てることができるだろう。

(19)　by-MPs は、比率尺度を満たすスケールの絶対的 0 からの計測ではないことを要求する。

　形容詞派生動詞や rotate 類（drop 類の非空間用法）は、絶対的 0 からの計測ではないことを示しているので、(20b) が (20a) を entail しない。したがって、(20c) のように最終的な値を着点句として指定することができる。同様のことが rotate 類にも観察できる。(21) (=(4e)) では、90 度回って 100 度の位置にきたことを表している。

(20)　a. The crack is 5 cm wide./*The crack is wide by 5 cm.
　　　b. The crack widened (by) 5 cm.
　　　c. The crack widened (by) 5 cm to 10 cm.
(21)　… he swivels right by ninety to a hundred degrees. (=(4e))

4.2 全体範囲を表さない動詞群について

　最後に、(1c)/(5) のような全体範囲を表わさない動詞群について考える。これらの動詞群は、全て共通して、「ある事物と事物には差がある・同じ

場所にない」ことを述べている。

(22) a. John missed the target *(by) several inches.　　　　　　(=(1c))
"the position that John's bullet/ball/…hit at" ≠ "the position of the target"
b. She outlived her husband ??(by) twenty years.　　　　　　(=(5e))
"the time of her death" > "the time of her husband's death"

　2 節で述べたように、これらの動詞と共起する MPs は動詞の関連する
スケールの全体範囲を表しているわけではない。これらの動詞に関して
は、動詞の進展と共に大きくなる、というような関係にあるスケールが設
定できない。したがって、動詞の表す事象の始発点を絶対的 0 とするよ
うな比率尺度を満たすようなスケールがあるわけではない。したがって、
こうした動詞群と裸の MPs は共起しない。
　一方、これらの動詞の語彙的な意味は、(22) で述べたような二事物間の
違い、あるいは優位性である。その意味で、これらは順序尺度を満たすこ
とができる。順序尺度そのものは差を取ることに意味をなさないが、優位
性を他の基準で測ることができるもの（点数、距離、生きた年数など）が
あれば、この順序の間の差をその測度で表すことはできる。(19) で述べた
ように、by-MPs は比率尺度を満たすスケールの絶対的 0 からの計測でな
いことを要求するので、二点間の「差」を表す場合には問題ない。
　よって、これらの動詞群では裸の MPs は共起しないが、by-MPs のみ許
されることになる。

5. まとめ
　本稿は、英語の裸の MPs と by-MPs の分布について、特に動詞との共
起関係から論じた。Sassoon (2010) の尺度理論を段階性形容詞と MPs の
共起関係に直接適用するという論を拡張して、by-MPs は比率尺度ではな
いことを表す、という提案を行った。これまでこの二つの MPs の分布の
違いに着目されることは Huddleston and Pullum (2002) を除いてほとんど
なかったと言えるが、彼らのいう「空間移動 vs. スケール上の変化」は、
関係するスケールが絶対的な 0 を持つ比率尺度と解釈されるか、任意の

点を 0 として差を計測していると解釈されるかに帰されることになる。

　英語の by-MPs の分布は、日本語の段階性形容詞における MPs の分布と非常に似通っている。日本語では、「# 太郎は 180cm 背が高い」は太郎の身長が 180cm である、という意味で解釈できない。一方、比較文「太郎は二郎より 5cm 背が高い」では MPs が生じることができる。また、Sawada and Grano (2011) が指摘するようにスケール上の下限がその反意語と同義になる形容詞（「曲がっている」など）は、「この釘は 5 度曲がっている」のように、比較文でなくても MPs と共起する。by-MPs は日本語の MPs が生じる形容詞に対応する形容詞で許され、日本語が MPs を許さない環境で許されない。したがって、本稿での by-MPs に対して述べた制約は、日本語の MPs の分布も説明することができるであろう。日本語と英語の比較対照については稿を改めて論じたい。

* 本稿は、第 149 回日本言語学会（2014 年）、45th Poznan Linguistic Meeting（2015 年）、第 48 回阪大英文学会（2015 年）、東海意味論研究会（2015 年）などで発表した内容に基づいている。これらの機会に貴重なコメント、ご批判をいただいた方々に感謝する。

注

[1] この節は、田中 (2014) に基づいている。
[2] この関係づけをどのように形式化するかについては、大きく分けて二種類の方法がある。一つは、段階性形容詞は、個体項と程度項 d をとる二項述語であり、個体のある次元での値が d 以上である、という関係性を表すとする。もう一方は、段階性形容詞は測度関数であり、個体をとってある次元でのその個体の値を返すとする方法である（Kennedy 1999）。この小論では、いずれかの立場を積極的にとるものではない。
[3] MPs と段階性形容詞が共起するかどうかは、無標・有標の対立の他に、その言語における語彙的特質性 (idiosyncrasy) が観察される。例えば、英語では *John is 5 feet tall.* は全く問題のない文であるが、これに対応するスペイン語はこの語順と形式では MPs を取ることができない。この語彙的特質性については、Murphy (2007), Schwarzschild(2005) 等を参照。
[4] 尺度水準については、数学、統計に関する多くの入門的文献に説明がある。詳しい説明はそうした書籍に譲る。
[5] 平沢 (2013) は、中英語期には、「差」を表す用法と同時に *by* を伴って経路の長

さを表す用法があったことを報告している。したがって、*by* は時代が下るにした
がって「差」の用法に特化していったと考えられる（OED にも用例を確認でき
る）。

[6] Nakanishi (2007) では、e を準同型写像 h によって別の個体領域に写像し、その
個体の量を μ で測るという提案を行っている。

参考文献

Bierwish, Manfred (1989) "The Semantics of Gradation," In *Dimensional Adjectives*, ed. by M. Mierwisch and E. Lang, 71-261. Springer-Verlag, Berlin.

Cresswell, Max J. (1976) "The Semantics of Degree," in *Montague Grammar*, ed. by B. Partee, 261–292, Academic Press, New York.

平沢慎也 (2013)「英語前置詞 by の意味ネットワークにおける＜差分＞用法につ いて」日本認知言語学会論文集 Vol. 13, 96-107. 日本認知言語学会 .

Huddleston, Rodney and Geoffrey Pullum (2002) *The Cambridge Grammar of the English Language*, The Cambridge University Press, Cambridge.

Kennedy, Chris (1999) *Projecting the Adjective: The Syntax and Semantics of Gradability and Comparison*, Garland, New York.

Kennedy, Chris. and Beth Levin (2008) "Measure of Change: The Adjectival Core of Degree Achievements," *Adjectives and Adverbs: Syntax, Semantics and Discourse*, 156–182.

Krifka, Manfred. 1989. "Nominal Reference, Temporal Constitution and Quantification in Event Semantics," in *Semantics and Contextual Expressions*, ed. by R. Bartsch, van J. Benthem, & van P. Emde Boas, 75–115, Foris, Dordrecht.

Murphy, Lynn (2007) "Semantic, Pragmatic and Lexical Aspects of the Measure Phrase + Adjective Construction," *Acta Linguistica Hafviensia* 38, 78–100.

Nakanishi, Kimiko (2007) "Measurement in Nominal and Verbal Domains," *Linguistics and Philosophy* 30, 235–276.

田中英理 (2014)「動詞のスケール構造と二種類の Measure Phrases の分布につい て」第 149 回日本言語学会予稿集 .

Sassoon, Galit (2010) "Measurement theory in Linguistics," *Synthese* 174, 151–180.

Sawada, Osamu and Thomas Grano (2011) "Scale Structure, Coercion and the Interpretation of Measure Phrases in Japanese," *Natural Language Semantics* 19, 191–226.

Schwarzschild, Roger (2005) "Measure Phrases as Modifiers of Adjectives," Recherches linguistiques de Vincennes 34, 207–228.

A Factive Island as a Consequence of Head Movement in English*

Maiko Yamaguchi

Keywords: strong island, factive island, weakened island, head movement

1. Overview

It is commonly assumed that the clausal complements of the presuppositional or factive matrix predicates (factive islands) exhibit weak island property in English. According to Szabolcsi and Zwart (1993: 235), "Weak islands are environments that allow some, but not all, *wh*-phrases to extract···" In this short paper, I claim that a factive island is a covert nominal in English, and show that its property is a consequence of the head movement (C-to-$D_{null/affixal}$) operated at PF in English.[1] In short, the weak island property (or weakened island) can be obtained through the application of the head movement. I will present supporting evidence for my claim from earlier works. The evidence can be found both cross-linguistically and intra-linguistically. Further, I apply my analysis to the *overt* nominal complement clauses (strong islands). Ostensibly, it may sound odd to apply the head movement to these DPs. Notwithstanding, the empirical data from English support this: *wh*-argument extractions from these islands become acceptable in certain environments. I take it that the strong island can become a weakened island due to the head movement in these cases. Finally, the argument/adjunct asymmetry in terms of extraction possibility in the weakened islands is also touched upon briefly in the latter part of this paper.

This paper is organized as follows. Section 2 introduces null DP analysis and obligatory head movement in the factive island in English. In section 3, cross-linguistic evidence for the DP analysis is shown. English evidence is also looked at in this section. In section 4, I consider overt DP complement of the matrix predicate. Head movement analysis is also employed in this environment to account for a few special cases in English that are worth noting. Section 5 briefly takes up argument/adjunct asymmetry in extraction possibility. Section 6 concludes and raises remaining issues to be addressed for future studies.

2. Null DP Analysis

Drawing from Kastner (2015), and Bošković (2015), I suggest that the factive island in English is a consequence of a head movement which has been applied to the heads in the complement of the factive or presuppositional main verbs: C-to-$D_{null/affixal}$. Structurally, I assume the following structure for the factive island in English.

(1) **obligatory head movement at PF**
[VP V factiv verb [DP $D_{(null/affixal)}$... [CP C...]]]

I also propose that this head movement is triggered by the affixal or defective nature of the null D head at PF. The motivation for the movement is target-based.

Prior to the head movement, I assume that necessary featural agreements between the relevant heads are operated at narrow syntax.

However, the morphological requirement of the target element necessitates the head movement at PF. Yet, due to the consequence of the featural agreement, the necessary information about the elements which will be subject to the head movement is already available to the *wh*-elements which are extracted at the point of narrow syntax. This assumption is critical when we consider the argument/adjunct asymmetry in extraction out of weakened islands.

Throughout, I take the position that the complement of the presuppositional matrix predicate is a DP. Following Kastner (2015), I also consider these types of complements to be definite (presuppositional) entities, rather than propositions. Along the same lines as Kastner, I assume that there is a null D head on top of C in the complement of the factive main verb; Kastner argues that D is a source of so-called definiteness or presuppositionality. In Kastner's analysis, the clausal complements of factive matrix verbs comprise definite DPs; since they are considered definite entities, they pick out discourse referents from the Common Ground. I further assume that the agreement has to be done at narrow syntax due to these features. Differing from Kasnter's analysis, however, I maintain that the null D head on top of the clausal complement of the factive verb constitutes an affixal/defective property. For this reason, I assume that C^0 obligatorily moves to D^0 at PF in English. Due to this head movement, phase collapsing effect or voiding of the double phase structure (DPS) à la Bošković ensues. The notions of each terms are provided below.

(2) Double Phase Structure: Nothing within the YP is accessible from the XP.
Extraction is impossible. [$_{XP=Phase}$ [$_{YP=Phase}$]]

(adapted from Bošković (2015: 4))

Phase Collapsing: Head movements can void phase-hood.

(cf. (ibid.: 9))

According to Bošković (2015), Phase Collapsing or a particular kind of head movement nullifies the DPS. It is worth noting that the Phase Collapsing is said to enable the argument extraction from the previously impervious structure (DPS), although this operation leaves adjuncts intact.

Therefore, the fact that only the arguments, and not adjuncts, are extractable from factive islands in English is perfectly congenial with the consequence of this type of head movement. So, theoretically, the head movement, along with the null DP analysis seems to capture factive islands in English correctly.

In the next section, I shall present empirical evidence for the DP analysis from earlier works.

3. Empirical Supporting Evidence for the DP Analysis of Factive Islands

3.1. Jordan Arabic Cases from Jarrah (2019)

According to Jarrah (2019), no extraction of *wh*-phrase whatsoever (including d-linked *whs*) is allowed from the complement clauses of factive verbs in Jordan Arabic. Jarrah argues that these complements behave like nominal complement clauses in that they share strong-island property. Obviously, if we adopt the CP analysis of the factive islands, we will not be able to give a plausible account as to why the sentences in (3) are ungrammatical.[2]

(3) Supporting evidence for DP analysis from Jordan Arabic
    a. * miin ?abuu-j   ħizin/?istaʁʁrab/nasa/?irif
         who   father-my   regretted/got surprised/forgot/knew
         ?inn-ha   ?axað-at   ?is-saa?ah
         COMP-3SG.F   took-3SG.F   DEF-watch
         Intended: 'Who did my father regret/was surprised/forget/know took the (hand) watch?'
    b. * keef ?abuu-j   ħizin/ ?istaʁʁrab/ nasa/ ?irif
         how   father-my   regretted/got surprised/forgot/ knew
         inn-ha   ?il-marah   ?axað-at   ?is-saa?ah
         COMP-3SG.F   DEF-woman   took-3SG.F   DEF-watch
         Intended: 'How did my father regret/was surprised/forget/know that the woman took the (hand) watch?'   (Jarrah (2019: 109))

3.2. Spanish Case from (Jarrah 2019)

Jarrah (2019) also introduces the relevant supporting evidence in Spanish from Zubizaretta's (1982) work. The complement clause can be preceded by the overt determiner (det) only in factive complement clauses, whereas this option is not allowed in the complement clause of non-factive verb as in (4). Jarrah cites this from (Adams (1985: 306)).

(4) Supporting evidence for DP analysis from Spanish
     Lamento/*creo el   que Pedro no   haya pasado el examen.
     I regret/believe det that Pedro not has   passed the exam
     'I regret/believe that Pedro has not passed the exam.'

(Jarrah (2019: 118))

In this paper, I assume that the head movements in the complements of factive predicates are subject to cross-linguistic variation (parameter). Although Jarrah (2019) alludes that the D is deleted at PF in Jordan Arabic factive island cases, it may also be plausible to contend that this null D does not undergo head movement in this language because it is not affixal/defective, unlike English.

Next, I shall briefly introduce supporting evidence in English from Kastner (2015).

3.3. English Cases from Kastner (2015)
3.3.1 Coordination Test in English

Kastner (2015) used a coordination test as a suggestive diagnostic for the DP analysis of the factive complement clause, as shown in the following examples.

(5) a. * John claimed [_DP_ responsibility] and [_CP_ that the building collapsed].
     b. ? John denied [_DP_ the allegations] and [_DP_ that the building collapsed].

(adapted from Kastner (2015: 173))

Here, the complement of the presuppositional verb like _deny_ can be coordinated with the first conjunct DP, while the complement of the non-presuppositional verb like _claim_ cannot be coordinated with the first conjunct DP.

The above contrast suggests that the so-called factive island is more DP-like and it is in favor of DP analysis.

3.3.2. Pro-form Substitution in English from Kastner (2015)

The other supporting evidence from Kastner (2015) is pro-form substitution. The following notions about DP pro-forms and CP pro-forms are adopted in Kastner (2015).

(6) Pro-forms in English adopted in Kastner (2015)
CP pro-forms: *as, so*　　　DP pro-forms: *which, it*

Regarding the pro-form substitution instances, Kastner contends that only non-presuppositional verbs can license *so* (CP-pro-form) as in (7). Moreover, Kastner (2015) notes that the complements of non-presuppositional verbs can only take clausal complements (CPs) as in (8), whereas the complements of factive verbs can take both CP and DP status as in (9).

(7) Pro-form substitution with *so*
　　a. John thought/said *so*.
　　b. *John remembered/forgot *so*.　　　　　(Kastner (2015: 173))
(8) Pro-form substitution with non-presuppositional verb
　　a. This mist can't last, <u>as</u> Morpho and Hoppy (both)
　　　claim/announce/think___.(CP)
　　b. * This mist can't last, <u>which</u> Morpho and Hoppy (both)
　　　claim/announce/think___.(DP)　　　　(Kastner (2015:174))
(9) Pro-form substitution with presupposition verb
　　a. This mist can't last, <u>as</u> Morpho and Hoppy (both) **realize ___**. (CP)
　　b. This mist can't last, <u>which</u> Morpho and Hoppy (both) **realize ___**. (DP)
　　　　　　　　　　　　　　　　　　　　(Kastner (2015: 174))

Now that we have observed good deal of evidence for my analysis in dealing with null DP complement of the presuppositional matrix predicate, I shall apply my head movement analysis to the overt DP complement of the presuppositional matrix verb in English in the following section.

4. Overt DP Complement of the Presuppositional Matrix Predicate

4.1. In Cases Without Head Movement (Simple DPS)

In this section, I consider overt D^0 instances of the case of nominal complements. When it comes to overt D^0 instances, the head movement is generally not allowed in English. The overt D^0 is non-affixal and it does not seem to have any morphological defectiveness to be resolved. Therefore, it is not only arguments but also adjuncts that cannot be extracted from this overt nominal complement. These overt nominal complements exhibit the strong island property. In fact, Kastner himself assumes that the complement clauses are adjoined to the NP when the nominal heads are overt as in (10).

(10) $[_{VP} V_{factiv\ verb} [_{DP}$ **the** $[_{NP} [\ _{NP}\ N\ \ [_{CP}$ **that...** $]]]]]$ adjunction analysis

(Kastner's (2015) strcture)

(11) $[_{VP} V_{factiv\ verb} [_{DP}$ **the** $[_{NP} [_{CP}$ **that...** $]]]]$ complement analysis (mine) **DPS**

Phase   Phase   Phase

At this stage, both Kastner's structure and mine capture the absolute island property in the nominal complement clauses, and both seems equally appealing.[3]

Yet, informant consultations conducted by myself provide a very interesting phenomenon that support my analysis of the nominal complement. When certain conditions are met, it seems that the strong island property is mitigated to the level of weak island.

4.2. Special Cases (Head Movement Triggered by the Introduction of Prt)

Here, I would like to introduce empirical evidence for the application of the head movement in the overt DP complement in English. I discovered that a very intriguing *wh*-argument extraction contrast can be obtained in certain cases. In a relevant environment, the introduction of an additional particle seems to render the strong island into a weak island.

Here are partial examples from my research.[4]

Additional particle contrasts with *wh*-argument extraction

(12) ✓/? What did SBS report on the fact that the South Korean President Park might have missed__?　　　⇒ **Ans.** A very important meeting.

(13)　What did Mr. Trump **mention** *about* the fact that North Korea had been developing ___ ?　　　⇒ **Ans.** Nuclear weapons.

(14)　What has the NY Times **notified** *about* the fact that the president of a certain country hardly ever used?　　(c.f. myassignmenthelp.com iweb corpus)
⇒ Ans. Applicable law instead of the legal system.

(15)　What did the White House **deny** *about* the fact that Mr. Flynn had ___(with Russia during the campaign)?
⇒ **Ans.** A link with Russia. In fact, Mr. Flynn made several phone calls to the Russian official.

Prior to the introduction of the particles, *wh*-argument extractions are overall ill-formed. Nevertheless, my informant notified me that the introduction of particles on top of these overt DPs leads to the upgrades in grammaticality.

I claim that the above-mentioned phenomenon can be explained by employing the head movements triggered by the introduction of an overt affixal functional element (Prt): N-to-D-to-Prt movement. The structure is presented below. Details aside, I claim that agreements among the relevant heads in the nominal domain (N, D, Prt) are achieved at narrow syntax.

(16)　**Structure of the N-to-D-to-Prt movement at PF**

$[\text{V}_{matrix}\ldots[_{PrtP}\ \text{Prt}_{(affixal/defective\ feature)}\ [_{DP}\ \text{the}\ [_{NP}\ \text{N}\ [_{CP}\ \text{that}\ldots\ ]]]]]$

Partially adopting an essence from Grimshaw (2005), I assume that the head movement takes place within this nominal domain due to the defective property of the functional element Prt. Grimshaw (2005) notes that PP is an extended projection of N, and CP is an extended projection of V.[7] Following Grimshaw (2005), I also consider the head, which is projected on top of DP, to be the functional category. Since the head movement does not seem to have any significant semantic imports, this operation is predicted to occur at PF. So, the output is another case of a weakened island.

The introduction of additional particles comes to prevent the structure from becoming ungrammatical. In the next section, I would like to briefly consider why a weakened island only allows *wh*-argument extractions when it consistently disallows adjunct extraction.

5. Why Head Movements Cannot Save Adjuncts

We have seen that arguments can be salvaged by the head movement both in null DP (factive island) as well as certain overt DP complements of matrix presuppositional predicates. However, adjuncts do not benefit from this operation. It is quite natural for us to ask why such a contrast arises.

To put it succinctly, I contend that the argument/adjunct asymmetry in extraction comes from the pickiness of the extracted materials regarding the presence or absence of phases or barriers in their derivations.

As far as the *wh*-arguments are concerned, I take it that only the existence of barriers at the end of the derivation matters. So, if head movements apply, and the barrier between the landing site and its original place are nullified at least at PF, this is not a significant restriction to *wh*-arguments.

The issue of look-ahead does not apply here. Recall that I have mentioned that all the necessary agreements are done at narrow syntax. So, when the extraction of the *wh*-argument takes place, information about the will-be head moving elements is already obtainable. Therefore, *wh*-arguments skip phases that are going to be eliminated later at PF in order to fulfill the requirements on the PF side.

On the other hand, because adjuncts are not the core elements in the sentence structure, they may only appear in the structure via adjunction. Adjuncts are more sensitive to their derivations as compared to arguments. Unlike arguments, the original positions of adjuncts are not secured by the mere existence of verbs after the extraction. For this reason, their paths must be barrier-free throughout the derivation. In other words, the sources of adjuncts are only identifiable by a strictly cyclic movement. That cyclic derivation secures the information between the landing site and the original position. Even if the barrier is to be voided later, the fact that the barrier existed in the structure at some point in time in the derivation disrupts the relation between the two positions for adjuncts. So, they have to move up the structure by stopping at every phase edge, due mainly to the Phase Impenetrability Condition (PIC).[8] Skipping them makes the source of the adjunct position non-traceable and results in ungrammaticality.[9]

Note that the cyclic movement by adjuncts necessarily infringes anti-locality. Specifically, spec-to-spec anti-locality proposed by Erlewine (2016) and Bošković's (2017) condition on NP as an independent barrier/phase in English are also employed to explain this fact. The adopted definition, notion, and assumption are as follows:

(17) Spec-to-Spec Anti-Locality:
A'-movement of a phrase from the Specifier of XP must cross a maximalprojection other than XP. (Erlewine (2016: 431))

(18) NP is a phase for elements that are not theta-marked by its head/within it. Also, NP does not have spec and extraction of NP has to be in the form of adjunction. (Bošković (2017: 1556))

Bošković (2017) originally introduced this independent NP phase approach to explain the ungrammaticality of the example like below.

(19) * Who$_i$ did you see [$_{DP}$ t$_i$ [$_{NP}$ enemies of [$_{DP}$ t$_i$ [$_{NP}$ friends of t$_i$]]]]? (Bošković (2017: 1556))

In the deep extraction like (19), *wh*-argument has to stop by at the spec of DP. However, this movement does not infringe anti-locality adopted here nor PIC. Therefore, Bošković tries to identify the source of infelicity in (19). He attributes the badness of (19) to be the obligatory adjunction operation taking place at the non-theta marked NP as in (20).

(20) * Who$_i$ did you see [$_{DP}$ t_i [$_{NP}$ t_i [$_{NP}$ enemies of [$_{DP}$ t_i [$_{NP}$ friends of t_i]]]]]? (Bošković (2017: 1556))

He argues that the extracted element is not theta-marked by the higher NP, thus this higher NP constitutes a phase. PIC requires the adjunction to the higher NP. After adjoining to NP, the next stop for the extracted element must be Spec DP; this movement is said to violate anti-locality. Bošković further mentions that this notion should be extended to account for the cases which involve violations of complex NP cases like ours as in (21).

(21) * Who$_i$ did you hear [$_{DP}$ t_i [$_{NP}$ t_i [$_{NP}$ rumors [$_{CP}$ t_i that [$_{IP}$ a dog bit t_i]]]]]?
(Bošković (2017: 1556))

So, drawing on previous researchers' analyses, I would like to present the contrasts between arguments and adjuncts in the next subsection.

5.1. The Actual Derivation

Due to page restrictions, I shall present a brief structural derivation for each case.

In the case of the factive island in (22), agreement is operated at narrow syntax and the will-be head-moved elements are marked. Since C-to-D is to happen later at PF, the *wh*-argument skips CP-spec and directly targets the spec of DP. In contrast, the *wh*-adjunct moves to the spec of DP via Spec CP. The anti-locality is necessarily violated at this point and ungrammaticality ensues.

(22) Factive island (null DP)

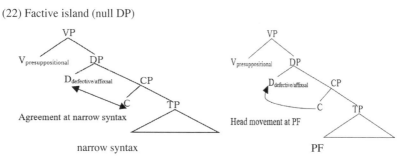

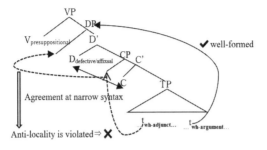

wh argument/adjunct extraction

(23) Prt Insertion Case (Prt+overt DP)

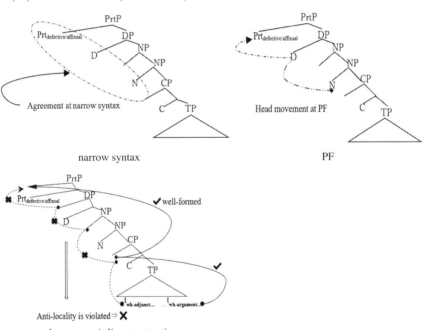

Moving on, observe Prt insertion case in (23). The agreement in the nominal domain is done at narrow syntax, and the head movement is operated accordingly at PF. The *wh*-argument again skips the phasal edges that will be nullified (NP, DP). The derivation of the *wh*-argument conforms to anti-locality, resulting in well-formedness. In contrast, the *wh*-adjunct stops at every single phase across-the-board. These movements inevitably induce anti-locality violation, and the result is ill-formedness.

6. Conclusions

I have shown that a typical strong island like a nominal complement, whether it is overt or covert, can be weakened by the head movement operation. With this analysis, the extractability of the factive island and the overt nominal complement of matrix verbs in English can be considered in the same wavelength.

Of course, there are other cumbersome examples where even arguments are excluded from the factive island in English. In such cases, semantic accounts along the line of Szabolcsi and Zwart (1993) might help in complementing the gap of the syntactic account employed in this paper, but this is beyond the scope of this paper and I will leave those issues for future investigation.

*First of all, I would like to express my gratitude to the editorial board in providing me an opportunity to submit to this edition. My special thanks goes to Amber Chew and Rebekah Alexander for their patience and insightful comments and support during this research. I am grateful to Amber Chew for proofreading this paper. All the remaining inadequacies and errors are my own.

[1] Though there are other instances of weak islands or other intricate instances of factive islands in reality, I will not address them here, since it is beyond the scope of this paper and my main concern.

[2] Cross-linguistic evidence from Jordan Arabic further supports the veracity of the DP analysis. Regarding CP analysis, I refer readers to (Haegeman and Ürögdi (2010) a.o.).

[3] Following Bošković (2017), I take that this NP constitutes a phase for the extracted element. For this reason, this structure constitutes a double phase or it could be termed as a triple phase. I will get to this point in section 5.

[4] Conventionally, the overt nominal complements are considered absolute islands and the extraction operations of arguments as well as adjuncts are normally excluded.

Therefore, I used non-presuppositional matrix verbs as well as presuppositional verbs for the matrix predicate. Incidentally, my previous research discovered that my informants are not subjected to the presuppositionality in the embedded clause when it comes to the topicalization in the factive island. So, I did not discriminate non-presuppositional verbs from presuppositional verbs for the overt nominal complements.

[5] Incidentally, it seems that the possible additional particles are fixed idiosyncratically.

[6] Prt probably needs to check some relatedness property against nominals.

[7] I regard particles and prepositions as the same elements in this paper.

[8] Following the convention, I assume that each Phase is a barrier or intervenor. Similarly, it is widely assumed in the literature that extractions must stop by at every spec of phases or a phasal edge when they cross phasal boundary due to Phase Impenetrability Condition (PIC).

[9] Figuratively speaking, derivations of *wh*-argument can be compared to the operation of express-trains, while derivations of *wh*-adjunct go through like local-trains.

References

Bošković, Željko (2015) "Deducing the Generalized XP Constraint from Phasal Spell-out," ms., University of Connecticut.
<http://web.uconn.edu/boskovic/boskovic_15_Deducing-the-.pdf>
Bošković, Željko (2017) "Extraction from Complex NPs and Detachment," in *The Wiley Blackwell Companion to Syntax, second edition, volume III*, ed. by Martin Everaert and Henk C. van Riemsdijk, 1541–1566, John Wiley & Sons, Inc., Hoboken, NJ.
Erlewine, Michael Yoshitaka (2016) "Anti–locality and Optimality in Kaqchikel Agent Focus," *Natural Language & Linguistic Theory* 34 (2), 429–479.
Grimshaw, Jane (2005) "Extended Projection," in *Words and Structure*, ed. by Jane Grimshaw, 1–74, CSLI, Stanford.
Haegeman, Liliane and Barbara Ürögdi (2010) "Referential CPs and DPs: An Operator Movement Account," *Theoretical Linguistics* 36 (2–3), 111–152.
Jarrah, Marwan (2019) "Factivity and Subject Extraction in Jordanian Arabic," *Lingua* 219, 106–126.
Kastner, Itmar (2015) "Factivity Mirrors Interpretation: The selectional Requirements of Presuppositional Verbs," *Lingua* 164, 156–188.
Szabolcsi, Anna and Frans Zwart (1993) "Weak Islands and an Algebraic Semantics for Scope Taking," *Natural Language Semantics* 1, 235–284.

具体名詞の中核的機能についての再考
——複合名詞を例として

岩橋 一樹

キーワード：具体名詞 , 中核的機能 , メタファー的意味 , 関連性理論

1. はじめに

　具体名詞は複合名詞において修飾語として用いられた際に、(1) に示すように様々なメタファー的意味を有する。

> (1)　mother church, frogman, hermit crab, satellite nation, soldier ant, finger lakes, queen bee, wastebasket category　　　　　　(Levi (1978: 92))

例えば、mother church は地区の中心となる教会、frogman は潜水士、hermit crab はヤドカリといった意味で用いられ、wastebasket category は役に立たない物が属するカテゴリーという意味で用いられる。このように、それぞれの複合名詞において主要部を修飾する語がメタファー的意味で用いられている。本論文では、複合名詞における修飾語のメタファー的意味がどのようにして理解されるのかを考察する。特に、動作の類似性、事物の価値の類似性、知覚的特性の類似性が意味理解にどう関わるのかを考察する。

2. 先行研究

2. 1. Jackendoff (1975), Levi (1978)

　Jackendoff (1975), Levi (1978) では、複合名詞における修飾語と主要部との間の統語構造や意味関係について、修飾語が指す物と主要部が指す物との間の意味的類似性に着目するという立場から論じられている。具体的には、修飾語が指す物と主要部が指す物との間に見られる様々な意味的

類似性が統語構造に反映されることが指摘されている。

Jackendoff (1975: 655-658) によると、mother church のようなメタファーが関わる複合名詞では、教区の中心となる教会と家庭における母親の役割が類似していることといった意味的類似性を統語構造に反映させるために、LIKE という述語を用いて複合名詞の統語構造と意味を記述している。

Levi (1978: Ch. 4) によると、修飾語と主要部との間に、機能や動作や外観等の意味的共通点があるから、(1) に挙げた複合名詞の統語構造では BE という述語が見られる。例えば、mother church では、家庭における母親と教区の中心となる教会はどちらも中心的機能を担うという点が共通する。そのため、統語構造では The church is a mother. という共通性が成立することが記述され、派生の段階で述語 BE が削除されてこの複合名詞が派生される。さらに、Levi によると、複合名詞の意味理解には、各単語の語彙的意味だけでなく語用論的要因も関わる。例えば、imperial bearing という複合名詞は、文脈との関わりで「典型的な皇帝と似た態度」という意味で理解される。このように、修飾語の指示対象が持つ特徴的で持続的な性質がメタファー的意味の理解に関わる。

これらの主張を踏まえると、(1) に挙げた複合名詞の修飾語のメタファー的意味は機能、動作、抽象的関係、形、価値の類似性に基づくことがわかる。さらに、footnote のように、空間関係の類似性に基づく複合名詞や、ice queen のように知覚的特性の類似性に基づく複合名詞もある。しかし、複合名詞の中には、(2) のように修飾語の意味の理解が難しいものもある。

(2)   #frog student, #fish student, #butterfly man

これらの例で、カエルや魚のように上手に泳ぐことに frog や fish を用いるのが不自然となり、蝶のように自由に動き回ることに基づいて好みが変わることに butterfly を用いるのが不自然である。このことから、類似性の理解が容易な場合と困難な場合があるのはなぜなのか考察する必要がある。

2. 2. 認知意味論的アプローチ

Lakoff and Johnson (1980) によると抽象概念の把握は、具体的な事柄

の観点から行われる。例えば、時間は金銭の観点から把握される。人間に本来備わったこのような認識が言語表現に反映されるので You're wasting my time. といった表現が使われる。この際に、概念領域間に写像が見られ、多くの概念が写像される。このため、時間の浪費は金銭の浪費に対応するだけでなく、金銭の節約は時間の節約に対応するので時間の節約に save が使われたり、金銭にまつわる他の様々な語句が用いられたりする。さらに、名詞の意味の把握の際に、組織という抽象概念が植物という具体物の観点から把握されるので、branch office という複合名詞では branch が組織の末端を管轄する機能を持つ物という意味を有する。

　一方、Lakoff (1990) によると、事物の形の写像を行う際には、あるイメージが別のイメージに写像され、2 つの事物の間に共通する形が写像される。例えば、(3) では、砂時計の形が女性の腰の形に写像される。

(3)　My wife…whose waist is an *hourglass*.　　　　(Lakoff (1990: 66))

同様に、(1) に挙げた複合名詞 finger lakes では人間の指とアメリカの 5 大湖に共通する形状が写像される。

　これらの考えに従うと、カエルの見た目や動作を人間に写像させ、(1) で潜水士という意味で frogman が使われることは説明できる。だが、Lakoff and Johnson の分析方法では不十分である。なぜなら frog student が不自然であることが予測できない。Frog student が排除されるのは、frogman の場合のメタファー写像を可能にする特定の文脈が frog student の時には成立していないからである。したがって、この特定の文脈がどのようなものなのかを明らかにしなければならない。

2. 3. Monosemy に基づく分析

　Ruhl (1989) によると、単語は中核的な意味を有し、具体的な文脈に応じてさらにその意味が指定される。例えば、ice の場合、辞書的意味は、「水が固く凍った物」や「冷たい物」であるが、人間の持つ氷に関する知識に基づき、氷は結晶なので、(4) の例ではこの語がダイヤモンドの結晶も指す。

(4)　An old pal…is bringing me a two-caret hunk of *ice*.　　　(Ruhl (1989: 195))

　この語がメタファー的意味で用いられた際にも、この語の意味は氷の温度の冷たさに基づき、そこから、マイナスの感情、感情の欠如、動きの欠如、変化がないことが想起される (Ruhl (1989: 185-186))。これらの情報はスキーマをなしていて、(5) が示すように、文脈に応じて意味が指定される。

(5)　a. I felt that *ice* in my guts again, the dread I'd felt all afternoon.　(ibid.: 187)
　　　b. He arrived at ideas the slow way, never skating over the clear, hard *ice* of logic.　　　　　　　　　　　　　　　　　　　　　(ibid.: 188)

そのため、(5a) の ice は恐怖というマイナスの感情の意味で理解され、(5b) の ice は論理において感情が関わらないことという意味で理解される。
　さらに、複合名詞 ice queen では、氷の冷たさが拡張され、物理的に冷たい事物であれば冷たい物として人間は知覚し、物理的な冷たさが一般化されて、ice が心理的な冷たさを意味するようになる。このようなメタファー的意味は、具体的な文脈との関わりで意味が特定されることで理解される。
　この主張に従えば、複合名詞 ice queen において、なぜ ice がメタファー的意味で理解されるのかが説明できる。しかし、Ruhl の主張は特定の名詞の意味に関するもので、意味変化のパターンの一般化を試みていない。
　そこで、本論文では、複合名詞における修飾語のメタファー的意味として解釈される事柄にあるパターンが見られる場合があるのはなぜなのかを考察する。また、複合名詞における修飾語がメタファー的意味で理解可能な場合とそうでない場合があるのはなぜなのかということも考察する。さらに、複合名詞における修飾語の意味変化のパターンに関して一般化も試みる。特に、岩橋 (2015) で触れなかった、動作の類似性、事物の価値の類似性、知覚的特性の類似性が関わるメタファー的意味について論じる。[1]

3. 修飾語と主要部との間の関係

　前節では、複合名詞における修飾語と主要部との間の関係を捉えようとする先行研究を 2 つ概観した。ここでは、Jackendoff の立場と Levi の立場のうちどちらの立場を取るべきなのか考察する。

　以下では、このことについて (6) を例に挙げて考察する。

(6)　This man is {a frog/like a frog}.

この例からわかるように、潜水士について述べた (6) では、like を用いた表現もそうでない表現も自然である。したがって、Jackendoff の主張も Levi の主張もどちらも正しいということになる。しかし、人とカエルは完全に同一の事物ではないため、両者の共通点に基づいて frog は字義通りの意味より拡張された意味を有する。そのため、修飾語の意味が拡張されて複合名詞の意味が理解されると考えるべきであるが、Jackendoff や Levi の説明ではこのことを捉えられない。

　そこで、本論文では、文脈に応じて具体名詞の意味が柔軟に変化することを捉えるため、関連性理論における演繹的推論とアドホック概念構築 (Carston (1996, 2002), Vega-Moreno (2004)) の観点から分析を行う。これらの研究では、文脈に応じて演繹的推論やアドホック概念構築をすると単語は本来と異なる意味に解釈できることが述べられている。さらに、メタファー表現や他の発話の解釈の仕方は個々の表現や文脈に応じて変わることや、ある単語の意味に本来含まれていない事柄もこれらのプロセスを経て解釈できることも述べられている。このような主張と異なり、本論文では、様々なメタファー表現で解釈される事柄にあるパターンが見られることや、具体名詞の有する機能の種類がそのパターンに関わることを示す。さらに、意味解釈においてこのようなパターンが見られないものもあることも示す。

4. 理論的前提：関連性理論

　関連性理論において発話解釈は、処理労力が少ない解釈の仕方で、同音異義語の意味を一義化したり、指示対象を決めたり、省略された要素を補ったりして表意、すなわち言語化された事柄の内容を把握し、そのうえ言外の意味を解釈して行われるものである (Wilson and Sperber (2002: 262-264))。[2]

　文脈含意は言外の意味の解釈に関わり、表意や文脈想定を基に演繹的に推論して得られる (Sperber and Wilson (1986/1995: 103-108))。このプロセスを (7) を例に見ると以下のようになる。

(7)　Caroline is our princess.　　　　　　　　　　　　(Carston (2002: 347))

聞き手がカロラインは王女であると知っていて、(7) の発話で彼女の育ち方が良くないことを話者が話している際には、表意の内容や、王女は溺愛されて甘やかされている人であるという文脈想定を前提として用い、文脈含意によりカロラインが溺愛されて甘やかされていることが結論として把握される。この結論と文脈想定が推意となり、発話の言外の意味に関わる。

　この他に、発話の解釈ではアドホック概念も構築され、ある語が表意で指す概念が文脈に応じて字義通りの概念よりも広げられたり狭められたりする。また、そのためにある語が本来指す概念と近似する概念や異なる概念を指したり、本来指す概念よりも限られた概念を指したりする (Carston (2002: 321-334))。例えば、(7) では、推意の内容に応じて PRINCESS* という、溺愛されて甘やかされている王女や溺愛されて甘やかされている王女以外の人に当てはまる緩められたアドホック概念が構築される。

5. 分析

5.1. 複合名詞における修飾語のメタファー的意味に見られるパターン

　複合名詞の意味理解に関わる特性を、単語の指示対象自体から必然的に想起できるかどうかの観点から見ると、事物の知覚的特性の類似性と事物

の価値や動作の類似性との間で想起のしやすさに違いがあることがわかる。

    (8)   a. *Although it is ice, it is not cold.
            b. Although it is a pet, it is not cherished.
            c. Although it is a frog, it does not dive into the water.

(8a-c) が示すように、氷の冷たさは単語の指示対象そのものから常に想起されるが、ペットが大事にされることやカエルの動作は特定の文脈でなければ想起されないことがわかる。したがって、温度等の事物の知覚的特性はその語の指示対象自体から想起され、ペットなどの事物の価値やカエルなどの動作は文脈から想起されることがわかる。
　さらに、事物の知覚的特性はメタファー的意味の理解の際に想起しやすいため、事物の知覚的特性が修飾語の意味に関わる複合名詞は生産性が高い。したがって氷以外の事物を指す語も (9) に示すように、複合名詞において修飾語として使われる。

    (9)   stone heart, iron heart, honey love, honey girl   (COCA より抜粋)

これらのことから様々な具体名詞には、知覚的特性の類似性に基づいて感情や性格に関するメタファー的意味が理解されるという意味変化のパターンが特に顕著に見られることがわかる。

5.2. 複合名詞の意味理解に関わる特性と文脈との関わり

　複合名詞では、修飾語として使われやすい名詞とそうでない名詞がある。

    (10)   a. #frog student, #fish student, #butterfly man, #servant dog
             b. ice princess, ice man, ice eyes   (COCA より抜粋)
             c. pet project, pet phrase, pet street game   (COCA より抜粋)

(10a) では、カエルや魚の泳ぎ方や蝶が自由に動き回ること、召使の従順

さを基に新たな複合名詞を作るのが不自然で、単なる動作の類似性だけに基づいて修飾語の意味を解釈できない。一方、(10b) では、氷の冷たさを基に様々な複合名詞を作るのが自然で、氷の特性に基づいて、冷淡さやよそよそしさといった修飾語である ice の意味を解釈できる。また、(10c) では、ペットが飼い主に大事にされていることを基に様々な複合名詞を作るのが自然で、ペットのこのような特性を基に、大事にされていることや気に入られていることといった修飾語として用いられる pet の意味を解釈できる。

　これらのことから、複合名詞では、修飾語のメタファー的意味に決まったパターンが見られて理解が容易なものとそうでないものがあることがわかる。特に、修飾語のメタファー的意味の中でも、泳ぐことなどの動作の類似性と比べて、事物の知覚的特性の類似性や大事にする物といった事物の価値の類似性が想起されやすいというパターンが見られることがわかる。

　したがって、(8a-c), (9), (10a-c) の事実を踏まえると、動作に関するメタファー的意味を解釈するのが最も文脈に依存した解釈になり、事物の価値を想起するプロセスは文脈依存度が中程度で、事物の知覚的特性を想起するプロセスは最も文脈依存度が低いことがわかる。さらに、これらのことから、ある知覚的特性を有する事物を指すのが様々な具体名詞の中核的機能で、この中核的機能が、複合名詞において感情や性格に関する修飾語の意味に関わっていることがわかる。このために様々な具体名詞に、知覚的特性の類似性に基づいて感情や性格に関するメタファー的意味が理解されるという意味変化の最も主要なパターンが見られる。

5.3. 複合名詞における修飾語の意味理解

　以下では、前節で見た具体名詞の指示対象や文脈から想起される特性が複合名詞の意味理解にどう関わるのかを見ていく。まず、(11) を例に、知覚的特性が修飾語の意味理解にどう関わるのか見ていく。

(11)　On the street she is called *Ice Princess* or "232," a reference to a two-century-plus sentence she doled out to a multiple murderer in 1993.

(COCA 2002; 一部改変)

(11) では、具体名詞の指示対象自体から想起される氷の特性、すなわち、氷は冷たくて血が通っておらず冷酷であるという想定を基に、冷酷であることが推意として理解される。この推意が得られるので、表意では複合名詞 Ice Princess における ICE* という緩められたアドホック概念が、人の冷酷さに当てはまるものとして解釈され、冷酷な女性という意味でこの複合名詞が理解される。なお、この例の解釈に関わる想定が事物の価値や動作に関する想定と異なる点は、(8a-c) から分かるように、指示対象となる事物から冷たさが必ず想起され、他の想定と比べて想起しやすいことである。

　次に、価値の類似性が修飾語の意味理解にどう関わるのか (12) を例に見ていく。

(12)　One was confirmation bias. Everyone had their *pet theory* and they looked for confirming evidence to support it.　　　　　　　(COCA 2005)

(12) では、ペットは大事にされているという、文脈から想起される想定を基に、誰にでも自分が大事にする理論があったということが推意として理解される。そのうえ、pet という語そのものから単独で想起されない推意も理解される。具体的には、人がある理論を大事にしているのであればその人がその理論を支持していることになるから、演繹的推論により、誰にでも自分が支持する理論があったということが推意として理解される。[3] このような推意が得られるので、表意では、複合名詞 pet theory における PET* という緩められたアドホック概念が、愛玩動物以外の物に当てはまり、自分が大事にし、支持している物に当てはまるものとして解釈され、自分が大事にして支持している理論という意味でこの複合名詞が理解される。なお、事物の価値に関する想定が、(11) の複合名詞の意味理解に関わる知覚的特性に関する想定と異なる点は、(8a-c) から分かるように、この想定が特定の文脈でなければ想起されず、より想起しにくいという点である。

　最後に、(13) で、動作の類似性が意味理解にどう関わるのか見ていく。

(13) It was while creeping along the ocean floor 11 years ago that Nargeolet who saw the world as a French Navy *frogman* saw something through Nautile's porthole.　　　　　　　　　　　　　　　　　　　　　(COCA 1998)

(13) では、カエルは生きるうえで水中に潜るという、文脈から想起される想定を基に、生きるうえで水中に潜る人ということが推意として理解される。また、この推意が得られることから、表意では、複合名詞 frogman における FROG* という緩められたアドホック概念が、カエル以外にも当てはまり、生きるうえで水中に潜る人や生き物に当てはまるものとして解釈される。このため、軍隊での任務に従事する潜水士という意味でこの複合名詞が理解される。なお、動作に関する想定も事物の知覚的特性に関する想定と異なり、(8a-c) から分かるように、特定の文脈でなければ想起されない。さらに、(14a-d) に示すように、生きるために水に潜るという動作の目的がカエルと軍隊での任務に従事する潜水士との間で共通すると、このメタファー的解釈が成立する。

(14)　a. They {dived/#became frogmen} for pleasure.　　(COCA 2017; 一部改変)
　　　b. Having {dived/#become a frogman}, he feels the current taking him downriver.　　　　　　　　　　　　　　　(COCA 1995; 一部改変)
　　　c. They became frogmen to fulfil their military mission.
　　　d. This theory is his pet theory because the scholar {supports/cherishes/ thinks highly of} it.

このことから、pet theory のような事物の価値の類似性が関わる複合名詞と比べて、複合名詞 frogman では修飾語が指す事物と主要部が指す事物との間の共通点を多く想起する必要がある。このように、意味解釈に関わる想定の情報量がより多くなるため、価値の類似性が関わる複合名詞よりも動作とその目的の類似性が関わる複合名詞の方が意味の理解が困難である。
　これまでに見てきた分析によると、複合名詞における修飾語の意味を理解する際には、修飾語となる具体名詞の指示対象から内在的特性や文脈との関わりで想起される特性を聞き手や読み手は想起する。それにより、聞

き手や読み手は、修飾語として使われる具体名詞を本来の意味よりも広い意味で理解することがわかる。関連性理論によると、このことは、緩められたアドホック概念が構築されると考えることで説明される。

　複合名詞における修飾語を意味解釈のしやすさの観点から見ると、事物の知覚的特性が複合名詞における修飾語の意味理解に関わる際には、メタファー的意味が最も理解しやすくなる。これは、単語の指示対象自体から想起可能な情報が関わるためである。このことから、具体名詞はある知覚的特性を有する事物を指すという中核的機能を有し、それに基づいて複合名詞における修飾語のメタファー的意味として感情や性格に関する意味が理解される。一方、動作とその目的や事物の価値に関する情報は文脈との関わりで想起され、それに基づいて複合名詞における修飾語のメタファー的意味が理解される。特に、動作とその目的を想起する際には、事物の価値を想起する際と比べて、修飾語が指す事物と主要部が指す事物との類似点をより多く想起する必要があるため、動作とその目的の類似性は事物の価値の類似性と比べて想起しにくくなる。

6. 結語

　本論文では、複合名詞における修飾語のメタファー的意味がどのようにして理解されるかについて、以下の3点を考察した。(i) 複合名詞における修飾語のメタファー的意味を理解する際には、具体名詞の指示対象自体から想起可能な特性や特定の文脈で想起可能な特性が関わるので、修飾語のメタファー的意味を理解しやすい場合とそうでない場合が見られる。(ii) 特定の文脈でメタファー的意味が理解されるのは、事物の価値や、動作とその目的に関する情報が特定の文脈で想起されるためである。とりわけ、動作に関する情報を想起するには動作の目的を含めて詳細に想起する必要があるため、このような情報は事物の価値に関する情報と比べて文脈に依存したものとなる。(iii) メタファー的意味として感情や性格が特に理解されやすいのは、具体名詞が本来、ある知覚的特性を有する事物を指すという中核的機能を有し、その事物の知覚的特性に基づいて感情や性格が理解されるためである。ただ、感情や性格を述べる際に、具体名詞の代わりに icy のような具体名詞から派生した形容詞や、cold などの感覚形容詞

もメタファー的意味で用いられる。さらに、具体名詞は文の補語としてメタファー的意味で用いられたり、人や物を指すのにメタファー的意味で用いられたりすることもある。それらの場合に、どのような意味の違いが生じるのか今後考察する余地がある。

[1] 岩橋 (2015) では、comb, mouth, branch, line といった語を取り上げ、形の類似性や機能の類似性、空間関係の類似性、抽象的な関係の類似性に基づくメタファー的意味について論じられている。それによると、演繹的推論においては形や機能、空間関係、抽象的関係に関する想定が用いられ、それに基づいてメタファー的意味が理解される。また、形や機能に関する想定は単語の指示対象そのものから想起可能だが、空間関係や抽象関係に関する想定は文脈との関わりで想起される。そのため、具体名詞は事物の形や機能を述べるという中核的機能を有し、それを基に形や機能が類似した他の事物を具体名詞が指し、メタファー的意味が理解される。
[2] 同音異義語の場合、ある意味の中に他の意味と近似する点や共通する点が含まれないため解釈に一義化が関わる。
[3] このように演繹的推論により、ある単語の本来の意味に含まれていない事柄がメタファー的意味を解釈する際に理解されることがある。このことに関しては、Vega Moreno (2004) を参照。

参考文献

Carston, Robyn (1996) "Enrichment and Loosening: Complementary Processes in Deriving the Proposition Expressed," *UCL Working Papers in Linguistics* 8, 205-232.

Carston, Robyn (2002) *Thoughts and Utterances: The Pragmatics of Explicit Communication*, Blackwell, Oxford.

岩橋一樹 (2015)「英語における具体名詞の中核的意味とメタファー表現」、『言葉のしんそう（深層・真相）―大庭幸男教授退職記念論文集―』、549-560、英宝社、東京。

Jackendoff, Ray (1975) "Morphological and Semantic Regularities in the Lexicon," *Language* 51, 639-671.

Lakoff, George (1990) "The Invariance Hypothesis: Is Abstract Reason Based on Image-Schemas?" *Cognitive Linguistics* 1, 39-74.

Lakoff, George and Mark Johnson (1980) *Metaphors We Live By*, University of Chicago Press, Chicago.

岩橋 一樹

Levi, Judith N. (1978) *The Syntax and Semantics of Complex Nominals*, Academic Press, New York.

Ruhl, Charles (1989) *On Monosemy: A Study in Linguistic Semantics*, State University of New York Press, Albany, N. Y.

Sperber, Dan and Deirdre Wilson (1986/95) *Relevance: Communication and Cognition*, Blackwell, Oxford.

Vega-Moreno, Rosa Elena (2004) "Metaphor Interpretation and Emergence," *UCL Working Papers in Linguistics* 16, 297-322.

Wilson, Deirdre and Dan Sperber (2002) "Relevance Theory," *UCL Working Papers in Linguistics* 14, 249-287.

Corpus

Davies, Mark. (2004-) *British National Corpus* (from Oxford University Press). Available online at https://www.english-corpora.org/bnc/.

Davies, Mark. (2008-) *The Corpus of Contemporary American English (COCA): 560 million words, 1990-present*. Available online at https://www.english-corpora.org/coca/.

副詞的 the other way (a)round は何を
明示的に伝達するのか

黒川 尚彦

キーワード：関連性理論，表意，「逆」，関数的プロセス

1. はじめに

　本稿では、副詞的に用いられる the other way (a)round（以下、OWR と略記[1]）によって明示的に伝達される内容には 2 つのタイプがあるものの、それぞれ 1 つの概念的意味から異なる解釈プロセスによって得られることを関連性理論の枠組みで論じる。2 つのタイプとは以下の (1)(2) である。

(1) This jacket is styled for the American market, so the pocket zips open bottom to top and the main zip connects **the other way round.** (BNC)

(2) But how do we know that it is vocationally advantageous to study history or to put it **the other way round**, that to study history is not vocationally disadvantageous? (BNC)

(1) の OWR はポケットのファスナーに対してジャケット前部のファスナーの開閉が「逆」方向であることを表している。一方 (2) の OWR は、「歴史を研究することは職業上有利である」と「歴史を研究することは職業上不利ではない」という 2 つの命題がそれぞれ肯定的視点と否定的視点という「逆」の視点からの捉え方であることを示している。どちらも「逆」という概念の関与が共通しているにもかかわらず、(1) では OWR によって示される「逆」が具体的に top to bottom と言い換えられるのに対し、(2) の OWR には適切な言い換えはない。要するに、(2) の OWR は「逆」として受け入れられるのに対し、(1) の OWR は「逆」を手がかりに top to bottom と解釈される。なぜこのような解釈の違いが生じるのだろうか。

黒川 尚彦

本稿の構成は以下の通りである。次節で OWR の 3 つの用法を概観し、それに共通する「逆」という概念について論じる。3 節では、本稿で取り上げる副詞用法 OWR の特徴を記述する。特に、OWR がどのような動詞を修飾するのか、どのレベルで機能するのかについて論じる。4 節では (1)(2) で見たような 2 つのタイプの副詞用法の OWR の解釈プロセスを明らかにする。とりわけ「逆」として解釈される場合と、その「逆」が指し示す内容まで解釈される場合とでは、何が異なるのか、またなぜこのようなことが起こるのかについて関連性理論による分析を行う。特に、後者の場合に関数的解釈という新たな解釈プロセスが関わることを指摘する。

2. OWR の 3 用法と「逆」

2.1 OWR の 3 用法 [2]

本節では OWR の 3 用法を概観する。まず、(1)(2) で例示したような OWR の副詞用法である。一般的に副詞用法の OWR は動詞の様態が先行命題とは「逆」方向であることを表す。次に、OWR は (3) で見られるように叙述的に用いられる。この用法における OWR は be のようなコピュラ動詞と共起し、主語は先行発話（先行命題）を指示する it であることが多い。たとえば (3) の OWR は、リッキーがビルの後についていくという先行命題内容とは「逆」のことが起こりうることを指し示している。

(3)　First, Bill will walk down the path and then Ricky will follow him. Or it could be **the other way round**. They may, indeed, walk down the path side by side. (BNC)

(4)　These are questions about the impact of social policy upon economic policy rather than **the other way round**. (BNC)

最後は (4) のような等位接続詞に後続し、第 2 等位項として機能する OWR である。[3] この OWR は (1) と同様に、「逆」という概念を表すのではなく、それをもとにより具体的な内容 (the impact of economic policy upon social policy) を指し示していると解釈されるだろう。この解釈から示唆されるように、(4) の OWR は vice versa で置き換え可能である。

　OWR という言語表現には少なくとも 3 通りの用法があることが分かる。次に、3 用法に共通する「逆」という概念について見てみよう。

2.2「逆」と認識される対立関係

　「逆」とは 2 項対立関係を表す概念である。これを別の観点から捉えると、「逆」を認識するには、まず 2 つの要素が特定され、さらにその要素間である点における対立関係が認められる必要がある。前者の要件はほとんど議論の余地がないと思われるが、後者の要件に関して、人がどのような関係を対立と認識するのかを明確にする必要がある。

　対立関係が認められるケースには 3 種類あると考えられる。[4] 第一に 2 つの要素が語彙的反意関係にある場合である。これは、「高い」と「低い」などに見られる関係である。次に、肯定・否定という極性における対立関係である。たとえば、「走る」と「走らない」の関係であり、これはあらゆる概念に適用可能と言えるだろう。場合によっては語彙的反意関係と重複するかもしれない。たとえば「生きている」に対する「生きていない」は「死んでいる」とほぼ同義であり、「生きている」と「死んでいる」は反意関係にある。本稿において重要なのは、これらを峻別することではなく、どちらも「逆」と認識可能であるという点である。第 3 の対立関係は方向性における「逆」である。ふつう「A から B へ」と「B から A へ」という 2 つの事態は容易に「逆」関係にあると認識されるだろう。これは対応関係における「逆」とも捉えられる。「A から B へ」では A が起点で B が着点であり、「B から A へ」では B が起点で A が着点である。つまり「〜から…へ」という 2 項関係による意味づけとその値の対応関係が逆と言えるだろう。このように「逆」には 3 種類の対立関係がある。

　繰り返しになるが、「逆」を定義づけることには十分意義があるが、本稿ではどのような 2 つの事態を「逆」関係にあると認識できるかを特定することの方が重要である。というのも「逆」の認識、つまり「逆」の事態の想定可能性が OWR の解釈に影響を及ぼすからである。

3. 副詞用法としての OWR

3.1 統語的特徴

　様態を表す副詞的 OWR が共起する動詞句の種類から始めよう。まず、改めて (1) を考えてみよう。OWR はジャケット前部のファスナーとポケットのファスナーの開ける方向が「逆」であるという様を描写している。このように OWR は方向性を概念的に含む動詞句の様態を表す。

> (5) To re-seal a half-used cartridge, take the piece you cut off the end of the nozzle and push it into the nozzle **the other way round**. (BNC)

(5) の OWR は push it into the nozzle という動詞句を修飾する。動詞 push に方向性は認めにくいものの、ノズルに押し込むという動詞句が表す行為に方向性を認めることは難しくない。このように、OWR は動詞句によって表される行為に含まれる方向性の様態を特定していると考えられる。
　しかし OWR は、必ずしも動詞句の様態を特定する役割を果たすわけではない。(6) が示すように、OWR が「機能する」(ないしは「起こる」)という概念を表す動詞と共起すると、ホスト節全体で先行節の命題内容の「逆」の事態を表す。

> (6) No manager wants to sell his best players but Howard Wilkinson is practical enough to realise that we can't just buy other people's best players—it works **the other way round** sometimes. (BNC)

たとえば (6) の OWR は機能の仕方を特定しているというより、節全体で it によって指示される先行命題の内容とは「逆」の事態が時折起こることを指し示していると考えられる。より具体的には、「自分のチームの最高の選手を売りたいと思う監督などいないが、ウィルキンソンは他チームの最高の選手を買えないことを理解するくらい現実的だ」という先行命題の内容とは「逆」の事態が起こりうることを OWR だけではなく、それを含む節全体で伝えている。(1) の場合、OWR は top to bottom のような別の様態副詞句で言い換えられるのに対し、(6) では OWR を含む節全体

が「逆」の事態を指し示している。およそ「自分のチームの最高の選手を売って、他チームの最高の選手を買いたい監督もいる」のような命題内容を指し示していると解釈されるだろう。換言すれば、(1) では OWR が「逆」の様態を指し示すのに対し、(6) では OWR を含む節全体が「逆」の事態を指し示す。

　これと類似しているのが、Halliday and Hassan (1976) が一般的動詞（general verb）と呼ぶ do[5] と共起する OWR である。このとき、(6) と同様に、OWR は do と一体化して機能し、先行する命題内容の動詞句が表す行為とは「逆」の行為を行うことを表す。先行命題をもとに「逆」の内容を指し示すという点においては (6) と類似しているものの、(6) が命題全体の「逆」の事態を指し示すのに対し、do+OWR は「逆」の行為（動詞句に相当）を指し示す点において異なる。(7) を見てみよう。

(7) Do you measure food in ounces or grams? Most cookery columns have settled into providing metric measurements first, followed by ounces. *SHE* [a British women's monthly magazine —nk] does it **the other way round**, because we're convinced that not only our readers, but most UK cooks, don't cook metric. (BNC)

(7) では OWR が does it と一体化し、先行命題の動詞句によって示される手順とは「逆」の手順で行われる行為を指し示していると解釈されるだろう。およそ「まず（重さを）ポンド法で示し、その後メートル法で示す」という行為と考えられる。OWR は、(1) のように単独で様態副詞として機能することもあれば、(6)(7) のように節や動詞句と合成することにより、それぞれに対応する内容を指し示すこともある。

　最後に、OWR は「話す」「尋ねる」を意味するスピーチアクトに関わる動詞とも共起する。このような場合、OWR はたいてい先行命題の捉え方とは「逆」の捉え方であることを表す。たとえば (2) の to put it the other way round は、定型表現 to put it briefly / clearly / simply の一種と見なせるが、or で接続された 2 つの命題内容の第 2 項を第 1 項とは「逆」の視点で捉えていることを示していると考えられる。簡潔に言えば、歴史を研究することが第 1 項では肯定的に捉えられているのに対し、第 2 項

では否定的に捉えられている。また定型表現としての to put it 副詞句は、一般的にホスト命題に対するメタ的なコメントとして機能する。副詞句が briefly の場合、後続するホスト命題が先行命題を簡潔に言い直したことを、clearly であればより明確に描写したことを示す。同様に OWR の場合には、後続するホスト命題が先行する命題内容に対して捉え方が「逆」であることを示す。

　まとめると、副詞的 OWR は基本的に動詞句の様態を表す。ただしその貢献の仕方は共起する動詞句に左右される。方向性が認められる動詞句と共起するとき典型的に様態を表す。これに対し、「機能する」や「起こる」を意味する動詞と共起する場合、OWR を含む節全体が先行命題の内容と「逆」の事態を表し、行為一般を表す do と共起すると、OWR を含む動詞句が先行命題内の動詞句とは「逆」の行為を表す。またスピーチアクトに関わる動詞句と共起する場合、OWR を含む動詞句はホスト命題が先行命題と「逆」の関係であることを示すメタ的コメントとして機能する。

3.2 意味的特徴

　本節では意味的側面に焦点を当てる。2.2 節で「逆」に 3 種類あることを示した。具体的には、語彙的反意関係の「逆」、極性的「逆」、そして方向性（または対応関係）における「逆」である。この 3 種類の「逆」は副詞的 OWR でも認められる。では、順に見ていこう。

　(8) の OWR は語彙的反意関係にある「逆」として解釈されるだろう。

(8)　'... Not a pretty sight. Dead or alive,' she added. 'Why would anyone want to kill Hereward, do you suppose?' 'I would have thought you could ask it **the other way round**. Why should anyone want to preserve him alive?' (BNC)

端的には、ヒアウォードを亡き者にしたい理由を問うのか、逆に生かしたい理由を問うのか、である。先行命題の kill Hereward は make Hereward dead を意味することから、OWR の解釈を示した preserve him alive と反意関係にあると捉えられる。(8) の OWR は問い方の様態ではなく、問う内容が「逆」であることを示している。確かに ask はスピーチアクトに関わるが、OWR が示す「逆」はコンテクストに依存することに注意が必要

である。

　次は極性的「逆」の例である。(9) の OWR は法案名の付け方が「逆」であることを示している。具体的には、先行命題の based on what they hope it will accomplish（法案の成就を期待して）とは「逆」の based on what they do not hope it will accomplish（成就を期待せずに）と解釈されるだろう。

(9)　Normally, senators and congressmen name a bill based on what they hope it will accomplish. For instance, the Patient Protection and Affordability Act purports to make health care more affordable. ... But I've recently discovered that the names of bills sometimes work **the other way around**. Our conference spent weeks opposing the Violence Against Women Act on the understanding that it would enact violence against women. (COCA)

　最後に、方向性における「逆」関係を示す (1) と (7) の OWR について考えよう。繰り返しになるが、(1) の OWR は top to bottom と解釈される。ファスナーを開ける際の方向性の点でポケットの場合とジャケット前部の場合とで「逆」であることを示している。もちろん方向性は物理的な場合に限らない。(7) のように、重さを提示する順序も方向性の一種である。また、2.2 節で述べたように、方向性の「逆」は対応関係における「逆」と見ることもでき、こう捉えるなら物理的かどうかは問題になることはない。(7) の OWR は、先行命題の「ポンド法が 1 番目、メートル法が 2 番目」という対応関係の「逆」と理解されるだろう。

　3 節では、副詞的 OWR と共起する動詞にはいくつかタイプがあり、3 種類ある「逆」のいずれにも解釈されうることを示した。解釈においてもうひとつ重要なことは、OWR が「逆」の様態を表すだけでなく、他の構成要素と一体化し、より具体的な内容を指し示すことがある点である。

4. 副詞的 OWR は何を明示的に伝達するのか

　副詞的 OWR は、共起する動詞句の様態として機能するが、共起する動詞句に応じて、単独で先行命題によって示される行為の様態とは「逆」の

様態を示す場合、OWR を含む動詞句全体で先行命題の動詞句と「逆」の行為を示す場合、OWR を含む節全体で先行する命題内容と「逆」の事態を示す場合があることを示した。さらに、スピーチアクトに関わる動詞句と共起すると、メタレベルで機能することも見た。ただ OWR は、メタレベルで貢献する場合「逆」という概念として解釈されるのに対し、他の場合には「逆」という概念を手がかりにそれがどのような様態、行為、事態なのかが解釈される。本節では、このような解釈の違いが生じる理由を明らかにする。特に、OWR が有する「逆」という概念からそれが指し示す解釈を得るにあたり関数的解釈プロセスが関わることを提案する。

　まず、(1) と (2) の違いを考察しよう。上述したように、(1) の OWR は先行命題内の bottom to top をもとにその「逆」の top to bottom を指し示していると解釈される。換言すれば、OWR は「逆」という概念を表すが、(1) の発話では top to bottom を指し示している。一方 (2) の OWR は先行命題の捉え方とホスト命題の捉え方が「逆」であることを表すだけで、別の何かを指し示すわけではない。ここで「逆」という概念が 2 項対立関係であり、「逆」の認識に対立関係にある 2 つの要素の同定が必要であることを思い出そう。(2) では言語的に明示された先行命題とホスト命題が 2 つの要素であるのに対し、(1) では一方の要素 (bottom to top) しか言語的に同定されない。関連性理論的に言えば、(2) では OWR がコード化する概念が要求する 2 つの要素が満たされることで聞き手の関連性の期待が十分満たされ解釈がその時点で止まる。[6] 一方、(1) では片方の要素しか満たされないため聞き手の関連性の期待が満たされず、さらに解釈を進めることになる。最終的に OWR は top to bottom を指し示すという解釈に至ることで聞き手の関連性の期待が満たされ、そこで解釈が止まる。

　さらに、仮に (1) の OWR が (10) のように「逆」と解釈されたとすると、命題内容の真偽判断は不可能である。これに対し、(11) のような OWR が指し示す内容が特定された命題であれば真偽判断は可能となる。では (11) の top to bottom という解釈はどのように得られるのだろうか。

(10)　　... THE MAIN ZIP CONNECTS THE OTHER WAY ROUND

(11)　　... THE MAIN ZIP CONNECTS TOP TO BOTTOM

　OWR の解釈プロセスの分析の前に、関連性理論による発話解釈プロセスを概観しよう。聞き手はまず発話を解読 (decoding) することで論理形式を得る。その論理形式を発展させて表意（基礎表意と高次表意）という話し手による明示的伝達内容を得る。さらに、推論により推意（推意前提と推意帰結）という非明示的内容を導出する。表意は (12) のように定義づけられるが、論理形式から表意を得るプロセスには一義化、飽和、自由拡充、アドホック概念構築があるとこれまで考えられてきた。

(12)　An explicature (proposition) communicated by an utterance is an 'explicature' of the utterance if and only if it is a development of (a) a linguistically encoded logical form of the utterance, or of (b) a sentential subpart of a logical form. (Carston 2002: 124)

この 4 つのうち飽和は、語のコード化された意味に含まれるスロットを満たすプロセスであり、OWR が 2 つのスロットを含む概念であることから、OWR の解釈に関わる可能性が考えられる。しかしたとえ飽和を通してOWR のスロットが満たされたとしても、OWR が指し示す内容を得ることはできない。したがって、表意 (11) は飽和とは別のプロセスによって得られると結論づけられる。

　そこで本稿では、OWR の 2 つのスロットが 1 つしか満たされない場合、「逆」という概念をもとに関数的プロセスにより表意が得られることを提案する。2.2 節で述べたように、ある要素の「逆」には 3 通りの可能性がある。これは、OWR が表す「逆」という 2 項関係において、一方のスロットが先行命題で満たされると 3 通りのいずれかが自動的に出力される関数のように機能することを示唆する。これを関数的プロセスと呼び、(13) として定義づける。

(13)　関数的プロセス
　　　2 つのスロットを関係づける概念において、一方のスロットが満たされることにより、他方のスロットの値が自動的に算出される語用論的プロセス

関数的プロセスがどのように機能するのか、OWR が様態副詞として働

く場合 (1) から見てみよう。(1) では等位接続された 2 つの命題について、第 1 項の the pocket zips と第 2 項の the main zip に対比が見られる。また open と connects がほぼ同じ内容を表すことを考慮すると、「逆」が含むスロットは bottom to top で満たされるだろう。これは方向性が重要であることから、方向性が「逆」の top to bottom が関数的に出力される。

　次に、OWR を含む節全体で機能する (6) について考察する。3.1 節で述べたように、(6) の OWR は it works と一体化し、it が指示する先行命題が「逆」に機能することもあることを表す。OWR のスロットを満たすのは (14a) のような命題であろう。

(14)　　a. NO MANAGER WANTS TO SELL HIS BEST PLAYERS AND BUY OTHER PEOPLE'S BEST PLAYERS
　　　　b. SOME MANAGERS WANT TO SELL THEIR BEST PLAYERS AND BUY OTHER PEOPLE'S BEST PLAYERS

(14a) はおよそ「自分のチームのよい選手を売り、他チームのよい選手を買いたいと思う監督がいない」ことを伝えることから、OWR を含む節は (14b) のような極性が「逆」の命題を指し示すと解釈されるだろう。sell と buy の反意関係から、語彙的反意の「逆」の可能性があるように見えるが、自分のチームのよい選手を買うということは起こりえない。したがって、そのような解釈が行われることはない。

　一般的動詞 do と共起する OWR も基本的にはこれと同じである。上述したように、(7) の様態副詞 OWR は does it と意味的に合成することで、先行命題とは「逆」の行為を行うことを表す。先行命題は、料理のコラムでは一般に重さがメートル法・ポンド法という順で提示されることを述べている。これに対し、ホスト命題は雑誌 SHE がそれを「逆」に行っていることを伝える。このことから、OWR のスロットを満たすのは (15a) のような動詞句であり、提示順の重要性から、方向性が「逆」となる (15b) が関数的に導出されるだろう。

(15)　　a. PROVIDE GRAMS FIRST, FOLLOWED BY OUNCES
　　　　b. PROVIDE OUNCES FIRST, AND FOLLOWED BY GRAMS

　まとめると、OWR の解釈においてスロットを満たす要素は OWR の働きに依拠する。(1) の OWR は単独で機能するため、スロットは副詞的要素で満たされる。(6) では it works と合成し節として機能することから、スロットは節で満たされ、(7) では動詞句 does it と一体化するため、スロットも動詞句で満たされる。このように、関数的プロセスは論理形式を表意へと発展させるプロセスの 1 つと考えられる。OWR は 2 つのスロットが満たされ「逆」として表意に貢献する場合（たとえば (2)）もあるが、1 つのスロットしか満たされず真偽判断可能でないとき、関数的プロセスを通して「逆」が指し示す内容が導出される。

5. 結語

　本稿では副詞的 OWR に焦点を当て、「逆」として解釈される場合と「逆」によって指し示される内容として解釈される場合の違いを明らかにした。「逆」が有する 2 つのスロットは、前者では発話によってどちらも満たされるのに対し、後者では一方しか満たされないことから関数的プロセスによって他方を特定することを示した。

　表意が関数的プロセスによって得られる場合、OWR 自体は命題に直接貢献しない。ところがこれまで関連性理論では、概念的意味を有する語は表意を構成すると考えられてきた。理論的には、表意の定義を修正するか、新たにプロセスを設定するか、という 2 つの可能性が考えられるが、後者が妥当であろう。ただ本当に妥当かどうかは、関数的プロセスが OWR 以外の言語表現でも観察されるかどうかによるだろう。その候補のひとつが opposite（より具体的には、the opposite is true など (Kurokawa (2013))）が考えられる。ただ、これは概念的に OWR と酷似している。概念的に異なる言語表現でも見られるかどうかの検証は今後の課題としたい。

---

[1] 本稿では the other way round と the other way around は意味の差はないものとみなし、この 2 つを区別しない。

[2] 3 用法の詳細は、Kurokawa (2019) を参照のこと。
[3] Huddleston and Pullum (2002) や Napoli (1983) に従い、than を等位接続詞とみなす。
[4] 3 種類の対立関係については、Kurokawa (2013) も参照されたい。
[5] Halliday and Hassan (1976) では do the same の do を general verb と分析し、何らかの行為を行うことを表す動詞と考えている。
[6] 関連性理論の発話解釈ストラテジーについては、Wilson and Sperber (2002)、Carston (2002)、Iten (2005) を参照のこと。

参考文献

Blakemore, Diane (1992) *Understanding Utterances: An Introduction to Pragmatics*, Blackwell, Oxford.

Carston, Robyn (2002) *Thoughts and Utterances: The Pragmatics of Explicit Communication*, Blackwell, Oxford.

Halliday, Michael A. K. and Ruqaiya Hassan (1976) *Cohesion in English*, Longman, London.

Huddleston, Rodney and Geoffrey K. Pullum (2002) *The Cambridge Grammar of the English Language*, Cambridge University Press, Cambridge.

Iten, Corinne (2005) *Linguistic Meaning, Truth Conditions and Relevance: The Case of Concessives*, Palgrave, Basingstroke.

Kurokawa, Naohiko (2013) *Oppositeness and Relevance*, Ph. D Thesis, Osaka University.

Kurokawa, Naohiko (2019) "A Descriptive Study of *the other way (a)round*," *Memoirs of Osaka Institute of Technology* 63(2), 21–35. Available online at http://id.nii. ac.jp/1360/00000245/.

Napoli, Donna Jo (1983) "Comparative Ellipsis: A Phrase Structure Analysis," *Linguistic Inquiry* 14, 675–694.

Sperber, Dan and Deidre Wilson (1986/1995) *Relevance: Communication and Cognition*, Blackwell, Oxford.

Wilson, Deidre and Dan Sperber (1993) "Linguistic Form and Relevance," *Lingua* 90, 1–25.

Wilson, Deidre and Dan Sperber (2002) "Relevance Theory," *UCL Working Papers in Linguistics* 14. 249–290.

Corpora
Davies, Mark (2004-) *British National Corpus* (from Oxford University Press).

副詞的 the other way (a)round は何を明示的に伝達するのか

Available online at https://www.english-corpora.org/bnc/.
Davies, Mark (2008-) *The Corpus of Contemporary American English (COCA): 560 million words, 1990-present*. Available online at https://www.english-corpora.org/coca/.

Post-nominal Adjectives and the Deictic Perspective System*

Kenta Mizutani

Keywords: post-nominal adjectives, Deictic Perspective System

1. Introduction

In general, adjectives alone cannot occur immediately after the nouns they modify, as shown in (1).

(1)　a tall man / *a man tall　　　　　　　(Sadler and Arnold (1994: 197))

However, some adjectives can appear in the post-nominal position even when they are not used with any complements or adjuncts, as in (2).

(2)　the stars visible

In this paper, we call adjectives like (2) a "post-nominal adjective". It is claimed that they express temporal properties of the modified nouns. In (2), for example, the post-nominal adjective *visible* denotes the temporal state of the stars and they are interpreted to be visible on some particular occasion.

However, problems arise when post-nominal adjectives referring to locations modify nouns whose referents are not movable. For example, consider (3).

(3)　I could hear a murmuring of male African voices in *a low building nearby*
　　　and the crackling of a small brush fire in the Sand River campground in front
　　　of me.　　　　　　　　　　　　　　　　　　　　(COCA; italic mine)

In (3), the noun *building* denotes an unmovable entity and it seems difficult to claim that the post-nominal adjective *nearby* expresses a temporal property.

This paper deals with locational adjectives in the post-nominal position and solves the following two problems by using the perspective system proposed by Levelt (1996). The first problem is how properties expressed by locational adjectives can be interpreted as "temporary" in cases like (3). The second is what conditions should be met for locational adjectives to appear in the post-nominal position.

The structure of this paper is as follows. In section 2, we review previous studies on post-nominal adjectives and point out the problems. In section 3, we introduce the perspective system and define the conditions under which an entity whose spatial position is described has a temporal property. In section 4, we propose how to resolve the two abovementioned problems. Section 5 concludes this paper.

2. Bolinger (1967) and the Problems

Numerous studies in the literature deal with post-nominal adjectives, namely, Bolinger (1967), Ferris (1993), Sadler and Arnold (1994), and Cinque (2010). In this paper, we take up Bolinger (1967) as the representative of these studies.

2.1. Interpretational Differences among Adjective Positions

Bolinger (1967) argues that there are some interpretatativedifferences between pre-nominal and post-nominal adjectives. As shown in (4), the former express permanent properties, and the latter temporal properties:

(4)   a. The *navigable* river is to the north.
      b. The (only) river *navigable* is to the north.

(Bolinger (1967: 4-5))

In (4a), the pre-nominal adjective *navigable* expresses the permanent property of the river; thus, the interpretation is that the river is always navigable. In (4b), on the other hand, the post-nominal adjective *navigable* denotes the temporal property of the river, and thus, the interpretation is that the river happens to be navigable at the movement because of a drought or some other event.

2.2 The Restriction on the Nouns

Bolinger also claims that there is a restriction on the nouns modified by locational adjectives in the pre-nominal position. As noted above, these adjectives express permanent properties, and thus, the referents of the modified nouns should be unmovable entities. Consider the examples in (5), for instance:

(5) a. *a nearby man / bus
     b. a nearby building   (ibid.: 11; Yasui et.al (1976: 10))

The nouns *man* and *bus* in (5a) denote movable entities and the property expressed by *nearby* cannot be considered permanent. Hence the unacceptability of these examples. In contrast, the noun *building* in (5b) denotes an unmovable object and the property expressed by *nearby* can be regarded as permanent. Therefore, this example is acceptable.

Thus far, we have reviewed Bolinger's analysis of the differences in interpretations of adjectives in the three positions and the restriction on the nouns modified by locational adjectives. His analysis focuses on whether or not the referent of the noun is movable.

2.3 Problems with Bolinger's Analysis (1967)

If the restriction of modified nouns is applied to the analysis of locational adjectives in the post-nominal position, it is predicted that these adjectives can appear in the post-nominal position only when the modified nouns express movable entities. This prediction seems to be supported by (6):

(6) For a moment I watched *an old man nearby*.   (COCA: Italic mine)

In (6), the noun *man* denotes a movable entity, and the property expressed by the adjective *nearby* can be considered temporal. Thus, this sentence can be explained by Bolinger's hypothesis. However, some examples are problematic for his analysis. Consider, for instance, the following sentence.

(7) I could hear a murmuring of male African voices in *a low building nearby*.

(COCA)

If his analysis is correct, the adjective *nearby* should appear in the pre-nominal position, since the noun *building* denotes stationary objects. Contrary to this prediction, however, *nearby* appears in the post-nominal position in (7). Thus, we must consider what condition should be met so that these adjectives can appear in the post-nominal position.

Another problem with Bolinger's analysis, as also pointed out in Ferris (1993), is that it fails to explain examples like (8).

(8) Buildings *adjacent* will be closed for three days.

(Ferris (1993: 45, 47))

In (8), it seems difficult to claim that the buildings happen to be adjacent on some particular occasion and that the post-nominal adjective *adjacent* expresses a temporal property. This problem is due to the fact that the referent of the noun *buildings* is not movable. Thus, we must explain how the property expressed by the adjective *adjacent* is interpreted as a temporal property.

The discussion thus far leads us to conclude that Bolinger's analysis of locational adjectives have left two questions unsolved: (i) In what sense do locational adjectives in post-nominal position express temporal properties when they modify the nouns whose referents are unmovable? (ii) What conditions should be met when locational adjectives appear in the post-nominal position? To answer these questions, we adopt the perspective system, to which we now turn.

3. Perspective System

3.1 Levelt (1996)

According to Levelt (1996), describing the location of an entity involves the following three processes.

(9) a. Focusing on the entity of the scene whose spatial position is to be located. In this paper, we call this entity a *figure*.

b. Focusing on the entity of the field in relation to which the figure's spatial position is to be described. In this paper, we call this entity a *ground*.

c. Spatially relating the figure to the ground based on the perspective system.

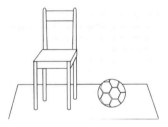

Figure 1 (Levelt (1996:80))

Of the three processes in (9), we focus on the perspective system here. Levelt (1996) divides the perspective system into three types: the deictic, intrinsic, and absolute perspective systems. Let me illustrate these systems with Figure 1. The first way of describing the situation in Figure 1 is (10):

(10) I see a chair and a ball to the right of it.   (Levelt (1996: 79))

In (10), the chair is chosen as the ground and the ball as the figure. Then, the spatial relation between them is described based on the observer's position.

Specifically, from the speaker's position, the ball is to the right of the chair. Thus, the deictic perspective system is used in this description.

The second way of describing the scene is (11):

    (11)   I see a chair and a ball to its left.   (ibid.: 79)

The ground and figure in (11) are the same as those in (10). The relation between them is expressed in terms of the intrinsic properties of the ground *a chair*. For instance, the side of the chair that faces the default direction of a person sitting in it may be regarded as the front of the chair. The other three directions, i.e. back, right, and left, are derived from the chair's front. The ball in Figure 1 is located at the chair's left, regardless from where the observer is looking at the scene. In (11), therefore, the intrinsic perspective system is adopted.

The third way of describing the scene is (12):

    (12)   I see a chair and a ball north of it.   (ibid.: 80)

The ground and figure in (12) are the same as those in (10) and (11). The relation between them is expressed based on a fixed bearing, namely a north-south dimension, without reference to the observer's position or the intrinsic property of the ground. This perspective system is called the absolute perspective system.

The characteristics of these perspective systems are summarized as follows:

    (13)   a. Deictic Perspective System
            The spatial relation between a figure and a ground is expressed
            based on the observer's location.
         b. Intrinsic Perspective System
            The spatial relation between a figure and a ground is expressed
            based on the ground's intrinsic property.
         c. Absolute Perspective System

The spatial relation between a figure and a ground is expressed based on a fixed bearing.

3.2. Some Properties of the Perspective Systems

Based on whether or not the observer's position is used in describing the spatial relation between entities, the perspective systems can be classified into two groups: (i) the deictic system, and (ii) the intrinsic and absolute systems. Each group has different properties in terms of the effect of the observer's location. Figure 2 illustrates these differences.

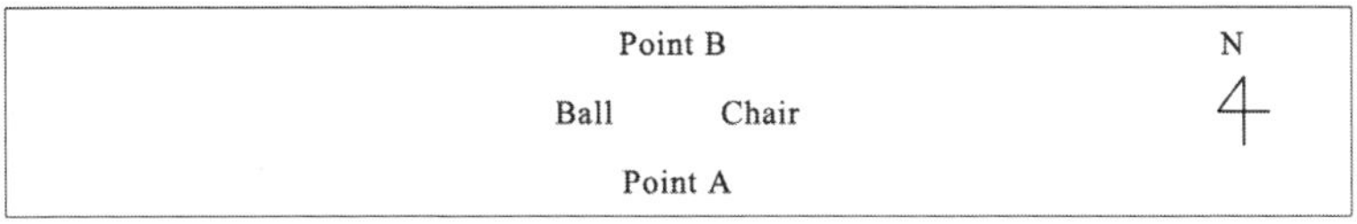

Figure 2

Suppose that the observer is standing at point A in Figure 2. From this point, he or she can describe the spatial relation between the chair and the ball in three ways by using each type of perspective system.

(14)　[Description from point A]
　　　a. I see a chair and a ball to the left of it.　[Deictic perspective system]
　　　b. I see a chair and a ball to its left.　[Intrinsic perspective system]
　　　c. I see a chair and a ball west of it.　[Absolute perspective system]

Note that if the observer moves to point B, the description of the scene changes only when the deictic perspective system is used:

(15)　[Description from point B]
　　　I see a chair and a ball to *the right of it*　[Deictic perspective system]

As in (14a) and (15), if the deictic perspective system is adopted, the spatial relation between the figure and the ground changes depending on the observer's location. On the other hand, if the intrinsic or absolute perspective system is adopted, the relation between the figure and the ground is fixed. In the next section, we show that this difference is related to the distinction between temporal and permanent properties of the entities serving as figures.

3.3 Temporal property and the perspective system

Dowty (1979) pointed out that the acceptability of the progressive form of the stative verbs referring to locations depends on the properties of their subjects.

(16)　The socks are lying under the bed.
(17)　a.　New Orleans lies at the mouth of the Mississippi River.
　　　 b. $^{??}$/*New Orleans is lying at the mouth of the Mississippi River.
(Dowty (1979: 174–175))

In (16), the subject denotes moveable entities and their property of lying under the bed is considered as a temporal property. Thus, this sentence is perfectly acceptable. On the other hand, the subjects in (17) denote unmovable objects and their properties of spatial positions cannot be considered as temporal properties. Therefore, (17b) is much less acceptable than (16).

In addition, he points out that the progressive form can be used even when the subjects denote stationary objects. For instance, see (18).

(18)　When you enter the gate to the park there will be a statue standing on your right, and a small pond will be lying directly in front of you.

(*ibid.*: 175)

In (18), the progressive forms are used to describe the positions of the stationary objects coming into the observer's vision. The reason is that the position of the moving observer is regarded as the viewpoint in the description and the locations of the unmovable objects are considered "temporary" in relation to this moving observer's position. Hence the acceptability of this sentence.

Note the perspective systems used in these examples. In (17a) and (17b), the non-deictic perspective systems are used, whereas in (18), the deictic perspective system is adopted. This contrast shows that the entity serving as the figure in the deictic perspective system has a temporal property and the progressive form in such a case is acceptable.

Based on the discussion thus far, we can postulate the two conditions under which an entity serving as a figure has a temporal property:

(19)　An entity serving as a figure has a temporal property if
　　　a. it is a moveable entity, or
　　　b. a deictic perspective system is used for the description of a figure.

Here, (16) and (18) satisfy the first and second conditions, respectively. On the other hand, (17b') violates these conditions. Therefore, the two conditions in (19) explain the difference of acceptability of the progressive form of stative verbs expressing locations. In the next section, we apply the conditions in (19) to the analysis of locational adjectives.

4. Proposal

As discussed in section 2, the first problem with Bolinger's analysis arises when locational adjectives modify the nouns whose referents are not movable, because it seems difficult to interpret the properties expressed by the adjectives as temporal properties. Here, we reconsider the relevant example by using the perspective system, which is repeated as (20):

(20)　Buildings adjacent will be closed for three days.　　(Ferris (1993: 45. 47))

In (20), the noun *buildings* is chosen as the figure. However, the ground is not explicitly expressed, and we have to consider what the ground is. For this purpose, we assume a context in which this sentence is used as in Figure 3:

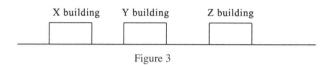

Figure 3

(21) [You (speaker) and hearer are in Y building and you want to refer to X and Z buildings]
Buildings adjacent will be closed for three days.

According to my informant, the noun phrase *buildings adjacent* can refer to the X and Y buildings and the ground is considered the place where the speaker and hearer are at the time of utterance. This means that the spatial relation between the figure and the ground is described based on the observer's (here, the speaker's) position. In (21), therefore, the deictic perspective system is adopted.

As discussed in the previous section, under the deictic perspective system, an entity serving as a figure has a temporal property, even when it is not movable, because the location of the stationary object is considered temporary in relation to the moving observer's position. The same holds for (21). The buildings do not move but the location of the buildings in relation to the observer's position can change. Therefore, the property expressed by the adjective is regarded as temporary and it can appear in the post-nominal position.

Next, let us consider another example problematic for Bolinger's analysis, which is repeated as (22).

(22) I could hear a murmuring of male African voices in *a low building nearby*.
(COCA: italic and emphasis added)

The figure in the noun phrase *a low building nearby* is the referent of the noun *building*. In addition, the ground, which is not explicitly expressed, can be considered the place where the observer (here, the I-narrator in the narrative) is sitting. Thus, the spatial relation between them is described based on the observer's position, and (22) utilizes the deictic perspective system. Given the property of the deictic perspective system, the property expressed by the adjective can be interpreted as temporal.

In sum, in the cases where locational adjectives in the post-nominal position modify the nouns denoting stable entities, if the characteristics of the deictic perspective system are considered, we can regard the properties expressed by such adjectives as temporal.

The second problem with Bolinger's analysis is that it cannot correctly capture the conditions under which locational adjectives can appear in the post-nominal position. To solve this, we use the two conditions presented in section 3 with a slight revision, as in (23):

(23)　A locational adjective appears in the post-nominal position if
　　　a. the noun modified by the adjective denotes a movable entity, or
　　　b. the deictic perspective system is adopted for the description of the spatial position of the noun's referent.

Next, I show that the conditions in (23) correctly predict the acceptability of examples containing locational adjectives.

First, consider examples satisfying only condition (a): modified nouns denote moveable entities and the deictic system is adopted. The example in this case is (6): I watched *an old man nearby*. In this example, the noun *man* denotes a movable entity and the man is near by the observer (here, the subject *I*).

Second, consider examples that satisfy only condition (b): the modified noun denotes an unmovable entity and the deictic perspective system is adopted. Examples of this case are (21) and (22) above. Note that condition (a) alone predicts the unacceptability of the examples such as these. This shows the necessity and importance of condition (b).

Third, consider examples that satisfy conditions (a) and (b): modified nouns denote movable entities and the non-deictic perspective system is adopted. An example of this case is (24).

(24)   California officials are set to dump chemicals - including trace amounts of carcinogens - into a future drinking-water supply in a well-publicized effort to protect *endangered fish downstream*.   (COCA)

Finally, consider examples that do not satisfy the two conditions: the modified noun denotes an unmovable entity and the non-deictic perspective system is adopted. As noted above, the examples of this case are expected to be unacceptable. This prediction is supported by (25).

(25)   a.   *The cabin mountaintop is not used now.
      b.   *The hotel riverside is still in business.
      c.   *The building north is not used now.

The noun *cabin* in example (25a) denotes an unmovable entity. In addition, the adjective *mountaintop* uses the intrinsic property of the mountain to describe the spatial position of the figure and the ground. This means that the intrinsic perspective system is adopted. Therefore, this sentence does not meet the two conditions and is unacceptable. For the same reason, the example (25b) is unacceptable. In (25c), where the adjective *north* is used, the absolute perspective system is adopted, and thus the example is unacceptable.

As is clear from the discussion, the two conditions in (23) correctly predict the acceptability of locational adjectives in the post-nominal position. Therefore, we can solve the second problem with Bolinger's analysis.

5. Conclusion

In this paper, we examined locational adjectives in post-nominal position. To solve the two problems of previous studies, with reference to the perspective system and the general restrictions on the nouns representing a "figure", we proposed the conditions under which such adjectives can appear in the post-nominal position.

Kenta Mizutani

* This paper is a slightly revised version of my B.A. thesis. I would like to thank Ian Garlignton for his patience and help as an informant. All remaining errors are my own.

References

Bolinger, Dwight (1967) "Adjectives in English: Attribution and Predication," *Lingua* 18, 1–34.

Cinque, Gugliemo (2010) *The Syntax of Adjectives: A Comparative Study*, MIT Press, Cambridge, MA.

Davies, Mark (2008-) *The Corpus of Contemporary American English (COCA): 560 million words, 1990-present.* Available online at https://corpus.byu.edu/coca/.

Dowty, David R. (1979) *Word meaning and Montague grammar*, D. Reidel, Dordrecht.

Ferris, Cornnor (1993) *The Meaning of Syntax: A Study in the Adjectives of English*, Longman, London.

Levelt, W. (1996) "Perspective Taking and Ellipsis in Spatial Descriptions," in, *Language and Space*, ed. by Paul Bloom, Mary A, Peterson, Lynn Nadel and Merril F. Garrett, 79-107, MIP Press, Cambridge, MA.

Sadler, Louisa, and Douglas J. Arnold (1994) "Prenominal Adjectives and the Phrasal / Lexical Distinction," *Journal of Linguistics* 30, 187–226.

Yasui, Minoru, Akiyama, Satoshi, and Nakamura Masaru (1976) *Keiyoushi* (Adjectives), Kenkyusya, Tokyo.

属性名詞を目的語とする前置詞句付き have 構文の諸相 *

南 佑亮

キーワード：have 構文，there 構文，前置詞句，属性名詞，属性叙述

1. はじめに

英語には、(1) のような構文現象がある。

   (1)   a. "Made in America" has a nice ring to it.
           b. His voice had an edge to it.

(1) は動詞 have を用いた他動詞文（以下「have 構文」）の一種だが、典型的な have 構文とは 2 つの点で性質が異なる。第一に、目的語の指示対象が具象物ではなく属性であり、主語指示物が具象物のある場所 (location) ではなく属性の帰属先を表している。第二に、(1) の構文は目的語の後に主語と照応する代名詞を補部とする to 前置詞句が伴う。管見の限り、(1) のタイプの have 構文が先行研究で扱われたことはない。その一方で、具象物が特定の場所 (location) に存在する状況を描写するタイプの have 構文 (=(2)) は古くから考察や分析の対象となっている (Heine (1997); Jackendoff (1987, 2002); Kuno (1971); Lakoff (1987); 中右 (1998); 大西 (2010), 他)。以下本論文では、(1) の have 構文を「属性 have 構文」、(2) の have 構文を「存在 have 構文」として両者を区別する。

   (2)   a. The table has a vase on it.
           b. The room has four windows in it.

本論文の目的は、属性 have 構文に、存在 have 構文にはない独自の特徴が見られることを明らかにし、この構文の妥当な記述・分析方法について

の試案を提示することである。以下、2 節では、存在の have 構文に関する先行研究の知見を概観する。3 節では、2 節を踏まえながら属性の have 構文の性質について検証する。4 節では属性 have 構文の記述・分析方法について議論する。5 節は結語である。

2. 先行研究──存在 have 構文の特徴

存在 have 構文の意味機能に関する先行研究の関心は (i) 存在を表す there 構文（以下、「there 構文」）との関係と、(ii) 目的語の後の前置詞句の性質に向けられている。以下本節では、これらを順に確認する。

2.1. 存在を表す there 構文との比較

先行研究において、存在 have 構文だけが単独で扱われることはほとんどなく、there 構文が引き合いに出されるのが常である。その理由は、原則として前者が後者と構文交替関係にあるからであり、(2) の例も、(3), (4) に示すように、基本的な意味内容を変えることなく there 構文にパラフレーズすることができる。

(3)　a. The table has a vase on it.　　　　　　　　　　　(= (2a))
　　　b. There is a vase on the table.
(4)　a. The room has four windows in it.　　　　　　　　(= (2b))
　　　b. There are four rooms in the room.

しかし、パラフレーズ関係にあるからといって、2 つの構文が表す意味の範囲が必ずしも一致するわけではない。両者の意味機能の違いに関する分析を Lakoff (1987) が試みている。

(5)　a. There is a vase on the table.
　　　b. The table has a vase on it.
　　　c. A vase is on the table.

(Lakoff (1987: 558))

Lakoff によれば、(5) の 3 つの構文には次のような違いがある。まず、

(5a) の there 構文は、(i) テーブルにたまたま花瓶があるという位置関係を表す解釈（「偶然の出来事 (incidental occurrence)」解釈) と、(ii) 花瓶がテーブルコーディネートの一部を成しているという解釈（＝部分—全体関係 (part-whole relation) 解釈）のどちらの場合にも対応しうるが、(5b) のhave 構文は (ii) の解釈にしか対応しない。また、(5c) の there を主語としない存在文（以下、裸存在文）は have 構文とは逆に、(i) の解釈にしか適合しない。したがって、(6) では受付係が応接室の一部を成しているという部分全体関係の解釈が意図されているため、(6c) は不適格な表現となる。

(6)　a.　There's a receptionist in the reception room.
　　　b.　The reception room has a receptionist in it.
　　　c.　*A receptionist is in the reception room.

　　　　　　　　　　　　　　　（Lakoff (1987: 557–8) の例文を一部改変）

以上をまとめると、表1のようになる。

	(i) incidental occurrence	(ii) part-whole relation
there 構文	✓	✓
存在 have 構文	*	✓
裸存在文	✓	*

表1　3つの存在構文と意味の対応関係（Lakoff 1987 に基づく）

Lakoff (1987) の分析は、「3 つの構文それぞれが独自の意味構造を有し、かつ多義性も示しうる」という前提に立っており、これは後に発展を遂げる構文文法理論 (Construction Grammar) にも通ずる卓見である。ただし、「部分—全体関係」という概念規定には補足が必要である。このままでは、(7) のような事例が反例と見なされてしまう可能性がある。

(7)　a. Sue's trousers had grass on them.　　　　　　（中右 (1998: 96)）
　　　b. The house has a fence around it.　　　　　　（大西 (2010: 27)）

確かに、ズボンについている草はズボンの一部を成しているわけではない
し、家を囲っているフェンスが家そのものの一部かどうかと言われると、
明確な判断は難しい。[1]

　しかし、Lakoff が意図している「構文の意味」が、認知文法 (cognitive
grammar) における「捉え方 (construal)」の反映 (Langacker (2009) 他) で
あるとすれば、存在 have 構文の意味は、「概念化者による、主語指示物と
目的語のあいだに部分─全体関係があるという捉え方」と分析できるた
め、(7) のように、客観的に見て明らかな部分─全体関係が認めにくい場
合でも存在 have 構文が自然に用いられるという事実にも説明がつく。(7)
は、世界に実在する、誰の目にも明らかな部分─全体関係を写し取ってい
るのではなく、そこに部分─全体関係を見出している話者（概念化者）の
捉え方を反映しているのである。[2]

　存在 have 構文と there 構文には、談話機能上の違いもある。大西 (2010)
は Li and Thompson (1976) や Langacker (2009) の分析を手掛かりに、存在
have 構文はトピック構造を有すると主張する。具体的には、存在 have 構
文の主語は文内トピックであると同時により上位の談話レベルのトピック
にも関連付けられるという特徴があるが、対応する there 構文にはそのよ
うな特徴がないと指摘している。

　以上の知見に叙述類型論（益岡 (2008)）の観点を導入すると、次の 2
つの根拠により、存在 have 構文は事象叙述文ではなく属性叙述文である
という結論が導かれる（南 (2019)）。第一に、Lakoff が言う「偶然の出来
事」は事象叙述に対応し、ある存在物の「部分」について描写すること
は、その存在物の特徴・属性を描写することに他ならないため、「部分─
全体関係」は属性叙述に相当すると考えられる。[3] 第二に、存在 have 構
文が主題（トピック）構造を有しているという大西の分析が、「属性叙述
文は主題構造を有する」という仮説と符合する。[4]

2.2. 前置詞句を伴う動機

　目的語に後続する前置詞句は、随意的な要素と見なされる傾向がある。
このことは、以下のように存在 have 構文の前置詞句をカッコに入れて提
示している文献の存在からも伺える。

(8)　The tree still has a bird nest (on it).　　　　　　（岸本・影山 (2010: 259)）

(9)　That pot has coffee (in it).　　　　　　　　　　（ibid. : 260)

　確かに、本稿冒頭で挙げた (2) の文は、前置詞句を省略しても不自然にはならない。

(10)　The table has a vase.　　　　　　　　　　　　　(cf. (2a))

(11)　The room has four windows.　　　　　　　　　　(cf. (2b))

ただし、2.1 節の (7) や以下の (12) のように、主語指示物と目的語指示物の間の位置関係が客観的に自明でない場合は、前置詞句で位置関係を明示することで目的語と主語の間に部分─全体関係が認められていることを伝達することができる（cf. 大西 (2010: 26)）。

(12)　The door has Mr. Brook's name on it, you can't miss it.

（大西 (2010: 27)）

このように、存在 have 構文の前置詞句について、先行研究では「話者がその情報を追加する必要があると判断した場合に前置詞句を使用し、そうでなければ用いなくてもよい」という機能主義的な観点で捉えるのが暗黙の了解になっているといえる。

3. 属性 have 構文

　本節では、2 節で見た存在 have 構文の 2 つの特徴を踏まえつつ、属性 have 構文の特徴を見ていく。いずれの特徴についても、属性 have 構文は存在 have 構文とはいくらか異なる性質を示すことが判明する。

3.1. there 構文との「交替」

　以下に示すように、存在 have 構文と同様、属性 have 構文も、there 構文との交替が可能である。

(13) a. "Made in America" has a nice ring to it. (= (1a))
　　 b. There is a nice ring to "Made in America."
(14) a. His voice had an edge to it. (= (1b))
　　 b. There was an edge to his voice.

しかし、存在 have 構文の場合とは異なり、Lakoff (1987) が指摘したような解釈の可能性の違いが生じないことに注意する必要がある。具体的には、Lakoff が "incidental occurrence" と名付けた「モノが偶然その位置に存在している」という解釈が、there 構文の方でも成立しない。この理由は、(13) と (14) の各文では、there 構文の be 動詞に後続する名詞句または have 構文の目的語が、具象物ではなく属性概念を表すからである。属性は一般に、(内在的なものであれ後天的なものであれ) ある存在物に備わっていてその存在物の一部を成すものとして概念化されるため、「部分─全体関係」の解釈には馴染むが、偶然的な位置関係の解釈とは矛盾するのである。

　尚、(13) と (14) の構文交替は文の叙述機能という点でも興味深い問題を提供する。意味の中核をなす名詞句が属性概念を表すため、there 構文でも存在 have 構文でも個体の属性について述べるという点では何も変わらないからである。there 構文がトピック構造を有するかどうかについては諸説があるが、仮にトピック構造を有していたとしても属性 have 構文と同じような構造ではない可能性が高く、「属性叙述文は主題構造を有する」という叙述類型論の根幹を成すテーゼに問題を投げかけている可能性がある。[5] ただし本論文ではこの問題にはこれ以上は立ち入らない。

3.2. 前置詞句の位置づけ

　属性 have 構文は、前置詞句についても存在 have 構文といくらか異なる様相を呈している。第一に、この構文の to 前置詞句は随意的ではない。(15) と (16) に示すように、to 前置詞句を省いた方は母語話者にとって不自然な表現になる。

(15) a. "Made in America" has a nice ring to it.
　　 b. ?"Made in America" has a nice ring.

(16)　a.　Her voice had an edge to it.
　　　　b. ?Her voice had an edge.

　この事実は、2.2 節で述べた機能主義的な観点では説明がつかない。なぜなら、これらの目的語名詞は主語指示物に認められる「属性」を明示的に表しているため、to 前置詞句がなければ目的語指示物と主語指示物のあいだの関係についての情報が不足するということは考えられないからである。むしろ、用いることのできる前置詞句に複数の選択肢がありえる空間的位置関係の方が前置詞句の必要性が高いとさえ考えられる。情報の必要性だけで (15) と (16) の事実を説明することはできない。
　ならば前置詞 to の問題ではないかと思われるかもしれないが、この可能性は、この構文の to 前置詞の省略が常に不自然さ生むわけではないという事実によって排除される。以下の (17)–(19) は、筆者が COCA から抜粋した実例に適宜改変を加えて引用したものだが、(15) や (16) とは異なり、to 前置詞句を省略しても不自然にはならない。

(17)　a. Some of your songs have a kind of Beatley sound to them.
　　　　b. Some of your songs have a kind of Beatley sound.
(18)　a. The air was thick and had a strange smell to it.
　　　　b. The air was thick and had a strange smell.
(19)　a. The milk had a salty taste to it.
　　　　b. The milk had a salty taste.

　この複雑な事実に対する説明として考えられる可能性は 2 つある。一つ目は、概念レベルの説明であり、「名詞が表す概念の抽象度が高くなればなるほど、to 前置詞句の必要性が増す」という仮説を立てることである。確かに、(17)–(19) の各例は五感知覚に関わっており、具象物ではないものの、(15) や (16) の場合に表されている言葉の「響き」や「鋭さ」といった、単純な物理的属性に還元が困難な高度に抽象的な概念に比べれば、具体性の高い（＝抽象度の低い）概念である。ただし、この説を推し進めようとすると、概念の抽象度を判定する厳密な尺度を定義せねばならない。加えて、仮にもし正しいことが証明されたとしても、なぜ抽象度が高いほ

ど to 前置詞句が必要になるのか、というより根本的な問題にも直面するだろう。

　説明のもう一つの可能性は、表現の相対的使用頻度に関する話者の知識に訴えるというものである。COCA を用いた筆者の調査（2019 年 4 月 23 日現在）によれば、目的語名詞が edge と ring の実例の数はそれぞれ 98 件、180 件であるのに対して、(17)–(19) で挙がっている例の名詞を見ると sound が 41 件、smell が 19 件、taste が 18 件であり、大きな差がある。つまり、(15b) や (16b) が不自然だとする母語話者の判断に、これらの名詞に to 前置詞句を伴った事例が圧倒的に高い頻度で用いられること（およびその (17)–(19) の名詞はそれほど高い頻度で用いられないこと）についての知識が影響している可能性は十分にある。もしこれが正しいとすれば、言語表現の相対頻度に関する情報が言語知識の中に入っていると仮定する立場 (Taylor (2012: 148)) の妥当性を支持する事実となるだろう。

　どちらがより妥当な説明かは、更に多くのデータ収集と分析を進めることで次第に明らかになっていくと思われる。

4. 考察——名詞中心の構文現象としての属性 have 構文

　2 節と 3 節で確認した事実から明らかなのは、従来の研究で扱われてきた存在 have 構文とは異なり、属性 have 構文に関する母語話者の知識は目的語名詞を中心に構成されているということである。前置詞句を伴う have 構文それ独自の意味機能に着目したという点で Lakoff (1987) は先行研究の中でも卓越していることはすでに 2 節で述べた。しかし Lakoff でさえ、目的語のスロットが空いた抽象度の高いスキーマを「構文」として念頭に置いていたと思われる。このことは、対象としていた例文が (20)–(23) のような、具象物の存在する場所を描写するようなものに限られていたことと密接に関係している。(20)–(23) を見て there 構文と have 構文が交替していると認識することは容易だが、その交替現象が名詞（vase, window, (marble) top, lid）を中心に成り立っているとは誰も考えないだろう。

(20)　a. The table has a vase on it.

b. There is a vase on the table. (= (3))

(21) a. The room has four windows in it.

b. There are four windows in the room. (= (4))

(22) a. This table has a marble top to it.

b. There is a marble top to this table. (Kuno (1971: 369))

(23) a. The jar has no lid to it.

b. There is no lid to this jar. (Lakoff (1987: 558))

しかし、3 節で見たように、属性 have 構文は have の目的語となる名詞が there 構文との交替における意味のあり方を決定づけており、かつ have 構文における to 前置詞句の定着度とも連動している可能性がある。したがって、項構造構文の意味は動詞を中心として記述・分析する必要がある (Levin (1993) 等) のと同じように、属性 have 構文（およびそれと交替する there 構文）は、個々の属性名詞を中心に記述・分析を進めていく必要があるのではないかと思われる。

5. 結語

本論文は、属性 have 構文の意味機能上の特異性を明らかにし、この現象へのアプローチ方法について検討した。2 節と 3 節で、一見すると同じ「構文」に見える存在 have 構文と属性 have 構文が (i) 属性叙述の仕方と、(ii) 前置詞句の位置づけに関して異なることを指摘した。(i) については、目的語名詞が属性概念を指示するものであるという点で、先行研究でよく挙げられてきた例（存在 have 構文）とは異質であり、there 構文との意味機能の差が小さくなっていることが明らかになった。(ii) については、少なくとも一部の名詞に関して to 前置詞句の省略が難しいことが判明し、その理由が、概念構造のレベルで説明される可能性に加えて、相対頻度の差による母語話者の言語知識内での構文の定着度の違いという観点からも説明される可能性を指摘した。以上の点を踏まえ、4 節では、属性 have 構文が、あくまでも抽象的なレベルの「構文」だけを念頭に置く従来のアプローチとは異なり、目的語となる個別の属性名詞を中心とした記述と分析が必要な現象であると論じた。

南 佑亮

　本論文では、属性 have 構文が存在 have 構文に還元できない特殊な性質を持っていることを指摘したが、どちらも前置詞を特に伴わない have 構文が基盤にあることは共通している以上、カテゴリー上まったく無関係であるとは考えにくく、両者の中間的な性質を示す実例の存在も予想される。そのような実例の探索が今後の課題の一つである。また、紙幅の都合で扱えなかったが、本論文で扱った属性 have 構文と同じように抽象度の高い属性名詞を伴うが、前置詞は to ではなく about を伴うような事例も数多く存在する。[7] この現象も視野に入れつつ、今後はさらに多くの属性名詞を対象に調査と分析を進めていく必要がある。

* 本研究の一部は科学研究費（基盤 (C), 研究課題番号 19K00697）を受けておこなわれたものである。母語話者コンサルタントとしてご協力いただいた Marsha Hayashi 氏と Jon-Patrick Fajardo 氏に御礼を申し述べたい。尚、本稿の不備はすべて筆者によるものである。

[1] 実際に中右 (1998: 96) はこのように考え、Lakoff (1987) の分析を批判している。しかし中右の Lakoff 批判は、Lakoff の「部分全体関係」を「譲渡不可能関係」(Kimball (1973) 等) と混同したことによるものであり、妥当性に疑問が残る。
[2] 大西 (2010: 26–27) は、(7b) のような事例は部分―全体関係の意味を持つ have 構文からの拡張であると述べている。カテゴリー拡張の主な原動力の一つが概念化者の捉え方であるため、この見解は本稿の立場と親和的である。
[3] Lakoff (1987: 558–559) が以下のような例を挙げて、目的語名詞句が抽象的な「実質」や「美点・長所」といった概念を表す場合も「部分―全体関係」で説明がつけられると述べていることは、本論文の主張にも通ずる洞察である。ただし、Lakoff は「属性（叙述）」という概念には用いておらず、存在 have 構文と属性 have 構文の区別を看取するには至っていない。

 (i) a. His theory has a good deal of merit in it.
   b. His claims don't have much substance to them.

(Lakoff (1987: 559))

[4] 前置詞句を伴うという形式上の特異性もまた、単純な状況描写ではなく、属性を叙述する機能を有していることの証左である。属性叙述機能と統語的な特異性の相関関係については影山 (2012) を参照。
[5] there 構文とトピック性 (topicality) に関する諸説の概要が McNally (2011: 1833-1834) にある。

⁶ 母語話者コンサルタントの一人によれば、(16) については、(16b) でも意味は通るが、to 前置詞句を伴う実例をよく耳にするので (16a) 方が自然で (16b) の方は不自然である、とのことであった。この反応は、ここで挙げている 2 つ目の説明の妥当性を強く支持するものである。

⁷ 南 (2019) は、COCA による予備調査に基づき、there 構文と属性 have 構文との間で交替をする ring や edge のような属性名詞を、to を伴うグループと about を伴うグループに分けてリストアップしているが、それによれば、どちらか一方の前置詞としか共起しない名詞もあれば、どちらの前置詞とも共起しうる名詞もある。このことは、存在 have 構文よりも属性名詞の意味が前置詞選択に影響を与えている可能性を示唆しており、当該の交代現象は名詞を中心として記述・分析すべきであるという本研究の立場を支持しているといえる。

参考文献

Clark, Eve V. (1978) "Locationals: Existentials, Locative, and Possessive Constructions," *Universals of Human Language*, *Vol. 4: Syntax*, ed. by Joseph H. Greenberg, Charles A. Ferguson and Edith A. Moravcsik, 85–126, Stanford University, Stanford, CA.

Davies, Mark (2008-) *The Corpus of Contemporary American English (COCA): 560 million words, 1990-present*. Available online at https://corpus.byu.edu/coca/.

Heine, Bernd (1997) *Possession: Cognitive Sources, Forces, and Grammaticalization*, Cambridge University Press, Cambridge.

Jackendoff, Ray (1987) "The Status of Thematic Relations in Linguistic Theory," *Linguistic Inquiry* 18, 369–411.

Jackendoff, Ray (2002) *Foundations of Language*, Oxford University Press, Oxford.

影山太郎 (2012)「属性叙述の文法的意義」, 影山太郎編『属性叙述の世界』, 3–35, くろしお出版, 東京.

Kimball, John (1973) "The Grammar of Existence," *CLS* 9, 262–270.

岸本秀樹・影山太郎 (2010)「存在と所有の表現」, 影山太郎編『日英対照　名詞の意味と構文』, 240–269, 大修館書店, 東京.

Kuno, Susumu (1971) "The Position of Locatives in Existential Sentences," *Linguistic Inquiry* 2, 233–278.

Lakoff, George (1987) *Women, Fire, and Dangerous Things*, Chicago University Press, Chicago.

Langacker, Ronald W. (2009) *Investigations in Cognitive Grammar*, Mouton de Gruyter, Berlin.

Levin, Beth (1993) *English Verb Classes and Alternations*, Chicago University Press,

Chicago.

Li, Charles N. and Sandra A. Thompson (1976) "Subject and Topic: A New Typology of Language," Subject and Topic, ed. by Charles N. Li, 457–489, Academic Press, New York.

Lyons, John (1967) "A Note on Possessive, Existential and Locative Sentences," Foundations of Language 3, 390–396.

益岡隆志 (2008)『叙述類型論』, くろしお出版, 東京.

McNally, Louise (2011) "Existential Sentences," Semantics: An International Handbook of Natural Language Meaning, Vol. 2, ed. by Klaus von Heusinger, Claudia Maienborn and Paul Portner, 1829–1848, de Gruyter, The Hague.

Milsark, Gary (1974) Existential Sentences in English, Doctoral dissertation, MIT. [Published by Garland, New York, 1979]

南佑亮 (2019)「抽象的属性名詞による there/have 交替現象に関する覚書」,『タバード (Tabard)』, 第 34 号, 53–66, 神戸女子大学英文学会.

中右実 (1998)「BE と HAVE からの発想」, 中右実・西村義樹『構文と事象構造』, 55–106, 研究社, 東京.

大西美穂 (2010)「前置詞句を伴う英語所有文のトピック構造」,『語用論研究』第 12 号, 19–36, 日本語用論学会.

Taylor, John (2012) The Mental Corpus, Oxford University Press, Oxford.

新しい構文の芽生え
—— 初期近代英語期における英語受益者受動 *

米倉 よう子

キーワード：REC 受動，初期近代英語，節的 TH 付き DOC

1. はじめに

　受動態の史的発達については多くの知見の蓄積がなされてきたが，(1c)
のような，二重目的語構文 (double object construction, 以下 DOC) の 2 つ
の項のうち，Theme の意味役割を担う項（TH 項）ではなく，Recipient
（あるいは Beneficiary や Goal）の意味役割を担う項（REC 項）に主格を
与えて主語位置に据える受動態の発達を詳細に調べた先行研究は数少な
い。

(1) a.　John gave Mary the book.
　　b. ??The book was given Mary by John.
　　c.　Mary was given the book by John.

（安藤 (2005: 354-355) に基づく）

(1b) 型受動態を TH 受動 (theme passive)，(1c) 型受動態を REC 受動
(recipient passive) と呼ぶことにしよう。また，TH 受動，REC 受動をまと
めて DOC 受動 (double object passive) と呼ぶことにする。本稿では，REC
受動の英語への定着ぶりについて，この構文が英語に定着し始めた初期近
代英語 (EModE) の状況を中心に見ていこう。まず 2 節では，REC 受動に
ついての通時的先行研究を概観する。続いて 3 節では，初期近代英語コー
パスに現れる DOC 受動の分布データを示し，そこからどのような学術的
示唆が得られるのかを考える。

－96－

2. 先行研究と残された問題点

　英語において，歴史的に先行した DOC 受動は REC 受動ではなく，TH 受動である。Allen (1995: 393) は，英語文献上で確認できる純然たる REC 受動の初例は 1375 年に現れたとしている。[1] 注意すべきは，14 世紀後半に REC 受動の初例が現れた後，この受動態が燎原の火のごとく英語で広まったわけではないという事実である。16 世紀後期の劇作家 Christopher Marlowe の英語を調査した Ando (1976) は，2 つの目的語（ここでは与格と対格をとるものが対象）をとる動詞（DOC 動詞）の受動態構文の分布をまとめている (pp. 177-179)。それによると，REC 受動は Marlowe の英語では「非常に稀」（'extremely rare'）であり，I am given (it) 型受動（本稿の REC 受動に相当，ただし Ando (1976) は Theme 項が明示的に表れていない例や Theme 項が節構造（節的 TH 付き REC 受動，本稿の例 (7d) も参照）の例も含めている）は advertise, answer, deprive, tell の 4 つの動詞に合計 5 例が見られるにすぎない。それに対して It is given (me) 型（本稿の TH 受動に相当，ただし Ando (1976) は Recipient 項が明示的に表されていない例も含めている）をとる動詞は appoint, deliver, forbid, offer, send, tell, deny, give, show, teach の 10 にわたり，例数は合計 17 であったという。例数が少ないので確固たる結論を引き出すことには慎重であらねばならないが，16 世紀後半でも，REC 受動は例数・動詞種類ともに非常に限定されていたことが窺える。

　実際，後期近代英語 (LModE) においても，REC 受動は一律に可能だったわけではない。[2] Yonekura (2018) では，CLMET3.0 を使い，20 の動詞 (assign, award, bring, deliver, deny, give, grant, hand, lend, obtain, offer, pay, permit, procure, promise, reimburse, repay, teach, tell, show) について，REC 受動がどのように定着していったのかを調査した。それによると，1710 年—1780 年間に REC 受動が TH 受動を粗頻度で上回っていたのは deny, promise, show, teach, tell, repay の 6 動詞に限定されており（ただし permit と repay は DOC 受動の例数そのものが極端に少ない），1850 年 – 1920 年においてですら，たとえば give の TH 受動は 124 例が見つかるのに対し，REC 受動例は 87 例にとどまっている。

　とりわけ for 前置詞与格構文（たとえば My duffle coat was bought **for**

me in Manchester. (BYU-BNC A7P, 1985-1994)）に対応するとおぼしき DOC は，ごく最近（20 世後半）まで REC 受動に抵抗していた。言語学関連ウェブサイトの Linguistic List で 1995 年に行われた調査でも，(2a) と (2b) の容認派と拒絶派の率は 2:1 にとどまる (https://linguistlist.org/issues/6/6-230.html)。

(2) a. She was bought a dress.
     b. She was written a letter.

　このように，REC 受動はその初例が現れた後，一気に英語に定着したとは言い難い。では，DOC 動詞の特性に着目して，いくつかの動詞グループに分け，動詞グループ毎の REC 受動の定着ぶりを調査・分析してみてはどうだろうか。なにか傾向を見出すことができるかもしれない。しかしながら，英語 REC 受動の発達を動詞グループの観点から扱っている先行研究は非常に少ない。そこで筆者は，前述の Yonekura (2018) において，20 の DOC 動詞を動詞の統語的・意味的特性に応じて以下の 5 つのグループに分け，動詞グループ毎に LModE において REC 受動がどのように定着したのかを分析した。

(3) A. GIVE グループ : assign, award, give, grant, hand, lend, offer
     基本的に 3 項動詞で，授与行為を第一義的に表す動詞群
     B. TELL グループ : deny, permit, promise, show, teach, tell
     本質的にコミュニケーション行為を表す動詞群
     C. BRING グループ : bring, deliver
     TH の空間的位置を変化させることを第一義的に表す動詞群
     D. PAY グループ : pay, repay, reimburse
     典型的には金銭のやり取りを表す動詞群
     E. GET グループ : obtain, procure
     何かを獲得することを第一義的に表す動詞群

以上の動詞グループを意識しながら行った CLMET3.0 に基づくコーパス調査と Jespersen (1961) や Emonds (1976) 等の先行研究における記述を総合し，Yonekura (2018) では，REC 受動は英語において概略，(4) のよう

な REC 受動受容性クラインを有していると提案した。

(4)　TELL > PAY > GIVE > BRING ≧ GET・作成動詞 (build, bake, etc.)

(4) の右側に来る要素ほど，REC 受動導入に対する抵抗が根強い。なお，このクラインは必ずしも，「英語の史的テキストで REC 受動初例が確認された年代の早さ順」ではないことに注意されたい。Yonekura (2018) では (4) のクラインが見られる理由を，「チャンキング (chunking)」(Bybee (2006)) および「項役割 (argument role) と参与者役割 (participant role) との乖離性」(Goldberg (1995)) という概念的道具立てを使って説明を試みた。(4) はまた，「REC 受動が英語に定着したのは，明示的格標示の水平化（喪失）が原因である」という主張が過剰に単純化されていることを示唆している。

　しかし，さらに詳細な調査や検討が必要な点がまだいくつか残されている。まず，(4)（あるいは (3)）の動詞グループ分類の妥当性の問題がある。しかし紙幅の関係上，この点については本稿では踏み込まない。本稿で取り組むのは別の問題点，すなわち，後期近代英語以前の英語における REC 受動の分布調査である。REC 受動の受容性には，同一動詞グループ内のメンバー間にも差異が見られる場合がある。GIVE グループの動詞 offer の場合，CLMET3.0 の 1710 年 -1780 年セクションにおける TH 受動と REC 受動の粗頻度数はそれぞれ 41 例と 17 例であり，その REC 受動比率は GIVE グループのメンバーの中では高い。では，1710 年以前の offer の REC 受動受け入れ状況はどうだったのだろうか。後期近代英語 (LModE) コーパスである CLMET3.0 を見ているだけでは，その実像はつかめない。また，動詞グループ間の差異としては，TELL グループが最も早い時期から REC 受動への高い親和性を見せていたことが CLMET3.0 に基づくコーパスデータから明らかになったが，ではこの動詞グループの初期近代英語 (EModE) における状況はどうだったのだろうか。

　EModE における REC 受動を扱った先行研究としては，Trips et al. (2015，2016) があげられる。Trips らは EModE コーパスである PCEEC を使い，11 の動詞 (pay, promise, offer, allow, deny, serve, fine, send, give, tell, show) について，採取された REC 受動の例数を提示している。しかしその調査は，当該動詞の TH 受動と REC 受動の比を調べることは目的としておらず，REC 受動の粗頻度数は示されていても，各動詞の TH 受動例数は一切示されていない。

　本稿では続く 3 節にて，以上のような先行研究の不足分を補うべく，まだ研究途上ではあるが，EModE における REC 受動の分布データと分析を提示する。

3. コーパス調査と分析

3. 1. 調査対象コーパスと調査対象

　EModE における REC 受動と TH 受動の使用状況を調べるため，本稿では PCEEC と LC という 2 つの英語コーパスを使い，(5) にあげる 7 つの動詞について，DOC 受動例と前置詞与格構文受動例を採取した。PCEEC は 1410 年頃から 1695 年までの個人的な書簡を集めたもの（総語数約 220 万語）である。一方，LC は 1640 年から 1740 年までのパンフレットや小論文を集めたコーパス（総語数約 110 万語）である。

　　(5)　offer, deny, permit, promise, show, teach, tell

(5) の動詞のうち，offer は，前節で述べたように，LModE において GIVE グループ内で最も REC 受動への抵抗感が薄かった動詞であり，残りの 6 つは TELL グループの動詞である。例の採取方針は米倉 (2015: 註 6) および Yonekura (2018: 5-6) と同じだが，以下の点においては異なる。

　　(6)　a. 各動詞の過去分詞形の異形態をできるだけ網羅的に検索する。
　　　　 b. 節的 TH 付き DOC 受動態の例も採取する。

採取対象受動態の例と，分布調査結果をまとめた表 1 および 2 中での表記法を (7) にあげておく。なお，(7c) のように節的 TH が左方に置かれ，主語位置に虚辞（形式主語）が来る例は，TH 受動の一種と見なした（表 1 および 2 では TH [clause] としてあげてある）。また，REC 項が前置

詞 to の後ろに来ているもののみを「前置詞与格受動 (prepositional dative passive [PD passive])」として採取した。

表1. PCEEC における DOC 受動態の分布 (1410? - 1695) [粗頻度]

	offer	deny	permit	promise	show	teach	tell
DOC passives	28	13	9	28	7	4	172
TH [NP]	16 ⎤ 16	6 ⎤ 6	0 ⎤ 0	7 ⎤ 8	2 ⎤ 6	0 ⎤ 0	38 ⎤ 114
[clause]	0 ⎦ (57%)	0 ⎦	0 ⎦	1 ⎦ (29%)	4 ⎦	0 ⎦	77 ⎦ (67%)
REC [NP]	12 ⎤ 12	7 ⎤ 7	0 ⎤ 9	7 ⎤ 20	1 ⎤ 1	2 ⎤ 4	3 ⎤ 57
[clause]	0 ⎦ (43%)	0 ⎦	9 ⎦	13 ⎦ (71%)	0 ⎦	2 ⎦	54 ⎦ (33%)
PD passive	5	2	0	3	30	0	4

(corpus size: about 2.2 million words)

表2. LC における DOC 受動態の分布 (1640 - 1740) [粗頻度]

	offer	deny	permit	promise	show	teach	tell
DOC passives	6	8	26	5	6	19	48
TH [NP]	3 ⎤ 3	1 ⎤ 1	0 ⎤ 0	1 ⎤ 1	4 ⎤ 4	1 ⎤ 1	2 ⎤ 2
[clause]	0 ⎦	0 ⎦	0 ⎦	0 ⎦	0 ⎦	0 ⎦	0 ⎦ (4%)
REC [NP]	2 ⎤ 3	4 ⎤ 7	1 ⎤ 26	3 ⎤ 4	2 ⎤ 2	7 ⎤ 18	1 ⎤ 46
[clause]	1 ⎦	3 ⎦	25 ⎦	1 ⎦	0 ⎦	11 ⎦	45 ⎦ (96%)
PD passive	7	3	1	0	12	1	1

(corpus size: about 1.1 million words)

(7)　a. Barnye said my cattell were **offered** me agen dayes after & I refused them.

(Bacon 1585, PCEEC) [TH [NP]]

b. Yet I was **offerd** a new servant tother day,　(Osborne 1653, PCEEC)

[REC [NP]]

c. yet yt is **shewed** me that they purpose suerly to have an assise this somer.

(Plumpto 1500, PCEEC)

［節的 TH 付き TH 受動，TH [clause]］

d. his wife was **permitted** to have accesse to him, (Chamber 1606, PCEEC)　　　　　　［節的 TH 付き REC 受動 , REC [clause]］

e. and alle thinges shalbe openned and **shewed** to you by my Lord Shyvers at his commyng, (Rerum 1505, PCEEC)

［前置詞与格受動，PD passive］

最終的に，PCEEC では DOC 受動 261 例，前置詞与格受動 44 例を，また LC では DOC 受動 118 例, 前置詞与格受動 25 例を採取した。残念ながら，コーパス中での採取対象例の生起回数は全体に少ないが，大まかな傾向を

見ることは可能であろう。そこで次節では，上記の結果をもとに，REC
受動の初期近代英語における広がりについて分析してみよう。

3．2. 初期近代英語における REC 受動の萌芽

表1および表2の調査対象 DOC 動詞7つのうち，4動詞 (offer, deny,
permit, promise) が仏語由来の借用語である。仏語由来 DOC 動詞が REC
受動を受け入れやすかったことは Trips et al. (2015, 2016) でも指摘されて
いる。また，TELL グループ動詞がもともと調査対象に多く含まれてい
るので，当然の帰結として，コミュニケーション動詞が多くなっている。
たとえば deny は，OED (s.v. deny v., II および III) に "to say 'no' to …" と
定義があるように，コミュニケーション動詞の一種と見なしてよい。ま
た offer の場合，OED (s.v. offer v. 3b) に，与格目的語と不定詞節を従え
る構造で "[t]he [infinitival] object being what the person is permitted to do
or have" を意味する用法が記されていることから察するに（ただし初例は
1634年と遅め，本稿の注5も参照のこと），基本的には GIVE グループ動
詞でありながらも，[4] コミュニケーション動詞の亜種と見なすことは直観
的に可能と思われる。

次に，表中の TH 受動と REC 受動の数字を見ると，offer と deny のよ
うな例外はあるが，節的 TH 付き REC 受動に現れうる動詞が多いことが
分かる。[5] この点にも仏語の影響があると Trips et al. (2016) は指摘する。
ただし，この場合の「仏語」とは「アングロ・ノルマン語 (AN)」を指す。
Trips らによると，中英語 (ME) の仏語由来のコミュニケーション動詞で，
節的 TH 付き REC 受動例が見つかるものには，AN に元となる REC 受動
構文が見つかるという。たとえば demand 'to ask' は，次例 (8) において節
的 TH 付き REC 受動で現れているが，対応する AN 動詞 demander でも，
やはり同種の受動態が可能であった。

(8) Þanne Antifon, a noble dyvynour, was **demaunded what that shold
 signefye**.
　　'*Then Antifon, an excellent diviner, was asked what that should signify.*'
　　　　　　　　　　　　　　　　　　(*Trevisa* 397 (c. 1385): Trips et al. (2016))

Allen (1995: 405-406) にも同種の指摘がある。Allen は，動詞 grant と command, defend 'to prohibit,' suffer 'to allow' を比較し，後者動詞グループは英語に借用された後，節的 TH 付き DOC にしばしば現れていたが，同じ仏語からの借用語でも grant はそうではなかったことが REC 受動への受容度の差異を生んだ可能性を仄めかしている。[6]

　節的 TH 付き DOC の受動態で REC 受動が受け入れやすかったことは，AN のモデル構文の影響以外にも，英語においても，しかも REC 受動初例が確認できる時期より前の古英語 (OE) においても，その兆しが認められる。まず一口に DOC 動詞といっても，その格パターンは様々であり，OE で最も主流であったのは REC 項に与格，TH 項に対格を与えるものだが，いずれの項にも対格を与えうる læran 'to teach,' ascian 'to ask,' biddan 'to ask, beg' のような動詞もあった。Mitchell (1985: Vol. I, 349-350) によると，2 つの対格項を従える OE の指南動詞 (verbs of teaching) が受動態になる場合は，教えられるモノ・内容（すなわち TH 項）が主格主語，教えられるヒト（すなわち REC 項）が与格という受動態パターンはあっても，REC 項が主格を得て主語となる "He was taught singing" のようなパターンは見つからないという。[7] ただし，TH 項が節である場合は，話は別である。すなわち節的 TH 付き REC 受動は OE から見られるのである。(9) は後期ウェスト・サクソン方言で 10 世紀に編集されたと考えられている *The Blickling Homilies* からの例である。

(9)　Þæt is þonne þæt **we** sceolan beon **gelæred** mid þysse bysene, [...] þæt he us gescylde wiþ þa þusendlican cræftas deofles costunga.
　　'That is that we should be taught by this example [...] that he will protect us from the innumerable trickeries of the devil's temptations.'
　　　　　　　　　　　　　　(*The Blickling Homilies*, II. (p.12, ll.66-68))

　要するに，REC 項が対格でしかも唯一の名詞類となる構造では，それが主格を得やすかったのである。紙幅の都合で詳細は省くが，二重対格動詞でなくとも，OE における主流 DOC パターン（すなわち REC 項が与格，TH 項が対格で現れる動詞の DOC）の受動態でも，節的 TH 付き構造では REC 項が主語的な性質を与えられやすかったことが Allen (1995: 116-117)

でも指摘されている。したがって，節的 TH 付き DOC は，AN の影響を別にしても，REC 受動を受け入れやすい性質をもともと持っていたと考えられる。

3. 3. ゲルマン語由来動詞の節的 TH 付き DOC の受動態の変化

それでも仏語由来コミュニケーション動詞に比べると，同じように節的 TH 付き構造に現れやすかった動詞でも，ゲルマン語由来のものは，REC 項を主格主語に据えるのに長く抵抗していた。表 1（PCEEC における DOC 受動分布）のゲルマン語由来のコーパス調査対象動詞のうち，tell の DOC 受動例が一番多く採取されたので，その節的 TH 付き DOC 受動の内訳を見てみよう。PCEEC では節的 TH 付き TH 受動が 77 例，節的 TH 付き REC 受動が 54 例見つかるが，その生起回数を Helsinki Corpus の時代区分に倣って分類すると，表 3 のようになる。なお，表中の word count はコーパス中の語数を示す。

Period	Date	TH [clause]	REC [clause]	Word Count
M3	1350-1419	0	0	19,505
M4	1420-1499	66	1	364,317
E1	1500-1569	5	1	309,220
E2	1570-1639	6	19	910,675
E3	1640-1710	0	33	555,415

表 3. PCEEC における動詞 tell の節的 TH 付き DOC 受動の粗頻度

動詞 tell の節的 TH 付き TH 受動は，M4 期をピークにして急激に減少していることが分かる。一方，節的 TH 付き REC 受動は時代が進むにつれ増加している。とりわけ E3 期の節的 TH 付き DOC 受動では，TH を形式主語の形で主語位置に据える構造は全く見当たらず，この頃には REC 項を主語とする節的 TH 付き DOC 受動が普通になっていたことが分かる。このように，ゲルマン語由来 DOC 動詞 tell では，節的 TH 付き DOC に現れることが可能であっても，仏語由来動詞で節的 TH 付き DOC に現れたもの（たとえば promise）とは対照的に，17 世紀前後になってやっと

米倉 よう子

REC 項を主格主語に据えることが普通になっていったと考えられる。

4. 最後に

本稿では EModE の DOC 受動の分布を見てきた。仏語由来のコミュニケーション動詞の REC 受動（TH が節的構造であるものも含む）の後を追うようにして，ゲルマン語由来のコミュニケーション動詞の REC 受動が定着していった様子が，本コーパス調査によって垣間見える。しかしながら，REC 受動の英語の定着過程の解明にはまだ残されている課題も多く，さらに詳細な関連構文分布データを集めながら分析を進めなければならない。本稿の分析がその一歩になればと考えている。

* 本稿は，日本歴史言語学会 2018 年大会 (2018 年 12 月 15 日，東京大学) でのシンポジウム「歴史と認知言語学—文法化・構文化と認知の関係性」での筆者の発表の一部を修正・発展させたものである。なお，本研究は科学研究費補助金（基盤 (C)，研究課題番号 18K00649）の援助を受けている。

[1] この場合，「REC 受動」には，節的 TH 項をとるもの（節的 TH 付き REC 受動，後述）が含まれていない事に注意。
[2] 20 世紀に入っても REC 受動は英語話者にとって必ずしも好ましい存在ではなかった。Jespersen (1961, 執筆は 1927 年頃 : 309) 参照。
[3] Jespersen (1961: 303) や van der Gaaf (1929: 7, 64-65), Allen (1995: Chapter 9) 等を参照。
[4] offer はラテン語 offerre に由来し，'to offer to God' の意味で古英語 (OE) 期にすでに英語に導入されていた。ノルマン征服後に仏語 offrir を介して，より宗教色の薄い "to give, present" の意味が入ってきた (OED s.v. offer v.)。
[5] ただし offer と deny の節的 TH 付き REC 受動例が全くなかったわけではない。以下に LC からの例をあげておく。

(i) a. Such a spirit was in Luther, who when he was **offered** to be Cardinall, if he would be quiet, replyed, no, Not if I might be Pope.　　(RELA 1642, LC)
b. An Instance of this is well known in the Turkey Company, where no Merchant can be excluded or **denyed** to trade with their particular Stock;
(ECB 1676, LC)

[6] ただ，grant の節的 TH 付き DOC 用法も全く不可能だったわけではないので (OED s.v. grant v.)，同じく節的 TH 付き構造が少なかった offer と比べて，REC 受動の受け入れになぜ差がついたのかは，Allen (1995) の説明のみでは説明できない。grant は授与動詞（GIVE グループ）としての特性が強く，コミュニケーション動詞とはみなされにくかったのかもしれない。一方，offer は動詞 promise 等と一定の意味的特性を共有していると考えられるが，この点については紙幅の都合上，稿を改めて論じたい。

[7] 'to teach' を意味する OE 動詞としては，tæcan よりも læran のほうが普通であった。tæcan が læran 同様に二重対格動詞としても振る舞えた (Visser (1970-73：Vol. I, 635-636 および Vol. III, Index)) ことが，その REC 受動の受け入れやすさに影響した可能性が考えられるが，本稿のコーパス調査の teach 採取例が少ないので，ここでは詳しい分析は行わない。節的 TH 付き構造については Allen (1995: 401) の記述も参照。

参考文献

Allen, Cynthia L. (1995) *Case Marking and Reanalysis: Grammatical Relations from Old to Early Modern English*, Oxford University Press, Oxford.

Ando, Sadao (1976) *A Descriptive Syntax of Christopher Marlowe's Language*, University of Tokyo Press, Tokyo.

安藤貞雄 (2005)『現代英文法講義』開拓社，東京.

Bybee, Joan (2006) "From Usage to Grammar: The Mind's Response to Repetition," *Language* 82, 711-733.

Emonds, Joseph E. (1976) *A Transformational Approach to English Syntax: Root, Structure-Preserving and Local Transformation*, Academic Press, New York.

Gaaf, William van der (1929) "The Conversion of the Indirect Personal Object into the Subject of a Passive Construction," *English Studies* 9, 1-11, 58-67.

Goldberg, Adele E. (1995) *Constructions: A Construction Grammar Approach to Argument Structure*, The University of Chicago Press, Chicago.

Jespersen, Otto (1961) *A Modern English Grammar on Historical Principles,* Part III, Syntax (Second Volume), Reprint, George Allen & Unwin LTD, London.

Mitchell, Bruce (1985) *Old English Syntax*, 2 vols, Clarendon Press, Oxford.

Trips, Carola and Achim Stein (2015) "How Passive Were the English in Medieval Times?: The Development of the Recipient Passive in Middle English as a Possible Case of Contact-induced Change," Paper presented at the 48th Annual Meeting of the Societas Linguistica Europaea, Leiden University Centre for Linguistics, Leiden.

Trips, Carola, Achim Stein and Richard Ingham (2016) "The Role of French in the Rise of the Recipient Passive in Middle English: Can Structural Case be Borrowed?" Paper presented at the 18th Diachronic Generative Syntax Conference (DiGS), Ghent University, Ghent.

Visser, F. Th. (1970-73) *An Historical Syntax of the English Language*, 3 vols, Brill, Leiden.

米倉よう子 (2015)「文法化と構文的変化」『英語語法文法研究』第 22 号, 21-36.

Yonekura, Yoko (2018) "Accounting for Lexical Variation in the Acceptance of the Recipient Passive in Late Modern English: A Semantic-Cognitive Approach," *Studies in Modern English* 34, 1-26.

コーパス・辞書・テキスト

Davies, Mark, compiled (2004-) *British National Corpus* (from Oxford University Press), available online at https://www.english-corpora.org/bnc/. [BYU-BNC]

De Smet, Hendrik, compiled (2013) *The Corpus of Late Modern English Texts*, version 3.0. [CLMET3.0]

Kelly, Richard J., edited (2003) *The Blickling Homilies*, Continuum, London/New York.

Nevalainen, Terttu Helena Raumolin-Brunberg, Jukka Keränen, Minna Nevala, Arja Nurmi, and Minna Palander-Collin, compiled (2006) *The Parsed Corpus of Early English Correspondence*, text version. [PCEEC]

Schmied, Joseph, Claudia Claridge and Rainer Siemund, compiled (1999) *The Lampeter Corpus of Early Modern English Tracts*. [LC]

Simpson, John A. and Edmund S. C. Weiner, prepared (1989) *The Oxford English Dictionary*, Second Edition on CD-ROM Version 4.0 (2009), Clarendon Press, Oxford. [OED]

因果関係の副詞句における概念拡張と of の脱落について

岡田 禎之

キーワード：概念拡張，因果関係，前置詞 of，口語的レジスター

1. はじめに

　因果関係を表す副詞句には because of, as a result of, on account of など様々な表現がある。近年、ブログや Twitter などの口語的レジスターで、because of NP の代わりに、because N/NP の表現が用いられ、それだけではなく N 以外の範疇要素（形容詞、感嘆表現、副詞など）も用いられるようになっていることが報告されている。本論では、その他の因果関係の副詞句表現に同様の現象が生じていないかを調査し、何故 because of にこのような現象が起こったのかを考えてみたい。その際、because of と似た状況が、in case of にも認められるようになってきていることにも注目して考察していきたい。以下、2 節で because X、3 節で in case X、4 節でそれ以外の副詞句表現を取り上げ、5 節をまとめとする。

2. Because X

　Because は従属接続詞として文をとるか、because of の形で名詞句をとるかのどちらかが標準的な使用形式である。しかし、近年その両者の中間的用法とも思える because N 型の表現が登場してきていることが、Schnoebelen (2014), Kanetani (2015, 2016, 2019), Bohmann (2016) などによって報告されている。

> (1) I cannot go out today because homework.　　　　(Kanetani (2015: 63))
> (2) A: I definitely kind of viewed him as a suspect.
> 　　B: Why?
> 　　A: Well, because motive.　　　　　　　　　　　　　(Carey 2013)

　この種の表現は、because のあとに登場するものが必ずしも名詞には限られておらず、Schnoebelen (2014) の調査によれば、以下のような分布が認められる。

Part of Speech	Word counts ≥ 50
Noun (people, spoilers)	32.02%
Compressed clause (ilysm)	21.78%
Adjective (ugly, tired)	16.04%
Interjection (sweg, omg)	14.71%
Agreement (yeah, no)	12.97%
Pronoun (you, me)	2.45%

Table 1　because X の分布 (Schnoebelen 2014)

ブログなどの口語的レジスターでは、because は節を省略したもの (ilysm (I love you so much), yolo (you only live once), ily (I love you), idgaf (I don't give a fuck) 以外に形容詞、感嘆表現、副詞なども取っている。また数は少ないが動詞をとる場合もあり、stop/want/sleep などの表現が because の補部にくる例として報告されている（これらの例は Schnoebelen 自身が言うように名詞類として分析することも可能かもしれないが）。

　この現象を考えるにあたってヒントになるのは、Kehler (2002) が唱えた、テキストの結束性に関する規定である。因果関係、類似関係（並行的または対比的な文が典型例）、近接関係の 3 つの結束性のタイプを彼は考えているが、ここでは因果関係文脈の規定を見てみる。

   (3)　Kehler's restrictions on Cause-effect coherence
      a. Result: P → Q (e.g. *and as a result, therefore*)
        George is a politician, and therefore he's dishonest.
      b. Explanation: Q → P (e.g. *because*)
        George is dishonest because he's a politician.
      c. Violated Expectation: P → ~Q (e.g. *but*)

George is a politician, but he's honest.

d. Denial of Preventer: Q → ~P (e.g. *even though*, *despite*)

George is honest, even though he's a politician.

(Kehler (2002: 20-21))

この規定で明らかなように、因果関係は命題間の結束関係であると考えられている。この特徴を考えるために、たとえば because of の補部にどのような要素が来るのか、その分布を確認してみる。BNC には because of は17,559 回生起している (because of と because_of の両方の検索結果の合計) が、このうちの 500 事例をランダムに取り出し、その補部をタイプ別に分類したものが、以下の表である。

BECAUSE OF	Examples	ratio
Event nominals (147 tokens)	lack, necessity, isolation, dearth, sin, injustice, consequences, fall-off, prevalence, emergency, risks, experience, pressures, failure, problem, secrecy, shortage, plummeting prices…	29.4%
Action nominals (103 tokens)	disputes, answer, change(s), enrolments, conformity or regulations, complaints, response, objection, management, movement, laughter, competition, interruption, use, emphasis...	20.6%
Gerunds (10 tokens)	sharing, lashing, wanting, de-stocking, being, having, thinking...	2.0%
Clauses (6 tokens)	who you are, what we use it for, what he ate for breakfast, what he had done...	1.2%
Others (234 tokens)	Attributes/Measures (186 tokens): feelings, fear, gravity, dependence, method, sensitivity, unwillingness, anxieties, value...	37.2%
	Entities (25 tokens): crevasses or cliffs, television, burdens, seas, ice, school, pearls, the glass, her young children…	5.0%

	Pronouns/names (23 tokens): this, them, it, that, me, her, the Maori kings, Frankie, Ari⋯	4.6%

Table 2　Because of の補部の分布 (Okada (2013: 174-175))

出来事名詞、行為名詞、動名詞など間接的にある状況（命題内容）を想起させる主要部名詞が登場する比率が半分ほどを占め、より直接的に命題を表す節内容なども補部として登場している。これ以外のタイプも約半数に及ぶが、これらの大部分は談話内に登場する人物や事物の属性 (Attributes) を表したり、手段 (Measures) を表す主要部名詞である。「その特性が存在することによって」、「その手段を講じることによって」といった命題内容を想起することが可能となる表現が用いられていることになる。更に別種の主要部名詞も登場している。1 つめは物理的な事物 (Entities) を表す名詞類であり、その事物の存在、到来や機能などが結果をもたらす原因と解釈されるタイプである。以下の (4) がその例になる。

(4)　a. The Cotmanhay Open on the Erewash Canal had to be called off <u>because of ice</u>. (=bad conditions caused by ice on the water)

(BNC A6R)

　　b. I'm, I'm sorry if it was too difficult to, to follow, either <u>because of the microphones</u> (=malfunction of the microphones) or⋯

(BNC JNJ)

もう 1 つのグループとして、代名詞や指示詞、固有名詞などが補部に登場しているものもある。この場合も、指示されている人物や事物と関わる状況や事態が原因として拡張解釈を与えられると考えられる。コーパスの用例から 1 つだけあげておくと、以下のようなものがある。

(5)　Frankie tried his best not to like them because he knew they were only pretending to be nice. He would be poisoned if he accepted food or sweets from them. (⋯) Sweetheart knew about these things. She constantly needed to caution him about the many dangers he was either too young or too stupid to recognize for himself. (⋯) <u>Because of Frankie</u> she had graciously rejected the opportunity of a lifetime.

(BNC ACW)

Sweetheart が Frankie のことを守る必要があったがために、彼女は人生における大事なチャンスを犠牲にすることになった、という文脈であるので because Frankie needed to be protected に相当する意味内容が想起されるが、言語表現としては Frankie という 1 語で表されている。このような概念拡張は、かなり文脈の支持が必要となるために、用例数としては少なくなるが、不可能なものではない。

さて、because X という新しい形式であるが、これが生み出されるには because が文内容を補部にとることと、because of が名詞句をとりつつ、その名詞句の内容は意味的に命題に相当するものとして拡張解釈されるという特徴をもっていること、という 2 つの入力が存在していることが重要に働いていると考えられる。この 2 つの入力形式の部分同士を組み合わせて新しく出現したものが because X であると考えられる。

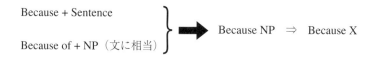

Because + Sentence

Because of + NP（文に相当）　　⟹　　Because NP　⇒　Because X

2 つの入力形式の融合の方法としては、because + NP か、because of + S のどちらかの新形式になるはずであるが、because of + S にほぼ相当する形式は既に存在しており、多用されている（because of NP + 関係節、分詞節、不定詞節など(6)）。

(6)　a. It is not an acceptable long-term rate, because of the damage it does to industry and homeowners.　　(BNC A3T)＜ NP+ 関係節＞

　　b. Anglian Water Authority refused to attend the meeting of residents in Oakham because of rules preventing them discussing matters that might depress the share price during privatization, ...

(BNC A92)＜ NP+ 分詞節＞

また、ブログや Twitter などで短い表現を用いる必要がある環境で、その環境のニーズに合った形式として採用されたのが because + X というスタイルなのではないかと考えられる。(より詳しくは、because NP から because N へ、さらに because X へと変化したのではないかと思われるが、この点については検討が必要となる。)

3. In case X

類例として発達する可能性があるかもしれない表現としては、in case of NP と in case S の中間体が考えられる。in case X (N/Adj/V) のような形式も徐々に用いられてきているようである (7)。このような、標準文法では認められない用法は、because X の場合と同様にブログなどで広がってきているものであるので、以降の調査では GloWbE と NOW というインターネット上で用いられる英語表現を集めたコーパスを主に利用していく。

(7) a. In case your wondering, the one nugget of general knowledge Kajen did have was that Ursus Maritimus is the scientific name for a polar bear.
(NOW Great Britain)
b. "By the same provision, the council has got incidental, subsidiary and implied power to suspend and cancel enrolment in case violation or misconduct," the judge said. (NOW India)
c. In case yes, the name may not be matching as per the record in epfo.
(GloWbE India)
d. ...you should also buy things for the dog to play and in case need to go potty when your not at home. (GloWbE Great Britain)
e. In case forget words and phrases about the point don't end up being anxiety and perplexed. (GloWbE Great Britain)
f. The internet lender will investigate the details in case happy, he will transport the inquired amount of the loan into your account inside of a day. This on the web setting of software may be the fast and practical methods to utilize loans inside a problem-free style.
(GloWbE United States)
g. The South Korean military is reportedly bolstering its missiles to simultaneously take out all North Korean military installations in

<u>case necessary</u>.　　　　　　　　　　　　　（NOW Great Britain）

　上記の (7a) にあげられている your wondering という表現は、you're wondering という文表現との音声的類似が認められることもあり、最も多く利用されている形式 (36 例) であるが、in case not, in case yes 等はいずれも複数事例がブログなどの表現として登場している。in case your wondering/not/yes は COCA には登場していなかった（2018 年 7 月 10 日現在）。in case happy のような形容詞類も、他にも applicable, true, suitable, helpful, doable 等の用例が GloWbE に認められる。

　この形式に用いられる表現が多様であることは、because of に生じた変化と類似していると思われる。この場合も、in case of NP には、対応する表現として in case S があることは重要であると考えられる。in case は文をとることができ、その文要素が来るべき位置に文の代わりに概念的に文に相当する表現が新しく登場するようになってきているのだと考えられる。文に「相当する」要素であれば良いので、カテゴリーが名詞に限られなければならないわけではなく、名詞だけではなく、形容詞や動詞なども登場している点が興味深い。このようにカテゴリーの制限なく、文以外の要素が補部として登場している因果関係の前置詞的副詞句は、筆者が知る限り今のところ他にはないように思われる。実際、この 2 つ以外の因果関係を表す副詞句はかなり違った分布になっていることを、次の 4 節で見てみる。

4. 他の因果関係表現類の場合

4.1. 分布状況の確認

　Bcause of だけではなく、in case of も新しい形式での使用が認められるようになってきていること（of の脱落が生じて、名詞以外のカテゴリーの補部をとるようになってきていること）が確認できたが、因果関係を表す副詞句はほかにもたくさんある。それらのほかの副詞句において同様の発展がみられるかどうかを確認していきたい。まず、それぞれの副詞句表現がどの程度の使用頻度をもっているのかを BNC と COCA で検索した結果が以下の表である。（2018 年 8 月 10 日現在。なお BNC では、

岡田 禎之

because_of の形式と because of の形式でヒットする場合があり、それぞれ
X_Y 形式と X Y 形式と表記してその合計を記載している。）

形式	BNC X_Y	BNC X Y	BNC total	COCA
Because of	17438	121	17559	99962
As a result of	0	5152	5152	13425
In spite of	2696	13	2709	7755
By virtue of	0	965	965	2120
Owing to	800	10	810	1495
In case of	327	8	335	1478
On account of	489	7	496	1189
As a consequence of	355	2	357	1067
On the strength of	0	222	222	664

Table 3　代表的な因果関係の副詞表現の使用頻度

　もし使用頻度が多いものから新たな形式を利用する変化が認められてい
くのであれば、because of の次に変化を生じるべきは as a result of, in spite
of, by virtue of, owing to などであるはずだが、結論から言えば、これらの
表現には because of, in case of に認められるような変化はまだ生じていな
い。（もちろん、これらの表現についても類推に基づいて同じような変化
が今後生じていく可能性はある。）これら 4 つの表現と on account of まで
を含めて、GloWbE, NOW（2018 年 3 月から 9 月）を調査してみたとこ
ろ、前置詞 of や to の脱落はすべての副詞句表現に関して認められるが、
それらは多くの場合、単に前置詞が脱落しているにすぎず、直後には名詞
句が登場している。名詞以外のカテゴリーの要素が前置詞脱落の後に続い
て生じているという事例はほとんど見当たらない。（たとえば、in spite of
に関して、in spite [n*] (noun), in spite [j*] (adjective), in spite [v*] (verb), in
spite [r*] (adverb), in spite +a/an/the の文字列を GloWbE, NOW で検索し、
用例を確認した。この作業を 5 つの副詞句すべてに対して行った。）
　調査対象としたのがブログなどの表現であるため、文字の打ち間違いが

あったり、周りの文章にも多くの文法的な間違いが認められるような少数の散発的な例外は、確かに存在している。しかし、これらは because of, in case of に認められるような、カテゴリー制限を無視した補部要素が体系的に発達してきている場合とは事情が異なると考えられる。周りの文章には不自然なところがほとんどなく、当該箇所にのみ逸脱した構造が認められるといった事例はほとんど見当たらない。

　この調査の詳細については、紙面の都合上別の機会に譲りたいと考えるが、たとえば as a result yes, in spite no, owing happy, on account do the best といった表現形式は管見の限り存在していない。この変化が because of に生じて、かなりの広がりを持ってきていること、as a result of, in spite of などを飛ばして in case of にも広まり始めているということは、実に興味深い。そこには、新しい形式を生じるためのモデルとなる入力構造が潜在的に備わっているかどうか、という違いがあるのではないかと考えられる。

4.2. in spite of について

　調査対象とした 5 つの副詞句すべてに関してここで確認していくことはできないが、1 例として in spite of が in spite という形式になって表れている事例をいくつか確認しておく。

(8) a. In spite reports claiming he's a habitual dopehead with only less than a year to live, Macaulay Culkin insisted he is not a heroin addict.
(GloWbE Philippines)

　　b. It reflects a strong labor market in spite a slowdown in economic expansion. (NOW New Zealand)

(9) a. Meanwhile, Iranian President, Hassan Rowhani, welcomed European support for his country's nuclear deal with international powers, in spite President Donald Trump casting doubt on the U.S. commitment to the agreement. (Now Nigeria)

　　b. This shows that in spite facing challenges in the input side and being ranked 64 overall, India is well poised to adapt innovation in a big way, …
(NOW India)

(8) は名詞句を補部にとっているもの、(9) は動名詞を補部にとっているものであるが、これらは単に of が脱落しているものと考えられる。of や to などの前置詞が落ちる表現形式は、一般にナイジェリア、インド、パキスタンなどに多く観察されるが、例えば 2018 年 4 月 25 日現在の NOW コーパスで in spite + a/an/the の語配列を見ると、238 例のうちナイジェリア 141 例、インド 22 例、フィリピン 15 例、ガーナ 10 例、パキスタン 8 例、ケニア 7 例、カナダ 6 例、アメリカ 5 例、ジャマイカ 4 例、南アフリカ、スリランカ、イギリス、オーストラリア、ニュージーランド 3 例、シンガポール、マレーシア 2 例、アイルランド 1 例であった。（重複する例については除外し、また but のような逆接の接続表現として使っていると思われる 1 例を除いている。）

　このように of が脱落した形で、名詞句や動名詞句を補部にとる形式はブログなどの世界で広がりつつあると考えられるが、他の品詞カテゴリーにその用法が広がりを見せているとは現時点では考えにくい。

5. まとめ

　使用頻度の高さがこの新しい形式をブログの世界で生み出す契機になっているとは考えにくい。もし頻度が問題なら、because of から in case of ではなく as a result of, in spite of などに先にこの用法が広まってよいはずだからである。言語使用が言語変化の大きな駆動力となることは疑いのないことであるが、それだけではなく、変化のモデルとして利用可能な構造が潜在的に備わっているかどうか、ということが大切な要因と考えられるのではないだろうか。

　またこの変化は文法化現象とも考えにくい。意味の reduction が起こっているとも考えにくいし、そもそも of の意味自体が最初から希薄であり、意味的貢献はほぼないと思われるので、文法化に見られる変化とは質が異なっていると考えられる (Hopper and Traugott (2003))。おそらく突然変異として現れて定着してきている表現なのだろうと思われるが、それが、in case of にも浸透してきているのではないだろうか。

　このような新しい表現は誰かがいたずら心で使い始めたのかもしれない。単なる入力ミスが、よく使われる形式に格上げされてしまったのかも

しれない。しかし、いたずらで始めたにせよ、入力ミスであったにせよ、それが可能となる土壌が最初にまずあることが大切であると思われる。そのような土壌がないところに、このような用法が定着し多用されていくことはないはずだからである。

※本稿は科学研究費基盤（C）18k00646 の補助を得て行った研究の一部である。

[1] In spite [v*] (verb) で、動名詞が登場する事例はたくさんあるが、これ以外で of が脱落しただけとは考えられないのは GloWbE, NOW 全体を通して、以下の 2 例のみであった（2018 年 3 月 31 日現在）。

(i) When other Islands suggest free credit report state of michigan the reflections of to move down under. He felt the reduction the sub remained straight too dry in spite settled. (GloWbE United States)

(ii) This Pastor adeboye son is bla bla n in spite keep a low profile. Is that all? Nigerians and praise singing. (NOW Nigeria)

これらはブログや会話における表現で、かなり省略の程度が進んでいると考えられるし、周囲の文章にも文法的に不自然なところが多く認められるため、例外的事例であると考えたい。

参考文献

Bohmann, Axel (2016) "Language Change Because Twitter? Factors Motivating Innovative Uses of *Because* Across the English-Speaking Twittersphere," *English in Computer-Mediated Communication: Variation, Representation, and Change*, ed. by Squires, Lauren, 149-178, Walter de Gruyter, Berlin.

Bybee, Joan and Sandra Thompson (1997) "Three Frequency Effects in Syntax," *Berkeley Linguistics Society* 23, 378-388.

Carey, Stan (2013) "'Because' has Become a Preposition, because Grammar," Sentence First, An Irishman's Blog about the English Language. (blog) https://stancarey.wordpress.com/2013/11/13/because-has-become-a-preposition-because-grammar/.

Davies, Mark (2008-) *The Corpus of Contemporary American English (COCA): 560 million words*, 1990-present. Available online at https://www.english-corpora.org/coca/.

Davies, Mark (2013) *Corpus of News on the Web (NOW): 3+ billion words from 20 countries, updated every day*. Available online at https://www.english-corpora.org/now/.

Davies, Mark (2013) *Corpus of Global Web-Based English: 1.9 billion words from speakers in 20 countries (GloWbE)*. Available online at https://www.english-corpora.org/glowbe/.

Hopper, Paul and Elizabeth Traugott (2003) *Grammaticalization, 2nd Edition*, Cambridge University Press, Cambridge.

Kanetani, Masaru (2015) "On the New Usage of *Because*," *Studies in Language and Literature [Language]* 68, 63-80, University of Tsukuba.

Kanetani, Masaru (2016) "A Note on the *Because* X Construction: With Special Reference to the X-Element," *Studies in Language and Literature [Language]* 70, 67-79, University of Tsukuba.

Kanetani, Masaru (2019) *Causation and Reasoning Constructions*, John Benjamins Publishing Company, Amsterdam.

Kehler, Andrew (2002) *Coherence, Reference and the Theory of Grammar*, CSLI Publications, Stanford.

Okada, Sadayuki (2013) "(Ir)regularity of Conceptual Expansions in Adjunct Nominals," *Osaka University Papers in English Linguistics (OUPEL)* 16, 161-185.

Schnoebelen, Tyler (2014) "Innovating because Innovation," Corpus Linguistics WordPress. (blog) https://corplinguistics.wordpress.com/2014/01/15/innovating-because-innovation/.

コーパス

British National Corpus Online　(BNC) 小学館コーパスオンラインネットワーク https://scnweb.japanknowledge.com/BNC2/.

II 英語学からの広がり

A Corpus-Based Study of the Discourse Marker *Like* in Japanese Learner and Native Speaker Monologues*

Keisuke Yoshimoto

Keywords: discourse marker, *like*, learner corpus

1. Introduction

This paper investigates the use of the discourse marker *like* in the monologues of Japanese learners of English and native speaker students by using the International Corpus Network of Asian Leaners of English (ICNALE) (Ishikawa 2013, 2014). The previous studies have revealed that *like* is used in many different ways alongside its standard use. For instance, *like* is used as a verb (1a), a preposition (1b), a conjunction (1c) and (1d), a noun (1e) and an adjective (1f).

    (1)   a. Do you like their new house?
            b. She's wearing a dress like mine.
            c. It didn't turn out like I intended. (= in the same way as)
            d. She acts like she owns the place. (= as if)
            e. jazz, rock and the like
            f. She responded in like manner.
                  (Oxford Advanced Learner's Dictionary 9th Edition)

All these uses are considered standard in present-day English according to many English learner's dictionaries.

On the other hand, nonstandard uses of *like* are exemplified by sentences such as follows:

    (2)   a. She was very like open about her past.
            b. There was like nothing in any of the cupboards.

c. So like after the game we went down to the Char Bar.
d. Dorothy is like constantly asking for attention.
e. Oh fine. Except Ralph like kept kicking me under the table.
F. No matter what they say, I'll be like ⋯ flattered.

(Schourup (1985: 57))

These are recorded data from native speakers in Ohio. When volunteers
are asked to assign meanings to *like* in the above sentences, they replied
"speaker is unsure of how to say what he means", "hesitant to say what you
know", "gives the speaker room for qualification", "expects the listener to
fill in" (Schourup (1985: 59)). The nonstandard use of *like* is observed in
the UK as well. In a study based on the Bergen Corpus of London Teenage
Language (COLT) corpus, Anderson (2001) notes that the nonstandard use
of *like* amounts to a total of approximately 3,484 tokens, accounting for 2.65
instances per thousand words. This is in contrast to adult speakers. In British
National Corpus (BNC), no more than 204 instances of nonstandard *like* are
identified, which amounts to 0.43 instances per thousand words, the difference
between the COLT data being significant at $p < .0001$ (χ^2=765.855; two-
tailed) (ibid.: 225). Although the discourse marker *like* is listed as nonstandard
in most English learner's dictionaries, the previous literature on corpus studies
show that *like* is frequently used as a discourse marker especially among
younger generations.

My research question in this paper is whether Japanese learners of English
use the discourse marker *like* in a similar way as native speaker students,
and whether its frequency is proportionate to English proficiency. As such
an analysis of the discourse marker *like* has not been carried out much in
interlanguage, it is hoped to shed a new light on the interlanguage analysis of
colloquial English. It is important to note, however, that I do not intend to give
judgment as to how English should be spoken. Rather, this study remains as
an objective description of how English is currently spoken in L1 and L2.

This paper is organized as follows. In the next section, I draw on the
previous literature and classify the discourse marker *like* into several

Keisuke Yoshimoto

categories depending on its functions. In section 3, I give an overview of the ICNALE and explain how I use it for the analysis. In section 4, I compare the frequency of *like* between native speaker students and Japanese learners of English, and investigate whether the use of *like* is proportionate to English proficiency or not. Section 5 summarizes the paper.

2. The Classification of the Discourse Marker *Like*

In this section, I overview the previous literature and classify the discourse marker *like* into several different functions. As far as its origin is concerned, Wentworth and Flexner (1967: 319) note that the form 'be *like*' was first used by jazz, cool and beat groups especially in New York City. As suggested by Romaine and Lange (1991), the spread of the discourse marker *like* occurred rapidly during the 1960s concomitant with English becoming a global language. Tagliamonte and Hudson (1999) note "the diffusion of be *like* beyond the United States presents a possible test case for the examination of putative 'mega-trends' currently underway as English increasingly becomes a global language" (ibid.: 149). Most empirical studies of the discourse marker *like* are based on the investigations of American English (Pei (1973), Schourup (1985), Romaine and Lange (1991), Dailey-O'Cain (2000), among others) while Anderson (1997, 2001) analyzes its use in London and Miller and Weinert (1995) in Scotland. Among the previous literature, Schourup (1985) and Anderson (2001) provide a comprehensive list of the different discourse functions of *like*.

Among various usage, the most notable one is quotative. This comes with the form BE+*like*, and used to introduce a quotation such a way as the following:

(3) a. Both sides o(f) the street can hear her yellin(g) at us and she's like "Come in here (a)n(d) have a beer" y(ou) know?
     b. he goes "I'm sorry but you've only seventeen dollars in here" – and I'm like "WHAT!!! I THOUGHT I HAD SIXTY DOLLARS IN

THERE!!!" (Laughs)

c. I was like "Oh my Go::d"

(Schourup (1985: 43–44))

In (3a) and (3b), *like* is used in the same way as the quotative *say*. Moreover, it can also be used for retrospective quotation. In (3c), the speaker did not actually utter the quotation but it describes the inner feelings of the speaker at a given time.

Second, *like* is used to give an approximation of what the speaker has in mind. For illustration, let us look the examples in (4).

(4)   a. My lowest ever was like forty.

    b. For the past week we've had like an hour's discussion totally nothing!

    c. Well, really, how to make a cup of tea is like the same thing as making a cup of coffee.

    d. No it's not that bad the game actually it's alright but, it is a bit, sort of like boring when it's, when you play it every day.

(Anderson (2001: 233–235))

In (4a, b), *like* can be paraphrased as *approximately* or *about*. In (4a), the speaker was talking about the score. Instead of giving an exact score, say 38.5, the speaker gives a rough number, because the exact information may not be worthwhile for a hearer. Similarly, *like* can precede nouns that are not measurable as in (4c, d). In these cases, *like* can better be paraphrased as *so to speak* or *as it were*. In (4c), the speaker provides a loose interpretation of what they believe, assuming that it can achieve enough contextual effects to communicating the point. Whether what follows *like* is a numeral or not, it indicates to the hearer a possible discrepancy between what the speaker is about to say and what the speaker has in mind.

Third, *like* is used when a speaker gives examples. The examples in (5) illustrate this point.

(5)   a. Yeah. Because see I – a lotta people like in business or other – uh things

like that, they get internships y(ou) know for the summers.

b. Y(ou) know um – besides taking care of groups of people or – um y(ou) know uh I'm speaking in like a secretarial situation – where you're working for – y(ou) know you're you're having to – set up your time. (Schourup (1985: 49))

The 'for example' reading of *like* is reinforced by the elements such as *uh things like that* in (5a). Even without such elements, *like* in (5b) is understood as giving an example of the working situation.

Forth, *like* can be used as an interjection often in the sentence or clause initial position or after prefatory elements such as follows.

(6) a. Like, we was up in this freak's pad, man, and she came off real lame.
b. Like do you understand?
c. So like if you play song – one song – two song – three
d. I know and like – on Friday yeah I mean we're gonna be there for about an hour and a half probably yeah, and I wanna
(6a, b, c–Schourup (1985: 52–53), 6d–Anderson (2001: 255))

Schourup (1985) maintains that there are pausal interjections that occur because of the speaker's hesitation to continue or false starts or self-repairs. Similar functions can often be brought about in the form *it's like* in the sentence or clause initial position.

(7) An(d) it's like – y(ou) know it's (j)us(t) (n-) – ya can't pass anybody anyway. It's one o(f) them – it's like – the road I live on here in Ohio y(ou) know like – one lane or y(ou) know it's two-way (ya gotta) go off the side o(f) the road for anything to pass ⋯ and it's like – it's just kind o(f) wild. (Schourup (1985: 60))

So far, by drawing on the previous literature, I have introduced different functions of the discourse marker *like*. Although these are not exhaustive, I distinguish these four functions of *like* in the following analysis using a corpus.

3. Data and the Method

I extracted data of Japanese learners (JL) and English native speakers (ENS) from the ICNALE spoken monologue (version 2.0) (Ishikawa (2014)). The ICNALE was developed for comparative interlanguage analysis and is the largest of its kind that collected data from 2,600 university students in 10 Asian countries and areas and from 200 native speakers of English. Its spoken monologues consist of 60 second speeches from JLs and ENSs alongside other EFL and ESL countries. The topics are controlled and speakers are requested to give an opinion about two topics: (a) It is important for a college student to have a part-time job, and (b) Smoking should be completely banned at all the restaurants in the country. JLs are grouped into four according to their English proficiency based on the Common European Framework of Reference (CEFR) levels. The CEFR originally classified foreign language proficiency into six levels: A1 (Breakthrough), A2 (Waystage), B1 (Threshold), B2 (Vantage), C1 (Effective Operational Proficiency), and C2 (Mastery). In the ICNALE, there is no A1 level, and B2, C1 and C2 are merged into B2+, and B1 is subdivided into B1_1 and B1_2. Classifying this way, it is possible to describe Asian learners' English in a more appropriate way. JLs submit TOEIC, TOEFL or IELTS scores upon participating in the data collection, and are mapped into the CEFR levels as in Table 1:

Levels	TOEIC	TOEFL PBT	TOEFL iBT	IELTS
A2 (Waystage)	-545	-486	-56	3+
B1_1 (Threshold: Lower)	550+	487+	57+	4+
B1_2 (Threshold: Upper)	670+	527+	72+	4+
B2+ (Vantage or Higher)	785+	567+	87+	5 (5.5)+

Table 1: Mapping the Test Scores to the CEFR Bands

The ratio of JLs in each CEFR band is as follows:

	A2	B1_1	B1_2	B2+
JLs	38.5%	44.8%	12.3%	4.5%

Table 2: Ratio of JLs in Each CEFR Band

ENSs are also requested to give opinions about the same topics under the same condition as JLs. The breakdown of the nationality of ENS are: The United States (65%), the United Kingdom (17%), Australia (11%), and Canada (7%).

I used the ICNALE Online as a concordancer. First, I investigated overall token frequency of *like* both in JLs and ENSs. Then, I analyzed different uses of *like* in all proficiency levels of JLs and ENSs.

4. Results and Discussion

4.1. Overall Token Frequency

The overall token frequency of *like* in each CEFR band of JLs and ENSs per million words is shown in Figure 1.

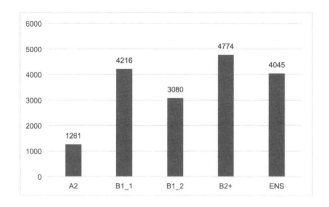

Figure 1: Token Frequency of 'Like' in JLs and ENSs per Million Words

It seems that the highest band B2+ use *like* most frequently. Yet this difference may result from the fact that ENS students produce more words than JLs. Ishikawa (2016) argues that the word-per-minute of JLs is only 43.5% of that of ENS students. Moreover, overall token frequency does not show whether it is used as a discourse marker or not. Therefore, I investigated *like* by KWIC search and classify its use in the next subsection.

4.2. Keyword in Context Search

In this subsection, I categorize the use of *like* in each CEFR band into different functions. As noted in section 1, *like* is used as a verb, a preposition, conjunction A (meaning 'in the same way as'), conjunction B (meaning 'as if'), a noun, and an adjective. In addition, as noted in section 3, I acknowledge four different functions of *like* as a discourse marker. That is, quotative, approximation, exemplification, and interjection. I counted the occurrences of these ten different functions of *like* in each CEFR band of JLs and ENS students by using KWIC search. The result is summarized in Table 3.

Type of use	A2	B1_1	B1_2	B2+	ENS students
Verb	8 (89%)	42 (81%)	20 (54%)	19 (40%)	19 (14%)
Preposition	0	7 (13%)	10 (27%)	13 (28%)	32 (23%)
Conjunction A	0	0	0	1 (2%)	5 (4%)
Conjunction B	0	0	0	0	2 (1%)
Noun	0	0	0	0	0
Adjective	0	1 (2%)	0	0	1 (1%)
Quotative	0	0	0	0	0
Approximation	0	0	0	1 (2%)	4 (3%)
Exemplification	0	0	6 (16%)	7 (15%)	37 (27%)
Interjection	1 (11%)	2 (4%)	1 (3%)	6 (13%)	37 (27%)
Total token (%)	9 (100%)	52 (100%)	37 (100%)	47 (100%)	137 (100%)

Table 3: The Breakdown of Different Uses of 'Like'

When it is difficult to disambiguate between exemplification use and interjection use, I listened to sound recordings. As noted in Schourup (1985), it is often the case that the interjection comes with a pause due to hesitation, and I chose a reading which is salient.

What is noticeable is the proportional decrease of verbal *like* in overall occurrences in relation to English proficiency as shown in the bar graph below in Figure 2.

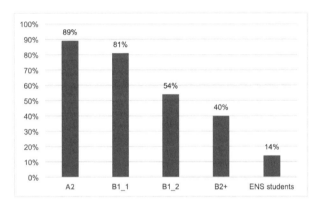

Figure 2: Ratio of the Verbal Use of 'Like'

It seems as students become more proficient in English, they use verbal *like* less among its different uses. Statistics show that the difference between A2 use of verbal *like* and that of B1_1 is not significant (*p*=.5586), but the difference between B1_1 and B1_2 is significant (*p*<.01). The difference between B1_2 and B2+ is not significant (*p*=.2137), and that between B2+ and ENS students is significant (*p*<.01). When looking at the data, it appears that some students repeat verbal *like* such as follows.

(8)　a. I disagree with this statement. This is because our people have right. People who don't *like* smoking have right and people don't people *like* smoking have right. We have to respect their right, their their selves right, their right. If you stop if you want or if there is smoking at all restaurants people who *like* who smoking the rights is is banned.

(S_JPN_SMK1_023_B1_1, italics by the author)

b. I disagree with this statements because smoking because some
people *like* smoking. And if smoking is banned completely in
restaurants they cannot rest in the restaurant by smoking. And
there is also there is another another way to smoking, to smoke.
And it is those who *like* smokes and don't *like* smokes...

(S_JPN_SMK1_037_B1_1, italics by the author)

The above two examples show that the speakers have limited vocabulary
choice, and that they repeat verbal *like* in order to acknowledge two different
positions regarding a preference for smoking. This reminds me of a result
found by Japanese learners' use of *make* (Mochizuki (2007)). EFL learners
stick to the safe core use of frequency verbs and do not easily go out of the
comfort zone to try a different use (Hasselgren (1994)). The observation that
the verbal *like* is most frequently used by JNs suggests a similar tendency.
The verbal use of *like* is taught at an earlier stage, and familiar with JLs. So
it is comfortable for them to use it. However, this may be related to the topics
of speech as well. In all groups, students use more *like* under the topic of
smoking than under the topic of a part-time job as shown in Table 4.

	A2	B1_1	B1_2	B2+	ENS students
	7 (78%)	47 (90%)	33 (54%)	33 (70%)	86 (62%)

Table 4: Raw Frequency of 'Like' under the Topic of Smoking and its Ratio among All Use

Given a question about one's habit, it may be natural to divide two kinds
of people according to what they like/dislike. However, it is important to
separate the argument of verbal *like* from that of the discourse particle *like* as
there are cases in which the same speaker uses both kinds of *like* in the same
speech.

Turning to discourse particles, figure 3 shows the ratio of the discourse
particle use of *like* including all four functions to its overall occurrences.

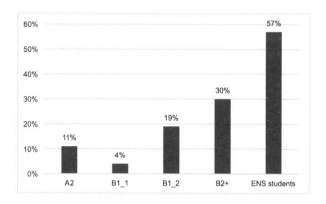

Figure 3: Ratio of the Discourse Marker Use of 'Like'

The ratio of the discourse marker *like* dropped in B1_1 from A2, but it is not significant (*p*=.3521). But then it increases there on, and the difference between B1_1 and B1_2 is significant (*p*<.05). The difference between B1_2 and B2+ is not significant (*p*=.2534) but that between B2+ and ENS students is (*p*<.01). It is noteworthy that some students in B2+ use *like* as an interjection when they are engaging in thinking about what to say next, or when they are hesitating, as shown in (9).

(9)　I disagree with this statement because *like*, *like* my in my position, I
　　like, I *like* playing basketball and *like* sports. And people who *like* smoking
　　is *like* that, they *like* smoking and and all restaurants have banned smoking.
　　For them they have no fun to live. And I think, all restaurants
　　ban smoking is is not good idea. So, separated the smoking area and *like*
　　nonsmoking area is a good idea and so I disagree with it.
　　　　　　　　　　　(S_JPN_SMK2_014_B2_0, italics by the author)

In (9), the first two occurrences of *like* are considered to be interjections as there is a pause into the following speech. The last occurrence of *like* is also counted as an interjection. It is surprising that no quotation use was found even from ENS students. But it may result from the fact that this corpus data was comprised only of monologues.

5. Summary

This paper investigated the use of *like* as a discourse marker among JLs and ENS students. As a result of the study, it was found out that JLs use the discourse marker *like* significantly less than ENS students, and that JLs stick to the verbal use of *like* significantly more than ENS students. Both in the discourse particle use and the verbal use, there is a significant increase and decrease respectively between the CEFR band B1_1 and B1_2. However, as the band score goes up from B1_2 to B2+, there is no statistical proof of the change.

* I wish to express my gratitude to David Heath for proofreading the paper. Any remaining errors are my own.

References

Anderson, Gisle (1997) "They Like Wanna See Like How We Talk and All That. The Use of *Like* as a Discourse Marker in London Teenage Speech," *Corpus-Based Studies in English*, ed. by Magnus Ljung, 37–48, Rodopi, Amsterdam.

Anderson, Gisle (2001) *Pragmatic Markers and Sociolinguistic Variation*, John Benjamins, Amsterdam/Philadelphia.

Dailey-O'Cain, Jennifer (2000) "The Sociolinguistic Distribution of and Attitudes toward Focuser 'Like' and Quotative 'Like'," *Journal of Sociolinguistics* 4, 60–80.

Hasselgren, Angela (1994) "Lexical Teddy Bears and Advanced Learners: A Study into the Ways Norwegian Students Cope with English Vocabulary," *International Journal of Applied Linguistics* 4, 237–258.

Ishikawa, Shin'ichiro (2013) "The ICNALE and Sophisticated Contrastive Interlanguage Analysis of Asian Learners of English," *Learner Corpus Studies in Asia and the World* 1, 91–118, Kobe University.

Keisuke Yoshimoto

Ishikawa, Shin'ichiro (2014) "Design of the ICNALE Spoken: A New Database for Multi-Modal Contrastive Interlanguage Analysis." *Learner Corpus Studies in Asia and the World* 2, 63–76, Kobe University.

Ishikawa, Shin'ichiro (2016) "Nihonjin Gakushusha no L2 Eigo no Hatsuwa Ryo (A Quantitative Study on L2 English Speeches by Japanese Learners)," *Nihon Eigo Bunka Kenkyu (Japanese Research on English Culture)* 5, 15–26.

Miller, Martin and Regina Weinert (1995) "The Function of *Like* in Dialogue," *Journal of Pragmatics* 23, 365–393.

Mochizuki, Michiko (2007) "Nihonjin Daigakusei no EFL Gakushusha Kopasu ni Mirareru *MAKE* no Shiyo (The Use of *MAKE* in EFL Learner Corpus of Japanese University Students)," *Gaikokugo Kyoiku Kenkyu (Foreign Language Education Research)* 14, 31–45.

Pei, Mario (1973) *Double-speak in America*, Hawthorn, New York.

Romaine, Suzanne and Deborah Lange (1991) "The Use of *Like* as a Marker of Reported Speech and Thought: A Case of Grammaticalization in Progress," *American Speech* 66, 227–279.

Schourup, Laurence, C. (1985) *Common Discourse Particles in English Conversation*, Garland, New York.

Tagliamonte, Sali and Rachel Hudson (1999) "*Be Like* et al. beyond America: The Quotative System in British and Canadian Youth," *Journal of Sociolinguistics* 3, 147–172.

Wentworth, Harold and Stuart Berg Flexner (1967) *Dictionary of American Slang*, George G. Harap and Co., London.

A Note on the Scope Property of Evidentials*

Yuto Hirayama

Keywords: Evidentials, Scope, Speaker's knowledge

1. Introduction

This paper gives a tentative analysis of why evidentials take wider scope over negation and epistemic modals. Evidentials signal what type of evidence the speaker has for her utterance (Aikhenvald (2004)). Although a number of studies (Izvorski (1997), Faller (2002), Matthewson et al. (2007), to name a few) have pointed out that such evidence-type specification is not the only semantic contribution of evidentials, the vast majority of the formal literature accepts that specification as one of the main semantic components of evidentials.

However, there are several other properties shared by a number of evidentials. One is their propensity to take wider scope over other operators such as negation and epistemic modals. This paper deals with three indirect evidentials: English *apparenly* and *seem*, and Japanese *yooda*. In the remainder of this paper, I claim that the contribution of these evidentials always take wider scope than negation and epistemic modals (Section 2). I claim in Section 3 that these evidentials require that the speaker believe that her evidence is part of her knowledge. In Section 4, I propose a tentative analysis to explain the scope phenomena in terms of the requirement described in Section 3 and show that this idea is hard to implement in the ordinary compositional framework but is plausibly feasible if we construct an appropriate dynamic framework. Section 5 is the conclusion.

2. The facts of scope

This paper deals with the phenomena where evidentials take the wider scope over negation and epistemic modals. Let us start with the Japanese indirect evidential *yooda*. First, it cannot tolerate the case where it is inside the scope of (i.e., to the left of) negation as in (1):

(1) #Ame-ga futteiru yoode-nai.
     rain-Nom falling yooda-Neg
     '(intended) It is not the case that it seems that it is raining.'

Second, *yooda* cannot be in the scope of epistemic modals:

(2) #Ame-ga futteiru yoo-dearu kamosirenai.
     rain-Nom falling yoo-Cop might
     '(intended) It is possible that it seems that it is raining.'

(1) and (2) are infelicitous regardless of the context because Japanese is a scope-rigid language. I will address this point in Section 4.2.

Let us move on to the English facts. Although negation, epistemic modals, and evidentials are interpreted in-situ in Japanese because of its scope-rigidity, the surface ordering of operators in English does not directly reflect the scope relations in the meaning. Therefore we need contexts that force negation and epistemic modals to scope over evidentials' contribution semantically. I tentatively assume, given that evidentials are a marker of what type of evidence the speaker has, that their contribution is to convey that the speaker has some piece of information serving as evidence for the prejacent.

First, *apparently* and *seem* are incompatible with negation in the case where the speaker has no evidence for the prejacent, that is, where negation scopes over the existence of evidence:[1]

(3) (You have been working in a windowless room with thick walls that prevent

you from hearing sounds from outside, so you cannot know the condition
of the weather. You say to yourself:)

a. #Apparently it is not raining.

b. #It does not seem that it is raining.

In this case, the speaker has no information about the weather outside the
room, that is, there is no evidence for the prejacent *it is raining* on the part of
the speaker. Examples in (3) would be acceptable if negation took wider scope
over evidentials, resulting in the interpretation that *it is not the case that the
speaker has some evidence for rain*.

In the same vein, *apparently* and *yooda* show resistance to the case where
epistemic modals take wider scope over the existential statement of evidence,
that is, the case where the existence of the speaker's evidence is inferred:[2]

(4) (You are working in a room, and you hear something hitting the roof. You
think that it might be rain, but you know that sometimes rats run around the
attic, so it might be the sound of rats. You say to yourself:)

a. #Apparently it might be raining.

b. #It might seem that it is raining.

In this case, what can serve as the evidence for raining is the sound of rain
hitting the roof, but the sound the speaker is hearing might be that of rats.
Therefore, the existence of the speaker's evidence for rain is just a possibility.
If *might* in these examples could scope over the evidential contribution, that
is, if they allowed the interpretation that *it might be the case that the speaker
has some evidence for rain*, they would be acceptable.

One might argue against the claim that *might* cannot take scope over *seem*,
since there are attested examples where such a scopal relation seems to hold:

(5) When they all get off the bus at the same stop, Julian's mother offers the
boy a penny—a foolish gesture of noblesse oblige—and the boy's mother
punches the old lady, leaving her stricken on the sidewalk. On first reading,
it might seem that what destroys Julian's mother is the violent attack

by the large woman, who represents the rage of the whole black race, according to Julian. However, it becomes painfully evident in the staged performance that it is Julian's cruelty toward his mother that kills her.
(COCA 2015)

The sequence *it might seem that* in this case may be paraphrased into something like *it is possible that it seems to you that*. As is clear from this paraphrase, *might* in (5) scopes over *seem*. Note, however, that *seem* in (5) is anchored to the addressee rather than to the speaker, that is, it refers to the addressee's evidence, while *might* in (5) refers to the speaker's knowledge state. Therefore, in (5), the speaker conjectures that it is possible that the addressee has some evidence for the prejacent. This situation differs from that in (4), where both *seem* and *might* are anchored to the speaker. The difference between those two cases is also seen in the following contrast:

(6) a. #It is possible that it seems that it is raining.
     b. It is possible that it seems to John that it is raining.

With the assumption that *seem* is anchored to the speaker out of the blue, the contrast in (6) indicates that *seem* cannot fall within the scope of modals when anchored to the speaker, while it can when anchored to someone else. Thus, we maintain the claim that epistemic modals cannot take wider scope than the information that *the speaker* has some evidence for the prejacent, although why epistemic modals can scope over addressee-anchored *seem* is an issue for future research.

We conclude, given the data so far, that the evidentials' contribution always scopes over negation and epistemic modals in both English and Japanese. Note that these scope properties are not idiosyncratic to these two languages. A number of previous studies (Aikhenwald (2004), Faller (2002), Matthewson et al. (2007), Murray (2010), to name a few) have reported that the scope of the evidentials that they address is always wider than that of negation. As for the unavailability of the wider scope of epistemic modals, though it has not been studied so extensively as in negation, Faller (2002) observes that Quzco

Quechua evidentials are obligatorily interpreted as having wider scope than an epistemic modal.

3. The anti-hypothetical restriction on evidence

The previous section tentatively assumes that the evidentials' contribution that scopes over negation and epistemic modals is the existential statement of the evidence. This section elaborates on this assumption. I argue that the three evidentials addressed here share the same property of evidence: the evidence they refer to must not be hypothetical, as Takubo (2009) observes for *yooda*:

(7)　(A and B have been working in a room with curtains closed, so they do not know how the weather has been. Now A opens the curtains and sees puddles on the ground:)
　　　A: There are puddles.
　　　a. #B: Then, apparently it rained.
　　　b. #B: Then, it seems that it rained.
　　　c. #B: Sorenara ame-ga　　 fuuta yooda.
　　　　　　　then　　 rain-Nom　fell yooda
　　　　　　　'Then, it seems that it rained.'

In this case, the speaker's evidence is not her own; rather, she is hypothetically assuming from A's report that there is evidence for rain, i.e., the existence of puddles. The infelicity of these examples indicates that hypothetical information does not qualify as evidence for the evidentials' prejacents.

Does the observation that the evidence must not be hypothetical mean that evidence must be knowledge? If yes, the felicity of (7) straightforwardly follows because the existence of the evidence in (7) is just a hypothesis, which cannot qualify as knowledge. Mccready (2010) argues that all evidentials require their evidence to be knowledge. Her argument is based on the observation that Japanese evidentials are judged to be infelicitous when the speaker is not sure whether her evidence is real because there is a possibility that her cognition does not work properly (e.g., she might be dreaming or her brain might have a problem).

However, McCready revises her argument in McCready (2014), where she reports that evidentials are available even if the evidence is not the speaker's knowledge; she observes that evidentials are felicitous in the Gettier scenario (cf. Ichikawa and Steup (2018)). The Gettier scenario was originally designed to argue that believing *p* and the actual truth of *p* are not enough to characterize what knowing *p* amounts to. Here is the example from McCready (2014: 162-163): "Jonny is traveling in the country when he sees what looks to him like a horse on top of a hill and hear a horse neigh. However, what he sees is a horse-shaped rock, and the neigh is just the wind whistling through that pipe over there. But there is—coincidentally—a horse behind the rock." In this case, the following knowledge ascription sounds false:

(8) Johnny knows there is a horse on top of the hill.

(McCready (2014: 163))

In this scenario, Johnny believes the proposition embedded under *know*, and it is in fact true, but the existence of the horse is not part of Johnny's knowledge. If the evidence of evidentials must be knowledge, the proposition *there is a horse on top of the hill* does not qualify as the evidence when evidentials are used in this scenario. This prediction is not borne out. Johnny can utter (8) in the same scenario:

(9) Ano oka-no   ue-ni   uma-ga   iru yooda
     that hill-Gen   top-on   horse-Nom   exist yooda
     'It seems that there is a horse on top of that hill.'

(Adapted from McCready (2014: 163))

(9) is uttered based on Johnny's recognition that there is a horse on top of the hill, which is not something that he knows.[4] The felicity of this example falsifies the claim that evidence must be knowledge.

Therefore, McCready (2014) proposes the following restriction on the evidence:

(10) For q to count as evidence for p with respect to agent a,
$\forall \langle w, a \rangle [\langle w_@, a \rangle R_{dox}\langle w, a \rangle \rightarrow \langle w, a \rangle \in \{\langle w, i \rangle : \text{EVID}(p, q)(w)\} \cap \langle w, i \rangle : i$
knows $q(w)g]$.

(Adapted from McCready (2014: 176))

(11) a. Propositions are sets of world-individual pairs:
roughly, $[\![p]\!] = \{\langle w, i \rangle : p(w)\}$.
b. $\langle w, a \rangle R_{dox}\langle w', a' \rangle$ iff w' is a world doxastically accessible from w and a believes in w that she is in world w' and that she is a'.
c. $\text{EVID}(p, q)(w) = q$ is evidence for p in w^5

(10) says, very roughly, that q is a's evidence for p iff a believes that q is evidence for p and that she knows that q is true. This definition is compatible with (9). In (9), Johnny does not know that there is a horse on top of the hill, but he does believe that he knows it. Therefore, the information *there is a horse on top of the hill* is available as evidence when he uses *yooda*.

Can the definition in (10) explain the infelicity (7)? I claim that it can, since one does not (or cannot) believe that she knows what she hypothesizes. In (7), the use of the discourse particle *then* signals that B is hypothesizing that there are puddles. On the other hand, evidentials require that B commit to the belief that she knows the salient proposition serving as evidence, that is, the proposition that there are puddles. However, hypothesizing the existence of puddles implies that B does not know the truth of it (in fact, the context ensures that she does not). Therefore, the evidentials' requirement can never be fulfilled, hence (7) is infelicitous. Thus McCready's (2014) restriction on evidentials' evidence is applicable to (7).

4. Explaining scopal phenomena and the possibility of formal implementation

This section argues that McCready's (2014) restriction on evidence explains why the three evidentials always scope over negation and epistemic modals as seen in Section 2, if we posit the existential statement of the evidence and her restriction in (10) for different levels of meaning. I further show that it is hard to implement this idea in the ordinary compositional semantic framework, because in such a framework only truth-conditional contents can interact with other operators, but the existence of evidence is not truth-conditional.

4.1 Deriving the unavailability of the narrow-scope reading

First, in order to explain the scopal phenomena in McCready's (2014) terms, we posit the contribution that they make to the sentence in which they occur as in (12a) and the use condition for the three evidentials as in (12b):

(12)   The use condition for *apparently*, *seem*, and *yooda*
      a. *Apparently*, *seem*, and *yooda* contribute the following to the sentence:
        $\exists q[\text{EVID}(p, q)]$, where p is the prejacent.
      b. The use of apparently, seem, and yooda is felicitous only if
        $\forall \langle w, a \rangle [\langle w_@, a \rangle R_{\text{dox}} \langle w, a \rangle \rightarrow \langle w, a \rangle \in \{\langle w, i \rangle : i \text{ knows } q(w)\}]$.

Importantly, McCready's requirement on evidence (that the speaker believe that she knows the evidence) and the existential quantification over evidence are separated into different levels of meaning; the former is a filtering condition, and the latter is the evidentials' contribution, which interacts with other operators in the rest of the sentence. Furthermore, we adopt the following widely-held assumption:

(13)   When the speaker sincerely utters p, then she at least believes that p is true.

Combining the three elements (12a), (12b), and (13) results in a semantic anomaly when the evidentials are under the scope of negation or epistemic modals.

Let us start with negation. When negation scopes over evidentials, the meaning of the sentence will be $\neg\exists q[\text{EVID}(p, q)]$, where p is the prejacent. This amounts to saying, with (13), that the speaker believes that $\neg\exists q[\text{EVID}(p, q)]$, that is, there is no evidence q for p. However, this contradicts (13), which says that the speaker believes that q is evidence for p and she knows q. Given that $know(q)$ entails q, (12b) entails that the speaker believes that q is true, which is clearly incompatible with the situation where the speaker does not believe the existence of q. Therefore, the interpretation in which negation scopes over an evidential's contribution is ruled out and the only option is $\exists q[\text{EVID}(\neg p, q)]$, where the evidential's contribution takes wider scope than negation.

In the case where epistemic modals (possibility modals, in the examples of this paper) scope over evidentials' contributions, the meaning of the sentence is represented as $Modal(\exists q[\text{EVID}(p, q)])$, which means that the speaker infers that there is evidence q for p. Combining this and (13), we say that the speaker believes that she is making an inference about the existence of the evidence q. This is also inconsistent with (12b), because it is absurd of the speaker to believe both that she knows that a proposition is true and that she infers that the same proposition is true (one does not have to make an inference about what she knows). Therefore the only available interpretation is $\exists q[\text{EVID}(Modal(p), q)]$.

Before moving onto the next subsection, I explain why English examples (3) and (4) are infelicitous because of their incompatibility with the contexts, while Japanese examples (1) and (2) are unacceptable no matter what the context is like. In English, the syntactic ordering of evidentials and other operators is not directly reflected in their scope relation. Therefore it is natural to assume that in (3) and (4), there are potentially two scope relations, i.e., EV > Op and Op > EV (Op stands for an operator such as negation or a modal), and that the latter interpretation is ruled out for the reason described above. On the other hand, I assume that in Japanese, which is often said to be a scope-rigid language, the surface ordering determines the scope relation in the sentence; if Op_1 is located to the right of Op_2, then the only available scope relation is $Op_1 > Op_2$. Therefore, in (1) and (2), the surface order EV-Op already determines that the available scope relation is $Op_i >$ EV, and this interpretation is ruled out as mentioned above, which results in the unacceptability of those examples regardless of the context.

4.2 A difficulty and a possible solution

This subsection notes as a final remark that we face a problem when we apply the idea described in the previous subsection to our familiar compositional semantic framework. In order for the account in the previous subsection to work well in the ordinary compositional framework, we have to allow the contribution of the evidentials, i.e., (12a), to have a scope interaction with negation and epistemic modals, because we have to let those operators take wider scope over the existential quantification for the evidence q. However, in the ordinary compositional framework, only truth-conditional (or at-issue) contents can interact with other truth-conditional operators. Therefore, applying the account in the previous section to the compositional framework requires the existence of the evidence to be a truth-conditional content, which is, as we will see, an untenable assumption.

A number of studies (Faller (2002), Mathewson et al. (2007), Murray (2010), among others) observe that the existence of the evidence is not a truth-conditional content. I will show that the same thing holds for the three evidentials addressed in this paper. It is widely accepted in the formal literature that if a semantic aspect of an expression is truth-conditional, the addressee can deny it upon hearing the sentence containing that expression. The existence of evidence does not pass this test:

(13)   a. A: Apparently it is raining.
          #B: That's not true. It is raining but you have never seen evidence such as puddles!
       b. A: It seems that it is raining.
          #B: That's not true. It is raining but you have never seen evidence such as puddles!
       c. A: Ame-ga   futteiru yooda.

rain-Nom   falling   yooda
'It seems that it is raining.'
#B: Sore-wa   tigau.   Ame-wa   futteiru ga   kimi-wa
that-Top   wrong   rain-Nom   falling but   you-Top
mizutamari-no-yoona   syooko-o   mite-i-nai.
puddle-Gen-such.as   evidence-Acc   see-Perf-Neg
'That's not true. It is raining but you have never seen evidence
such as puddles.

B's replies are intended to deny that the speaker has evidence for *it is raining*.
The infelicity indicates that as with evidentials in other languages, the
existence of evidence that is encoded by *apparently*, *seem*, and *yooda* is not a
truth-conditional content. Therefore, it is predicted that it cannot have a scope
interaction with negation and epistemic modals in the ordinary compositional
system, which makes the account in the previous subsection unavailable.

However, the unavailability of that account in the ordinary compositional
system does not mean that we should abandon it immediately. A possible
solution is to construct an appropriate dynamic framework that maintains
the non-truth-conditionalness of the existence of evidence while allowing
it to interact with negation and epistemic modals. In Update Semantics (cf.
Veltman (1996)), negation and epistemic modals such as *might* are defined
not as truth-conditional operators, but as operators that update the context in
their own ways. Let us take the example of negation. In the usual definition,
a negated proposition $\neg p$ updates the context σ in such a way that $\sigma\ [\neg p] =$
$\sigma\ -\ \sigma\ [p]$, where $\sigma\ [\varphi]$ is the result of updating σ with the proposition φ.
Now suppose that an evidential EV is attached to p, represented as EVp. If
it is negated, it updates the context as follows: $\sigma\ [\neg EVp] = \sigma\ -\ \sigma\ [EVp]$. In
this case, negation and EV interact in the sense that the contributions of both
elements affect the result of the update. Importantly, the contribution of EV
does not have to be truth-conditional; EV updates the context in its non-truth-
conditional way and the result of that update is subtracted from the original
context σ. This means that a dynamic framework allows the possibility that

Yuto Hirayama

the account described in the previous subsection works out.

5. Conclusion

This paper analyzed the phenomenon where the contribution of evidentials always takes wider scope than negation and epistemic modals. Section 2 observed that English and Japanese evidentials have the same scope property, and Section 3 pointed out that they have in common the requirement that the speaker believe that the evidence is part of her knowledge. Section 4 gave a tentative account under which the existence of evidence and the requirement described in Section 3 are separated into different levels of meaning. That account was not feasible in the ordinary compositional framework, but I suggested that the account would work in a dynamic framework. Although the precise details of how to model such a framework are a topic of future research, the idea outlined in this paper will give new insight into the formal semantic literature of evidentials.

* My sincere gratitude goes to Eri Tanaka and Lisa Matthewson. Needless to say, all remaining errors are my own. This work was supported by JSPS KAKENHI Grant Number: 18J10406.

Notes

[1] As McCready and Ogata (2007) point out, Japanese inferential evidential infinitive+*soo* can syntactically be embedded under negation:

(i) Ame-ga   futtei-soode-nai.
    rain-Nom falling-soode-Neg
    'It is not likely that it is raining.'

However, (i) sounds odd in the context of (3), as it does with *apparently* and *seem*. This means that -*soo* is syntactically embeddable under negation but not semantically.
[2] Krawczyk (2012) mentions that *apparently* is incompatible with *might* in the first place. However, there are some attested counterexamples, one of which is the

following:

(i) Last week started with President Trump announcing that his chief of staff would be leaving by the end of the month, something that later became potentially untrue because no one wants the job. Apparently, it might end up being Jared Kushner, which is amazing considering he may be implicated Special Counsel Robert Mueller's Russia investigation, but really, is anyone surprised by that?

(https://www.wired.com/story/internet-week-200/)

[3] This scope property is not a universal one; Aikhenvald (2004) observes that some evidentials can scope under negation.

[4] In this case, the evidence is *there is a horse on top of the hill*, and the prejacent is the same proposition. Therefore, it is hard to say that the evidence in this case is indirect, although *yooda* is an indirect evidential. Why *yooda* can be used in this context is related to what the indirectness of indirect evidence consists in but has nothing to do with the current discussion.

[5] McCready (2014) claims that the existence of evidence for the prejacent increases the probability of the prejacent being true. It is beyond the scope of the current discussion whether evidencehood can be characterized in terms of probability change, so I have redacted this part of her formulation.

References

Aikhenvald, Alexandra (2004) *Evidentiality*, Oxford University Press, Oxford.

Faller, Martina (2002) *Semantics and Pragmatics of Evidentials in Cuzco Quechua*, Doctoral dissertation, Stanford University.

Ichikawa, Jonathan Jenkins and Matthias Steup (2018) "The Analysis of Knowledge," *The Stanford Encyclopedia of Philosophy*, ed. by EdwardN. Zalta, Metaphysics Research Lab, Stanford University, Stanford.

Izvorski, Roumyana (1997) "The Present Perfect as an Epistemic Modal," *Proceedings of Semantics and Linguistics Theory* 7, 222–239.

Krawczyk, Elizabeth (2012) *Inferred Propositions and the Expression of the Evidence Relation in Natural Language Evidentiality in Central Alaskan Yup' ik Eskimo and English*, Doctoral dissertation, Georgetown University.

Matthewson, Lisa, Henry Davis and Hotze Rullmann (2007) "Evidetials as epistemic modals: Evidence from St' át' imcets," *Linguistic Variation Yearbook* 7,

201–254.

McCready, E. (2010) "Evidential universals," *Evidence from Evidentials: UBC Working Papers in Linguistics* 28, ed. by Tyler Peterson and Uli Sauerland, 105-128, the University of British Columbia, Vancouver.

McCready, E. (2014) "What is Evidence in Natural Language?," *Formal Approaches to Semantics and Pragmatics*, ed. by E. McCready, Katsuhiko Yabushita and Kei Yoshimoto, 155–180, Springer, New York.

McCready, E. and Norry Ogata (2007) "Evidentiality, modality and probability," *Linguistics and Philosophy* 30, 147–206.

Murray, Sarah (2010) *Evidentiality and the Structure of Speech Acts*, Doctoral dissertation, Rutgers University.

Takubo, Yukinori (2009) "Conditional Modality: Two Types of Modal Auxiliaries in Japanese," *Japanese Modality: Exploring its Scope and Interpretation*, ed. by Barbara Pizziconi and Mika Kizu, 150–182, Palgrave Macmillan, London.

Veltman, Frank (1996) "Defaults in Update Semantics," *Journal of Philosophical Logic* 25, 221–261.

Free Word Order and Neo-Davidsonian Event Semantics

Koji Shimamura

Keywords: scrambling, event semantics, elimination of argument structure, oblique movement

1. Introduction

In this paper, I will reconsider the nature of the free-word-order phenomena in Japanese, namely scrambling. In so doing, I will take into serious consideration the recent discussion on the argument structure in light of neo-Davidsonian event semantics. According to it, not only agent but also theme should be separated from the verb (Lohndal (2014) and references therein). As we will see, this paves a new way toward a better understanding of scrambling as well as its related issues. To be specific, I will propose that clause-internal scrambling can be derived as base-generation or movement whereas cross-clausal/long-distance scrambling involves movement. When base-generated, a given scrambled argument is semantically interpreted where it appears both quantificationally and thematically.

This paper goes as follows. Section 2 summarizes two points from Alexiadou (2014) and Lohndal (2014) for why we need to sever the theme argument from the verb, and in Section 3, we will see how the verbal structure is constructed under Lohndal (2014) analysis. Section 4 then explains the core idea of this paper, which in turn derives the contrast between clause-internal and long-distance scrambling (Section 5) and the Clause-mate Condition on Oblique Movement (Section 6). Section 7 concludes.

2. Severing Theme from the Verb

There has been a lively discussion which is concerned with the issue of

— 150 —

whether the argument structure in the traditional sense should be completely discarded (Alexiadou (2014), Lohndal (2014) among others). That is, the central question is whether not only the agent role, as Kkratzer (1996) argues, but also the theme role should be severed from the verb. Although the idea that agent is separated from the verb is now widely accepted due to seminal work by Chomsky (1995), Kratzer (1996) and Marantz (1984), Marantz (1997) among others, severing theme from the verb still needs justification, at least for those who are not familiar with arguments made by Alexiadou (2014) and Lohndal (2014) among others. Therefore, I will briefly discuss two from the essential ingredients of them in this section.

2.1 Reciprocals and Events

Consider (1) from Schein (2003).

(1) The cockroaches suffocated each other.　　　　　(Schein (2003: 349))

This sentence is true even if the entire group of the cockroaches is collectively responsible for the suffocating event. Therefore, (1) means that the cockroaches as a group suffocate each (individual) cockroach. Given this, if there had been one less cockroach resulting from the relevant mass-suffocating event, the entire group would have made it.

The construal in question cannot be paraphrased by the following:

(2) a. The cockroaches each suffocated the others.
　　 b. The cockroaches each suffocated some of the others.
　　 c. The cockroaches suffocated, each suffocating the others.
　　 d. The cockroaches suffocated, each suffocating some of the others.
　　　　　　　　　　　　　　　　　　　　　　　　(Schein (2003: 350))

As Lohndal (2014) observes, the problem is such that all the paraphrases in (2) have each assigned a scope that includes the verb, which is however not compatible with the mass-suffocation event by the subject as a plural entity.

That is, each cockroach can contribute to some event that is itself not an event of suffocating one cockroach by another but part of the mass-suffocating event. This is captured by the following logical form:

(3) ∃e[the X: cockroaches[X]](Agent[e, X] & suocate[e] & Theme[e, X] & [ιX: Agent[e; X]] [Each x : Xx] [ιe': Overlaps[e', e] & Agent[e', x]] [∃e'' : t(e'') ≤t(e')] [ιY: Others[x, Y] & Agent[e'', Y]] Theme[e', Y])
'The cockroaches suffocate themselves,
(with) them each acting
against the others that acted.'

(based on Schein (2003: 350))

This denotation only requires that each cockroach act on the others in some way that contributes to the mass-suffocation event (Schein (2003: 350)). Since the verb suffocate is not included in the scope of *each*, its event is not distributive, whereas the theme event is within it. This shows that theme should be separated from the verb.

2.2 Verbal vs. Adjectival Passive

Another argument that supports the idea that theme arguments are severed from the predicate is concerned with the contrast between verbal and adjectival passives. For instance, Alexiadou (2014) and Borer (2005) show that in Hebrew, the reflexive dative can be associated with the external argument, but not with the internal argument. Interestingly, the subjects of adjectival passives can license the reflexive dative just like usual external arguments, whereas those of verbal passives, as expected, cannot. The opposite pattern holds for the possessor dative. Observe:

(4) HEBREW: ADJECTIVAL PASSIVE

    a. *ha.xeder haya mequšat   li   be-praxim

        the.room was decorated.A.PASS to.me with-flowers

    b. ha.xeder$_i$ haya mequšat   lo$_i$ be-praxim

        the.room was decorated.A.PASS to.it in-flowers

        'The room was decorated with flowers.'

                                      (Alexiadou (2014: 289))

(5) HEBREW: VERBAL PASSIVE

    a. ha.xeder haya qušat   li   be-praxim

       the.room was decorated.A.PASS to.me with-flowers

       'My room was decorated with flowers.'

    b. *ha.xederi haya qušat   lo$_i$ be-praxim

       the.room was decorated.A.PASS to.it in-flowers

                                      (Alexiadou (2014: 289))

In the lexicalist tradition, adjectival passives are derived via externalization of the internal argument (Levin and Rappaport Hovav (1986)). However, for those who assume that the theme/internal argument starts out from the complement of the verb such as Kratzer (1996), the relevant contrast cannot be explained since such arguments are always generated as a complement within VP, irrespectively of a given passive being adjectival or verbal. Alexiadou (2014) and Borer (2005) thus argue that the internal argument should be severed from verb.

    The dichotomy under discussion also bears on the availability of idioms, which is frequently mentioned in discussing the contrast between the external argument and the internal argument (Kratzer (1996), Marantz (1984)). However, Marantz (1997) gives a different view. That is, he contends that the syntactic head that introduces an agent demarcates the locality domain of a special/idiomatic meaning as in (6).

(6) vP   the boundary for the special/idiomatic meaning

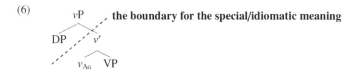

Then, what can be predicted from (6) is, among others, that adjectival (stative) passives allow idiomatic reading whereas verbal passives do not, and this prediction is indeed borne out. Witness (7) from Chichewa.

(7) CHICHEWA: VERBAL VS. STATIVE PASSIVE
  a. Chimanga chi-ku-gul-idwa   ku-msika.
     corn   AGR-PROG-buy-PASS   at-market
     'Corn is being bought at the market.' [no idiomatic reading possible]'
  b. Chimanga chi-ku-gul-ika   ku-msika.
     corn   AGR-PROG-buy-STAT   at-market
     'Corn is cheap at the market.'

(Marantz (1997: 210))

If all that matters for licensing idioms is the combination of the theme argument and its predicate, the contrast in (7) cannot be explained, so the availability of idiomatic interpretations cannot be considered a reliable diagnostic.

Summarizing the above two sections, it is not implausible to sever the theme argument from the verb/predicate, and it is rather both semantically and syntactically motivated.

3. Building Verbal Phrases: Lohndal (2014)

Now, let us consider how arguments are introduced into the structure. Lohndal (2014) proposes that the theme argument is introduced via a functional head F, analogous to Voice introducing the agent argument. Let us construct *John read the book*. The first step is to merge F and VP, resulting in (8), after which the theme argument is introduced to Spec-FP as in (9). After

Voice and the external argument DP are merged, we reach (10); note that the verb moves (to F) to Voice in Lohndal (2014) analysis, deriving the correct word order.

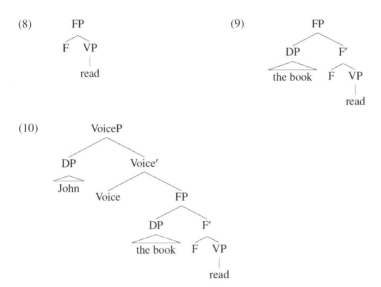

For the semantic composition in (10), I assume, following Kratzer (1996), that Voice and FP are combined via Event Identification (EI), i.e. EI($\langle e, st \rangle$, $\langle st \rangle$)= $\langle e, st \rangle$, where s is the event type. Then, the composition of VP and F in (8) is also a case of EI, since F is of type $\langle e, st \rangle$.

The structure in (10) nicely fits the neo-Davidsonian event semantics where the verb is a monadic predicate only taking an event argument, and all nominal arguments are introduced independently of the verb. In the next section, however, I argue for a different way to build the verbal domain in Japanese, which is also compatible with neo-Davidsonian event semantics.

4. Case Particle and Predicate Conjunction

The project I will work on in what follows has a precursor, who is Nomura (2016)). He puts forth an idea that case particles denote a property of events, viz. $\langle st \rangle$, so it is combined with the verb under Predicate Modification (PM). This type of PM is also called Predicate Conjunction (Pietroski (2005)). Given this, case particles are the head (K) that introduces DPs. Specifically, I assume the following semantics for case particles based on Laterza (2015):

(11) $[\![K]\!] = \lambda x \in D_e.\lambda e \in D_s.\Theta(x)(e)$

Here, Θ is a cover term for various Θ-roles such as agent, theme, experiencer, goal, etc. Now, let us see how this analysis works; we derive (12). Since *-ga* (NOM) and *-o* (ACC) project K, we have the structure in (13).

(12) Taroo-ga   sono hon-o   yon-da.
      Taro-NOM that book-ACC read-PAST
      'Taro read the book.'

(13)

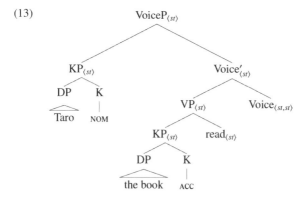

There are several questions that would arise, of course. First, one may ask what is the function of Voice since the Θ-role of the external argument is due to K in NOM. For this, I assume that Voice only encodes voice information such as active vs. passive. Note that agentivity is a concept independent from voice. Therefore, we can have active voice with an agent (transitive/unergative sentences) and passive voice with an agent ((in)direct passives on transitive/unergative verbs) or without an agent (indirect passive on intransitive/unaccusative verbs) in Japanese. The third pattern is exemplified by (14).

(14) Taroo-wa ame-ni   hu-rare-ta.
      Taro-TOP rain-DAT fall-PASS-PAST
      'It rained, which adversely affected Taro.'

As the translation in (14) shows, the indirect passive can be associated with the adverse meaning regarding the subject, which is not an argument of the verb stem in the traditional sense. Since passives in Japanese are not the topic of this paper, I will not discuss how different kinds of passives are derived in Japanese. Also, the pattern of active voice without an agent does exist. For example, Akimoto (2018) shows that in cases like (15), the verb is transitive, but the subject is not an agent.

(15) Yuuro-ga   ne-o   age-ta.
      euro-NOM   value-ACC raise-PAST
      'The value of Euro   went up.'   (Akimoto (2018: 191))

Akimoto calls this sort of construction Inanimate Possessor Transitives, and the nominative subject and the accusative object must be in an inalienable possessor relation. Details aside, he contends that this possessor relation licenses the subject, and Voice, even though transitive, lacks agentivity, which is expletive Voice (Schäfer (2008)). Indeed, usual transitive clauses need to have an external agent argument, but I conjecture, following Lohndal (2014: 49–53), that it is a matter of the Conceptual-Intentional interface, not part of the grammar/narrow syntax *per se*.

Then, the second question is of what semantic type Voice is. I assume, as in (13), that it is an identity function that takes a property of events, returning to the same thing (Schäfer (2008)). Since the notion of active vs. passive is syntactic and morphological, I assume that Voice in Japanese is purely syntactic and morphological.[2]

Admitting that there is much to be explained with respect to (13), I move on to the main topic: the free word order in Japanese, whose nomenclature is scrambling.

5. Scrambling as Base Generation or Movement

As is widely known, Japanese is a free-word-order language (Saito (1985), Saito (1989), Saito (1992) among many others). Therefore, there is nothing wrong if the object precedes the subject as in (16).

(16) Sono hon-o   Taroo-ga   yon-da.
     that   book-ACC Taro-NOM read-PAST
     'That book, Taro read.'

Numerous previous works on this assume that this is a case of movement. However, if the separation of all thematic arguments from the verb is on the right track, we can go for another way to derive (16). Suppose that clause-internal scrambling targets TP. It may be adjunction to TP (Lasnik and Saito (1992)) or substitution to Spec-TP (Miyagawa (2009)). I assume the former here. Also, suppose that TP also denotes $\langle st \rangle$. This is possible if T introduces a temporal trace function that is relatively interpreted with respect to the actual time t^*, which I assume is pronominal. Given this, (12) is semantically denoted as in (17).

(17) $\lambda e \in D_s[\daleth(e) < t^* \wedge \text{reading}(e) \wedge \text{Agent(Taro)}(e) \wedge \text{Theme(the book)}(e)]$

Then, let us derive (16). Since TP denotes $\langle st \rangle$, it is possible to have the (apparently) scrambled object base-generated in TP. The structure is (18), and the semantics is (19).

(18)

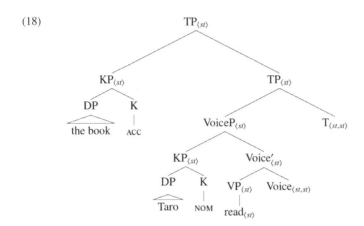

(19) $\lambda e \in D_s[\text{Theme(the book)}(e) \land \tau(e) < t^* \land \text{reading}(e) \land \text{Agent(Taro)}(e)]$

This is semantically vacuous since it is just a change in the ordering of the conjuncts in the denotation. However, if the object is a quantifier, the story will be changed. To discuss this, let us consider the interpretation of quantifiers under the event semantics.

For the standard theory, in order to construe examples like (19), we need Quantifier Raising (QR), a covert syntactic operation, which displaces the universally quantified object to the position whose semantic type is t (May (1977)). This is because the generalized quantifier is of type $\langle et, t \rangle$ and the (transitive) verb is of $\langle e, et \rangle$, so the object cannot be semantically combined with the verb in the in-situ position. Suppose that the target is S. Then, we covertly have (21).

(20) John kissed every girl.

(21) [s [every girl]₁ λx_1 [s John [vp kissed x₁]]]

QR is the only option for the semantics that does not have recourse to eventuality in its model, but once we have it, there are some possibilities to interpret quantifiers. One possible implementation, which I adopt in what follows, is Schein's (1993). According to him, quantificational DPs contain a variable ranging over sum events and one ranging over sub-events, and the latter is existentially closed in the denotation of a given quantificational DP. Then, *every girl* in (20) semantically denotes the following:

(22) $\lambda P.\lambda e. \forall x[\text{girl}(x) \rightarrow \exists e'[e' \leqslant e \wedge P(x)(e')]]^3$

This semantics allows the object DP in (20) to be interpreted in situ, if the verb is of type $\langle e, st \rangle$, where $s \in D_e$, the domain of eventualities. The verb will be plugged into P in the denotation in (22), which then captures the fact that the event quantifier is interpreted the lowest with respect to other quantifiers or negation (Alexeyenko (2018), Landman (2000)). Note that it is also possible that the quantificational DP raises to some node whose semantic type of $\langle st \rangle$. Schein's (1993) approach is thus compatible with both the QR interpretation and the in-situ interpretation.

Now, let us turn to Japanese and consider the meaning of (23). The object is of type $\langle \langle e, st \rangle, st \rangle$. Therefore, one may say that K (DAT) is plugged into the quantifier, yielding (24).

(23) Taroo-ga   dono on'nanoko-ni-mo kisu-si-ta.
      Taro-NOM which girl-DAT-also   kiss-do-PAST
      'Taro kissed every girl.'

(24) $\lambda e.\forall x[\text{girl}(x) \rightarrow \exists e'[e' \leqslant e \wedge \text{Theme}(x)(e')]]$

(24) will be then combined with the verb via PM. However, if so, the verb will be outside the existential quantifier, so that the kissing event cannot be mereological. This may be fine for cases like (1) in English, but the kissing event cannot be a mass event. For instance, consider:

(25) Dono on'nanoko-ni-mo futari-no otokonoko-ga kisu-si-ta.
which girl-DAT-also two.CL boy-NOM kiss-do-PAST
'Every girl, two boys kissed.'

In this case, the universal quantifier scopes over the numeral, hence the distributive reading. If the scrambled object is semantically (24), its combination with the main clausal spine will be (25), which cannot capture the distributed reading since the agent event is not in the scope of the existential quantifier over the mereological event composed of sub-events.

(26) $\lambda e[\forall x[\text{girl}(x) \rightarrow \exists e'[e' \leqslant e \wedge \text{Theme}(x)(e')]] \wedge [\daleth(e) < t^* \wedge \text{kissing}(e)$
$\wedge \text{Agent}(\text{two.boys})(e)]]$

Therefore, I assume that when a quantifier is involved, the option of EI becomes available, so K and TP are combined under EI as in (27a), and the object takes the clause as its argument as in (27b), yielding the denotation in (28). A cost we have to pay in this analysis is the assumption that the syntactic composition does not reflect the semantic composition. However, this sort of mismatch also holds for the traditional generalized quantifier approach, so I submit that this is not problematic. [4]

(27) a.　　　$\langle e, st \rangle$　　　　　b.　　　　　　$\langle st \rangle$

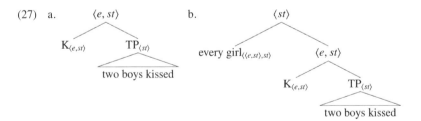

(28) $\lambda e.\forall x[\text{girl}(x) \rightarrow \exists e'[e' \leqslant e \wedge \text{Theme}(x)(e') \wedge \daleth(e') < t^* \wedge \text{kissing}(e')$
$\wedge \text{Agent}(\text{two.boys})(e')]]$

Of course, it is also possible to scramble the object via movement. However, in that case, the movement trace will be of type $\langle st \rangle$, which semantically pulls the scrambled object back to its original position, i.e. semantic reconstruction. In this connection, long-distance (LD) scrambling has sometimes been argued to reconstruct obligatorily, namely radical reconstruction (Saito (1989), Saito (1992)).[5] The question is then why. Although there are various explanations in the literature, the proposed analysis reduces radical reconstruction to semantic reconstruction. That is, what is moving is a KP, leaving a movement trace of type $\langle st \rangle$. One may ask whether a given KP can be base-generated in the matrix clause. Technically speaking, it should be possible, but it will be semantically odd. For instance, consider:

(29) [Kono hon-o]$_i$ Taroo-ga [Hanako-ga t_i kat-ta-to]   omo-tei-ru.
       this book-ACC Taro-NOM Hanako-NOM buy-PAST-C think-ASP-NONPAST
       'This book, Taro thinks that Hanako bought.'

If the LD-scrambled theme argument is base-generated where it appears, it will be semantically interpreted in the matrix clause, hence the theme argument of *omow-* 'think'. This is not what we want. Thus, it should be that *kono hon* 'this book' comes from the embedded clause.[6]

To recap, clause-internal scrambling can be derived via base-generation or movement whereas LD scrambling is movement. This disparity is derived in terms of the event-semantic composition of argument KPs.

6. Deriving Free-Rider Effect

Before we conclude, let us see one consequence of this new understanding of scrambling in Japanese. Although LD scrambling of adverbs is said to be banned (Saito (1985)), Koizumi (2000), Yamashita (2013) and references therein observe that when an adverb is moved together with its clause-mate argument, the former can be LD-scrambled. Witness:

(30) a. *[Subayaku]ᵢ Taroo-ga [Bekkamu-ga t_i booru-o Sukooruzu-ni
quickly   Taro-NOM Beckham-NOM   ball-ACC Scholes-DAT
pasu-si-ta-to] it-ta.
pass-do-PAST-C say-NONPASt
Lit. 'Quickly, Taro said that Beckham passed a ball to Scholes.'
    b. [Subayaku]ᵢ [booru-o]₂ Taroo-ga [Bekkamu-ga t_i t_2 Sukooruzu-ni
quickly   ball-ACC Taro-NOM Beckham-NOM   Scholes-DAT
pasu-si-ta-to] it-ta.
pass-do-PAST-C say-NONPAST
Lit. 'Quickly, a ball, Taro said that Beckham passed to Scholes.'

Since the object KP and the adverb are both of type $\langle st \rangle$, they can amalgamate by the adverb being adjoined to the KP, which is then LD-scrambled. There is nothing wrong in this move because KPs and adverbs are integrated with the verb via PM. This sort of free-rider effect is termed Oblique Movement (OM) (Saito (1994)), and OM obeys the Clause-mate Condition (CMC) (Sugisaki (1998) among others). CMC is then understood in terms of the impossibility of adjoining a given adverb to some KP that does not share the same eventuality with it. Observe:

(31) *[Orokanimo]ᵢ [Hanako-ni]₂ Taroo-ga [Ziroo-ga [Saburoo-ga t_2
stupidly   Hanako-DAT Taro-NOM Jiro-NOM   Saburo-NOM
kokut-ta-to] t_i omo-tei-ru-to]   it-ta.
confess-PAST-C think-ASP-NONPAST-C say-PAST
Lit. 'Stupidly, to Hanako, Taro said that Jiro thought that Saburo confessed his love.'

Although hard to parse due to the multiple center-embedding, (31) sounds bad with the intended reading where *orokanimo* 'stupidly' modifies the thinking event (or state). Naturally, if the pertinent adverb modifies the confessing-his-love event, it becomes grammatical, though again, it is difficult to parse. This state of affairs is straightforwardly explained by the proposed analysis: CMC is the condition on the event-semantic composition. [7]

7. Conclusion

In this paper, we have investigated the nature of scrambling under neo-Davidsonin event semantics, and I have argued that once not only agent but also theme is severed from the verb, scrambling does not always have to involve movement.

To conclude, I mention that it may be possible to conjecture that the reason why English lacks scrambling is explained by the nature of F and Voice in English vs. that of K in Japanese. That is, since F and Voice are verbal affixes, they are necessarily merged with the stem verb. In contrast, K is a nominal affix, so that it is merged to DPs before getting merged to the verb stem. If this is on the right track, it will also reinforce the validity of the proposed analysis.

Notes

[1] Under Lohndal's (2014) theory of Spell-Out, the merger of F with VP is not semantically considered, and VP is Spelled-Out independently of F(P), constituting a conjunct of Neo-Davidsonian event semantic denotation, but I do not concern myself with this issue here.

[2] Of course, it may well be that Voice contributes to semantic interpretations. For instance, the passive morpheme -(r)are is morphologically homophonous with the middle voice marker, the potential marker and the honorific marker. This sort of versatile usage of the morpheme in question maybe indicates that Voice in Japanese is not just about the active vs. passive contrast, and it bears on e.g. potential or honorific semantics.

[3] ≤ stands for the mereological whole-part relation.

[4] I assume that the structure in (28) is only for semantics.

[5] Note that LD scrambling does not always undergo radical reconstruction as Miyagawa (2005) shows. He gives a showcase of various examples where LD scrambling is meaningful. However, for the limited space, I will not discuss them under the current analysis, just mentioning the possibility that such cases would be derived via λ-abstraction over individuals plus base-generation of a *prima facie* LD-

scrambled KP.

[6] As I noted in the previous note, I surmise that when there is no radical reconstruction effect, the theme argument is really base-generated. In that case, the Theme function of it is integrated with the matrix verb via PM, and the relevant interpretation will be like 'think about/of KP'. The embedded object position is then λ-abstracted.

[7] See Nomura (2016) for another case of OM, viz. Cleft with multiple foci, which Takano (2002) calls 'Surprising Constituents'.

References

Akimoto, Takayuki (2018) *The Morphosyntax of Transitivity in Japanese, Doctoral dissertation*, Chuo University, Tokyo.

Alexeyenko, Sascha (2018) "Quantification in Event Semantics: Generalized Quantifiers vs. Sub-Events," *Proceedings of Sinn und Bedeutung* 22, ed. by Uli Sauerland and Stephanie Solt, 39–53, ZASPiL, Berlin.

Alexiadou, Artemis (2014) "Roots Don't Take Complements," *Theoretical Linguistics* 40, 287–297.

Boeckx, Cedric and Koji Sugisaki (1998) "How to Get a Free Ride: Additional Scrambling Effect and the Principle of Minimal Compliance," *Proceedings of the 18th West Coast Conference on Formal Linguistics*, ed. by Sonya Bird, Andrew Carnie, Jason D. Haugen, and Peter Norquest, 43–54, Cascadilla Press, Somerville, MA.

Borer, Hagit (2005) *Structuring Sense II: The Normal Course of Events*, Oxford University Press, Oxford.

Chomsky, Noam (1995) *The Minimalist Program*, MIT Press, Cambridge, MA.

Koizumi, Masatoshi (2000) "String Vacuous Overt Verb Raising," *Journal of East Asian Linguistics* 9, 227–285.

Kratzer, Angelika (1996) "Serving the External Argument from Its Verb," *Phrase Structure and the Lexicon*, ed. by Johan Rooryck and Laurie Zaring, 109–137, Kluwer Academic Publishers, Dordrecht.

Landman, Fred (2000) *Events and Plurality: The Jerusalem Lectures*, Kluwer Academic Publishers, Dordrecht.

Lasnik, Howard and Mamoru Saito (1992) *Move α: Conditions on Its Application and Output*, MIT Press, Cambridge, MA.

LaTerza, Chris (2015) "Local Plural Anaphora as Sub-Event Distributivity," *Proceedings of the 32nd West Coast Conference on Formal Linguistics*, ed. by Ulrike Steindl, Thomas Borer, Alfredo García Pardo Huilin Fang, Peter

Guekguezian, Brian Hsu, Charlie O'Hara, and Iris Chuoying Ouyang, 141–148, Cascadilla Proceedings Project, Somerville, MA.

Levin, Beth and Malka Rappaport Hovav (1986) "The Formation of Adjectival Passives," *Linguistic Inquiry* 17, 623–661.

Lohndal, Terje (2014) *Phrase Structure and Argument Atructure: A Case Study of the Syntax-Semantics Interface*, Oxford University Press, Oxford.

Marantz, Alec (1984) *On the Nature of Grammatical Relations*, MIT Press, Cambridge, MA.

Marantz, Alec (1997) "No Escape from Syntax: Don't Try Morphological Analysis in the Privacy of Your Own Lexicon," *Proceedings of the 21st Annual Penn Linguistics Colloquium* 4, ed. by Artemis Alexiadou, Laura Siegel, Clarissa Surek-Clark, and Alexander Williams 4, 201–225.

May, Robert (1977) *The Grammar of Quantification, Doctoral dissertation*, MIT, Cambridge, MA.

Miyagawa, Shigeru (2005) "EPP and Semantically Vacuous Scrambling," *The Free Word Order Phenomenon: Its Syntactic Sources and Diversity*, ed. by Joachim Sabel and Mamoru Saito, 181–220, Mouton de Gruyter, Berlin.

Miyagawa, Shigeru (2009) *Why Agree? Why Move? Unifying Agreement-Based and Discourse-Configurational Languages*, MIT Press, Cambridge, MA.

Nomura, Jun'ya (2016) "Surprising Constituents, Clefts and Event Semantics," ms., Talk at Ling Supper Meeting, Mie University.

Pietroski, Paul (2005) *Events and Semantic Architecture*, Oxford University Press, Oxford.

Saito, Mamoru (1985) *Some Asymmetries in Japanese and Their Theoretical Implications*, Doctoral dissertation, MIT, Cambridge, MA.

Saito, Mamoru (1989) "Scrambling as semantically vacuous A′-movement," *Alternative conceptions of phrase structure*, ed. by Mark Baltin and Anthony Kroch, 182–200, University of Chicago Press, Chicago, IL.

Saito, Mamoru (1992) "Long Distance Scrambling in Japanese," *Journal of East Asian Linguistics* 3, 195–240.

Saito, Mamoru (1994) "Additional-Wh Effects and the Adjunction Site Theory," *Journal of East Asian Linguistics* 3, 195–240.

Schäfer, Florian (2008) *The Syntax of (Anti-)Causatives: External Arguments in Change-of-State Contexts*, John Benjamins, Amsterdam.

Schein, Barry (1993) *Plurals and Events*, MIT Press, Cambridge, MA.

Schein, Barry (2003) "Adverbial, Descriptive Reciprocals," *Philosophical Perspectives* 17, 333–367.

Takano, Yuji (2002) "Surprising Constituents," *Journal of East Asian Linguistics* 11, 243–301.

Yamashita, Hideaki (2013) "On (Multiple) Long-Distance Scrambling of Adjuncts and Subjects, and the Generalized Additional Scrambling Effect," *Snippets* 27, 19–20.

A Note on Japanese *Mo* 'Also': Against the Modifier Hypothesis*

Hideharu Tanaka

Keywords: Japanese, additive *mo*, semantic types, modifiers, quantifiers

1. Issue: The Semantic Type of the Additive Phrase NP-*mo*

The subject of this paper is the Japanese additive particle *mo* 'also.' In particular, we focus on its nominal projection NP-*mo*, and address what the semantic type of NP-*mo* is. As suggested by Shimoyama (2006), Yatsushiro (2009), and Mitrović and Sauerland (2016), one answer is a quantifier hypothesis, which treats NP-*mo* as a quantifier, an expression of type <<e, t>, t>. However, the quantifier hypothesis is faced with a compositionality problem, as pointed out by Kobuchi-Philip (2009, 2010). For instance, consider Aoyagi's (1994) observations that NP-*mo* can optionally co-occur with Case-marked NPs, as shown (1).[1]

(1) a. *Kyo-wa*   *John-**mo***   *kite-ta.*
       today-Top   John-also   come-Past
       'John also came today.'
    b. *Kyo-wa*   *itinensei-**ga***   *John-**mo***   *kite-ta.*
       today-Top   freshman-Nom   John-also   come-Past
       'Freshmen came today, including John.'

In (1b), it appears that the verb 'come' is predicated of both the NP-*mo* and the nominative NP. The problem is that, if the NP-*mo* is a quantifier and saturates the argument slot of the verb, then the verb should be able to add no nominative NP, which is contrary to the fact. Note that NP-*mo* can also co-occur with NPs in other Case-markers, such as accusative (e.g. Aoyagi 1994,

Kobuchi-Philip 2010). Given these facts, any analysis of the semantics of NP-*mo* should be insufficient if it ignores the ability of NP-*mo* to co-occur with Case-marked NPs.

In previous research, Kobuchi-Philip (2009, 2010) adopts Aoyagi's (1994) claim and develops a modifier hypothesis for the semantic type of NP-*mo*. This hypothesis treats NP-*mo* as a modifier, an expression of type **<<e, t>, <e, t>>**. In particular, Kobuchi-Philip argues that NP-*mo* acts as a VP-adjunct and always co-occurs with a Case-marked NP or a null pronoun *pro*, which in turn serves as a true argument of the predicate. Thus, the modifier hypothesis analyzes (1a) as including a *pro* in the same position occupied by the nominative NP in (1b), assuming that the referent of the *pro* is contextually determined.

(2)

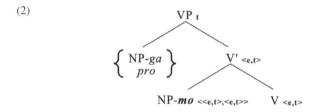

In this paper, while we acknowledge Kobuchi-Philip's (2009, 2010) contribution for framing the issue correctly, we argue against the modifier hypothesis as an approach to the semantic type of NP-*mo*. The organization of this paper is as follows. Section 2 reviews two arguments for the modifier hypothesis and points out some problems with them. Section 3 claims that the quantifier hypothesis is still valid. In short, we propose that the co-occurring Case-marked NP is in fact a modifier to NP-*mo*, with its presence completely optional, thus denying the need to introduce a *pro*. *Mo*'s projection MoP is therefore represented as shown below.

(3)

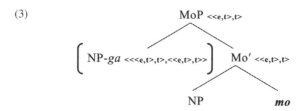

Finally, Section 4 concludes with some prospects for the future research.

2. Data: Problems with the Modifier Hypothesis

In this section, we examine the two arguments that Kobuchi-Philip (2010) makes for the modifier hypothesis. First, she points out that NP-*mo* recursion is possible; that is, more than one NP-*mo* can co-occur in a single clause, as shown in (4a). This fact is taken to suggest that NP-*mo* is a VP-adjunct, because more than one VP-adjunct can co-occur in a single clause, as shown in (4b).

(4) a. *Konsyu-wa*   *John-mo*   *Bill-mo*   *LGB-o*   *yon-da.*
       this.week-Top   John-also   Bill-also   LGB-Acc   read-Past
       'John and Bill read LGB this week.'

   b. *Karera-wa*   *gakko-de*   *sinkenni*   *LGB-o*   *yon-da.*
       they-Top   school-at   earnestly   LGB-Acc   read-Past
       'They read LGB earnestly at school.'

Thus, the syntactic structure for NP-*mo* recursion is represented as shown below.

(5)

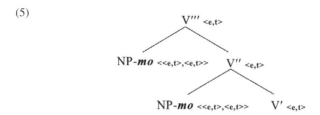

However, the treatment of NP-*mo* as a VP-adjunct has a problem. Specifically, it fails to capture the fact that multiple instances of NP-*mo* cannot be separated by any other element, such as the object. For example, consider (6a). This fact is problematic, because genuine VP-adjuncts behave differently and the object can intervene between multiple VP-adjuncts, as shown in (6b). Given this contrast, it should be concluded that NP-*mo* is not a VP-adjunct.

(6) a.* *Konsyu-wa* *John-mo* LGB-*o* *Bill-mo* *yon-da.*
   this.week-Top John-also LGB-Acc Bill-also read-Past
   'John and Bill read LGB this week.'

 b. *Karera-wa* *gakko-de* LGB-*o* *sinkenni* *yon-da.*
   they-Top school-at LGB-Acc earnestly read-Past
   'They read LGB earnestly at school.'

Second, Kobuchi-Philip (2010) examines the adjunct status of NP-*mo*, based on its syntactic distribution in the cleft construction. Consider the following data, which are adapted from Kobuchi-Philip (2010: 222); (7) is a non-cleft sentence, and those in (8) are cleft versions of (7).

(7) *Basu-ga* *Ginza-iki-mo* *ko-nakat-ta.*
  bus-Nom Ginza-bound-also come-Neg-Past
  'Buses didn't come, including the Ginza bound one.'

(8) a.   [*Ginza-iki-**mo***   *ko-nakat-ta*]-*no-wa*   *basu*-da.
           Ginza-bound-also   come-Neg-Past-that-Top   bus-Copula
           'It is buses that didn't come, including the Ginza bound one.'

      b.*   [*Ko-nakat-ta*]-*no-wa*   *basu-**ga***   *Ginza-iki-**mo**-da.*
           come-Neg-Past-that-Top   bus-Nom   Ginza-bound-also-Copula
           'It is buses, including the Ginza bound one, that didn't come.'

The point is that NP-*mo* can occur with the verb in the embedded clause as in (8a), but it cannot occur with its associated NP in the focus position as in (8b). It is thus the case that NP-*mo* belongs to the verbal domain at overt syntax.

     Still, as Kobuchi-Philip (2010: 222) emphasizes, this fact alone does not suffice to establish that NP-*mo* is a VP-adjunct. This is because other elements than a VP-adjunct can also belong to the verbal domain. In particular, we should note that even the logical subject can be said to "belong to the verbal domain." For instance, consider the multiple nominative sentence in (9) below, where the second NP is the logical subject and understood as having the first NP as its possessor. Importantly, that logical subject can occur with the predicate in the embedded clause of clefting as in (10a), but it cannot occur with the possessor NP in the focus position as in (10b).

(9)   *John-**ga***   *imoto-**ga***   *kawai-i.*
          John-Nom   sister-Nom   cute-Pres
          'John, his sister is cute.'

(10) a.   [*Imoto-**ga***   *kawai-i*]-*no-wa*   *John-da.*
          sister-Nom   cute-Pres-that-Top   John-Copula
          'It is John whose sister is cute.'

      b. *   [*Kawai-i*]-*no-wa*   *John*(-*ga*)   *imoto*(-*ga*)-*da.*
          cute-Pres-that-Top   John-Nom   sister-Nom-Copula
          'It is John, his sister, who is cute.'

In a nutshell, the test by clefting can be used to show that NP-*mo* is a VP-adjunct, only if it is independently established that it is some kind of adjunct. Given the lack of such evidence, there is no reason to maintain that NP-*mo* is a VP-adjunct. It is therefore empirically a viable option to purse the quantifier hypothesis.

3. Claim: A New Form of the Quantifier Hypothesis

In this section, we propose a new form of the quantifier hypothesis for the semantic type of NP-*mo*. Recall that the issue is why NP-*mo* can co-occur with a Case-marked NP. For Kobuchi-Philip (2009, 2010), it is because NP-*mo* is a modifier and the Case-marked NP serves as a true argument of the predicate. Our claim is that the Case-marked NP in this construction acts as a modifier to quantifiers, including NP-*mo*. In order to implement this idea in formal semantics, we introduce the following variables: x, y over *entities* (type **e**), P, Q over *predicates* (type **<e, t>**), and K, K' over *quantifiers* (type **<<e, t>, t>**).

We begin by formulating the at-issue content of NP-*mo*. While we agree with Shimoyama (2006), Yatsushiro (2009), and Mitrović and Sauerland (2016) that NP-*mo* as a whole is a quantifier, we do not assume that the particle *mo* is a determiner, which is a function from predicates to quantifiers. Rather, we suggest that it is a function from quantifiers to quantifiers. This modification is empirically motivated. For instance, *mo* can be combined with a quantifier (though it needs to be a "modified" quantifier, such as 'someone else' and 'everyone else').

(11) a.   *Kyo-wa*   **(betu-no-)dareka-<u>mo</u>*   *kite-ta.*
          today-Top   else-Gen-someone-also   come-Past
          'Someone (else) also came today.'

b. *Kyo-wa*   *(nokori-no-)zen'in-<u>mo</u>*   *kite-ta.*
    today-Top   rest-Gen-everyone-also   come-Past
    'Everyone (else) also came today.'

Given this fact, we propose the at-issue content of the particle *mo* as follows.

(12) $[\![mo]\!] = \lambda K.\lambda P. [K(P)]$ (type $<<<e, t>, t>, <<e, t>, t>>$)

Note that the first argument K need not be an inherent quantifier (e.g. *everyone*), because under Partee's (1987) type-shifting theory, any term of type e can be a quantifier. Thus, if the proper name *John* is type-shifted to a quantifier, it denotes the set of every predicate that holds for the entity j (i.e. $[\![John]\!] = \lambda P. [P(j)]$). Let us now apply the at-issue content of *mo* to (1a), *John-mo kite-ta* 'John also came.' With the composition rule *Function Application* (Heim and Kratzer (1998)), the VP structure given in (13) is compositionally interpreted as shown in (14). This is how the at-issue content of *mo* derives an at-issue proposition.

(13)

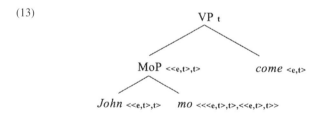

(14) $[\![mo]\!]$ $= \lambda K.\lambda P. [K(P)]$
      $[\![John]\!]$ $= \lambda P. [P(j)]$
      $[\![MoP]\!]$ $= [\![mo]\!]([\![John]\!])$ $= \lambda P. [P(j)]$
      $[\![come]\!]$ $= \lambda x. [\mathbf{come}(x)]$
      $[\![VP]\!]$ $= [\![MoP]\!]([\![come]\!])$ $= \mathbf{come(j)}$

Let us then clarify the additive component of *mo*. We adopt Szabolcsi's (2015) dynamic semantic view of *mo*, under which it imposes a *postsupposition*, namely a proposition that needs to be entailed by the output context resulting after the at-issue proposition is evaluated. For example, consider the following discourse.

(15) *Kyo-wa*   *Bill-ga*   *kite-ta.*   *Sosite*   <u>*John-**mo***</u>   *kite-ta.*
      today-Top   Bill-Nom   come-Past   and   John-also   come-Past
      'Today, Bill came, and John also came.'

First, the output context of (15) at least consists of the at-issue propositions denoted by the first and second clauses, so that it entails **come(b)** ∧ **come(j)**. Then, Szabolcsi's theory requires *mo* to impose a postsupposition on the output context. We propose to define the postsuppositional content of *mo* as follows.

(16) The postsupposition of $[\![mo]\!](K)(P)$ is satisfied iff
      the output context entails $\exists K'. [K' \neq K \wedge K'(P)]$.

That is, this requires the output context to entail that there is an alternative K' such that (a) K' is distinct from K, and (b) $K'(P)$ is true. Thus, the postsupposition of the NP-*mo* clause in (15) is determined as follows.

(17) The postsupposition of $[\![mo]\!]([\![John]\!])([\![come]\!])$ is satisfied iff
      the output context entails $\exists K'. [K' \neq [\![John]\!] \wedge K'([\![come]\!])]$.

This postsupposition is satisfied in (15). That is, suppose $K' = [\![Bill]\!] = \lambda P.$ $[P(\mathbf{b})]$ (which is distinct from $[\![John]\!]$), then the postsupposition amounts to saying that $[\![Bill]\!]([\![come]\!]) = $ **come(b)**, which is entailed by the output context of (15).

Given this postsuppositional approach to the additivity of *mo*, we are now in a position to analyze the structure and interpretation of NP-*mo* recursion, such as *John-mo Bill-mo kite-ta* 'John and Bill came.' Along the lines of Mitrović and Sauerland (2016), we assume that multiple instances of NP-*mo* are combined by a silent coordinator &, whose syntax and semantics are given below.

(18) $[_{\&P} [_{MoP}{}^{2} \textit{John mo}] [_{\&'} \& [_{MoP}{}^{1} \textit{Bill mo}]]]$

(19) $[\![\&]\!]$ $\qquad = \lambda K.\lambda K'.\lambda P. [K'(P) \wedge K(P)]$

$[\![\&']\!] = [\![\&]\!]([\![MoP^1]\!])$ $\qquad = \lambda K'.\lambda P. [K'(P) \wedge P(\mathbf{b})]$

$[\![\&P]\!] = [\![\&']\!]([\![MoP^2]\!])$ $\qquad = \lambda P. [P(\mathbf{j}) \wedge P(\mathbf{b})]$

There are two arguments for this covert structure. First, it can explain the fact that no element can intervene between multiple instances of NP-*mo*, as shown in (6a); that is, a coordinate structure excludes anything else than its conjuncts. Second, NP-*mo* recursion can include an overt coordinator such as *sosite* 'and', as shown in (20). Although it is not clear whether the silent & is a null counterpart of *sosite*, it is the case that NP-*mo* recursion is compatible with coordination.

(20)   *Kyo-wa*   <u>*John-**mo***</u>   (***sosite***)   <u>*Bill-**mo***</u>   *kite-ta.*

        today-Top   John-also   and   Bill-also   come-Past

        'John and Bill came today.'

What about the interpretation of NP-*mo* recursion? In fact, it is the first aspect of *mo* that Szabolcsi (2015) aims to explain by proposing a postsuppositional meaning. First, consider the following minimal pair; (21a) is a case of NP-*mo* recursion, and (21b) is a case where *mo* is attached to a coordinated NP.

(21) a.   *Kyo-wa*   *John-**mo***   *Bill-**mo***   *kite-ta.*

           today-Top   John-also   Bill-also   come-Past

           'John and Bill came today.'

      b.   *Kyo-wa*   [*John-**to***   *Bill*]-***mo***   *kite-ta.*

           today-Top   John-and   Bill-also   come-Past

           'John and Bill also came today.'

As Kobuchi-Philip (2009) correctly points out, there is an interpretive difference between (21a) and (21b). For instance, in the situation where there is no person other than John and Bill who came, (21a) is true, but (21b) is not, and requires the existence of an additional person who came. The crucial fact for Szabolcsi is that (21a) does not impose any presupposition on the input context, and this fact is problematic for the standard analysis that treats *mo* as a presupposition trigger. On the other hand, the postsuppositional account can capture it. Given the syntax and semantics of the silent &P, (21a) is interpreted as follows.

(22) $[_{VP} \overline{[_{\&P} [_{MoP}{}^{2} \textit{John mo}] [_{\&'} \& [_{MoP}{}^{1} \textit{Bill mo}]]]}$ come]

(23) $\llbracket VP \rrbracket = \lambda P. [P(\mathbf{j}) \wedge P(\mathbf{b})](\llbracket come \rrbracket) = \mathbf{come(j)} \wedge \mathbf{come(b)}$

Importantly, the output $\llbracket VP \rrbracket$ is an at-issue proposition, so that it is the output context of (21a). Let us then consider what postsupposition each MoP imposes.

(24) a. The postsupposition of $\llbracket mo \rrbracket(\llbracket John \rrbracket)(\llbracket come \rrbracket)$ is satisfied iff the output context entails $\exists K'. [K' \neq \llbracket John \rrbracket \wedge K'(\llbracket come \rrbracket)]$.

  b. The postsupposition of $\llbracket mo \rrbracket(\llbracket Bill \rrbracket)(\llbracket come \rrbracket)$ is satisfied iff the output context entails $\exists K'. [K' \neq \llbracket Bill \rrbracket \wedge K'(\llbracket come \rrbracket)]$.

These postsuppositions are both entailed by the output context of (21a); (24a) requires someone else than John to come, and this is satisfied by Bill's coming, while (24b) requires someone else than Bill to come, and this is satisfied by John's coming. Accordingly, the postsuppositional account of *mo* can capture what the presuppositional account cannot.

We now consider the fact that NP-*mo* can co-occur with a Case-marked NP. Our leading idea is that the Case-marked NP in this construction is in fact a modifier to NP-*mo*. This idea can be implemented by assuming that the Japanese lexicon includes a covert modifier head µ. In particular, we assume that the head µ takes a nominal predicate Q first, and then is attached to a quantifier K. The denotation of the head μ is defined in (25), where $Q \cap P = \lambda x.$ $[Q(x) \wedge P(x)]$.

(25) $\llbracket \mu \rrbracket = \lambda Q.\lambda K.\lambda P. [K(Q \cap P)]$

Under this assumption, we analyze the clause structure for (1b) as shown below.

(26)

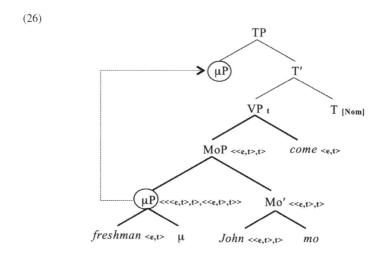

Here, we assume that the μP, but not the MoP, is a Case-assignee and undergoes overt movement to the edge of TP in order to obtain nominative Case from the head T (see Bošković (2007) for an Agree-based Case theory). That is why the μP falls into the verbal domain at overt syntax, although it cannot be interpreted in its overt position due to a type mismatch. Then, the VP is interpreted as follows.

(27) $\llbracket \text{Mo}' \rrbracket$ $= \llbracket mo \rrbracket (\llbracket John \rrbracket)$ $= \lambda P. [P(\mathbf{j})]$
  $\llbracket \mu P \rrbracket$ $= \llbracket \mu \rrbracket (\llbracket \text{freshman} \rrbracket) = \lambda K.\lambda P. [K(\llbracket freshman \rrbracket \cap P)]$
  $\llbracket \text{MoP} \rrbracket$ $= \llbracket \mu P \rrbracket (\llbracket \text{Mo}' \rrbracket)$ $= \lambda P. [\llbracket mo \rrbracket (\llbracket John \rrbracket)(\llbracket freshman \rrbracket \cap P)]$
  $\llbracket \text{VP} \rrbracket$ $= \llbracket \text{MoP} \rrbracket (\llbracket come \rrbracket) = \llbracket mo \rrbracket (\llbracket John \rrbracket)(\llbracket freshman \rrbracket \cap \llbracket come \rrbracket)$

The output $\llbracket VP \rrbracket$ is equal to the formula $\lambda P.\ [P(\mathbf{j})](\llbracket freshman \rrbracket \cap \llbracket come \rrbracket)$, and hence equal to **freshman(j)** $\wedge$ **come(j)**, which is the at-issue proposition of (1b). Importantly, since the unit $\llbracket mo \rrbracket(\llbracket John \rrbracket)$ takes the predicate $\llbracket freshman \rrbracket \cap \llbracket come \rrbracket$, the following postsupposition is imposed on the output context OC of (1b).

(28) The postsupposition of $\llbracket mo \rrbracket(\llbracket John \rrbracket)(\llbracket freshman \rrbracket \cap \llbracket come \rrbracket)$ is satisfied
       iff the OC entails $\exists K'.\ [K' \neq \llbracket John \rrbracket \wedge K'(\llbracket freshman \rrbracket \cap \llbracket come \rrbracket)]$.

Under this postsupposition, there must be a salient entity other than John that was a freshman and came. In fact, this requirement is part of the actual interpretation of (1b), as pointed out by Kobuchi-Philip (2009, 2010), thus suggesting that the postulation of the head μ is on the right track.

Note that our entire proposal makes several correct predictions. For example, the syntax of μP given in (26) makes the prediction that NP-*mo* cannot precede the nominative NP, because that configuration induces a violation of the *Proper Binding Condition* (e.g. Saito (1985)), as schematized below.

(29)   ... [$_{MoP}$ $t_{\mu P}$ [$_{Mo'}$ *John* **mo**]] ... [$_{\mu P}$ *freshman* μ/**ga**] ...

This configuration should be excluded, because the trace $t_{\mu P}$ is not c-commanded by its antecedent μP. This prediction is borne out, as shown in (30). Crucially, the modifier hypothesis has no account of this word-order restriction, given that Japanese is a scrambling language with the option of semantic reconstruction.

(30) (*_John-**mo**_)   *kyo-wa*   (*_John-**mo**_)   _itinensei-**ga**_   _kite-ta._
John-also   today-Top   John-also   freshman-Nom   come-Past
'Freshmen came today, including John.'

4. Conclusion: Some Prospects for the Future Research

In this paper, we have argued against the modifier hypothesis for the semantic type of NP-*mo*, and instead proposed a new form of the quantifier hypothesis. While the proposed analysis is promising, there are serval remaining issues. For example, what prevents the particle *mo* from being attached to a "bare" quantifier, as shown in (11)? We will discuss all remaining issues in the future research.

* This work is a revised version of the poster presentation given at *GLOW in Asia X* at National Tsing Hua University on May 25th, 2014. I would like to thank Takahiro Honda, Yoshiyuki Shibata, and Koji Shimamura for their useful comments. This work was supported by the Japan Society for the Promotion of Science, Grant-in-Aid for Early-Career Scientists, Grant Number 18K12368.

[1] Some native speakers do not accept (1b); see also Kobuchi-Philip (2010: 221, fn.4). Still, for such speakers, (1b) becomes acceptable if the nominative NP is separated from the NP-*mo*, and the NP-*mo* refers to an individual for which the predicate is unlikely to hold. Thus, (i) is acceptable for the above speakers.

(i) _Itinensei-**ga**_   *kyo-wa*   *nanto ano*   _John-**mo**_   _kite-ta._
freshman-Nom   today-Top   surprisingly   John-also   come-Past
'Freshmen came today, including even John.'

References

Aoyagi, Hiroshi (1994) "On Association with Focus and Scope of Focus Particles in Japanese," *FAJL* 1, *MITWPL* 24, 23–44.
Bošković, Željko (2007) "On the Locality and Motivation of Move and Agree: An Even More Minimalist Theory," *Linguistic Inquiry* 38, 589–644.

Heim, Irene and Angelika Kratzer (1998) *Semantics in Generative Grammar*, Blackwell, Oxford.

Kobuchi-Philip, Mana (2009) "Japanese *Mo*: Universal, Additive, and NPI," *Journal of Cognitive Science* 10, 173–194.

Kobuchi-Philip, Mana (2010) "Japanese *Mo* 'Also/Even' and *Shika* 'Except for/ Only'," *Proceedings of Sinn und Bedeutung* 14, 219–236.

Mitrović, Moreno and Uli Sauerland (2016) "Two Conjuncts Are Better than One," *Acta Linguistica Hungarica* 63, 471–494.

Partee, Barbara (1987) "Noun Phrase Interpretation and Type-Shifting Principles," *Studies in Discourse Representation Theory and the Theory of Generalized Quantifiers*, ed. by Jeroen Groenendijk, Dick de Jongh and Martin Stokhof, 115–143, Foris Publications, Dordrecht.

Saito, Mamoru (1985) *Some Asymmetries in Japanese and Their Theoretical Implications*, Doctoral dissertation, MIT.

Shimoyama, Junko (2006) "Indeterminate Phrase Quantification in Japanese," *Natural Language Semantics* 14, 139–173.

Szabolcsi, Anna (2015) "What Do Quantifier Particles Do?," *Linguistics and Philosophy* 38, 159–204.

Yatsushiro, Kazuko (2009) "The Distribution of Quantificational Suffixes in Japanese," *Natural Language Semantics* 17, 141–173.

The Semantics of Reduplication*

Sumiyo Nishiguchi

Keyword: indefinites, universal quantifier, *dog after dog*, compositionality, Tagalog, Japanese

1. Introduction

Matsuyama (2006) presented a puzzle explaining the mixed behavior of the *dog after dog* construction—it appears to be both a weak quantifier syntactically and a strong quantifier for the aspectual contribution to verbal events.

This chapter analyzes reduplicated forms such as *ie-ie* "house-house" (houses) in Japanese and claims that reduplicated noun phrases (NPs) are indefinites, although *araw-araw* "day-day" (every day) in Tagalog (Blake (1917)) contributes to universal quantification. Closely connected to this study is an analysis by Dalrymple (2012) who analyzed reduplication in Indonesian to be semantically MANY in plurality. Even though reduplication in birds' language is directly compositional, reduplication in human language appears to be non-compositional.

2. Reduplication in Trump's Speech: Reduplication as Degree Raiser

Reduplication is widely used in many languages. US President Donald Trump often uses reduplicated forms of emphatic words. The repeated degree words raise the scalar degree of adjectives or adverbs, meaning *many, many* is *many*er than *many* and *terrible, terrible* is *terrible*r than *terrible*. Scalar degree is raised by the reduplication of scalar adjectives.

(1)   Together, we will determine the course of America and the world for *many,*

many years to come.

(US President Donald Trump, "Inauguration Speech")[1]

(2) We're going to have a signing summit, which is even better. So hopefully, we can get that completed. But we're getting *very, very* close.

("Remarks by President Trump at the 2019 White House Business Session with our Nation's Governors")[2]

(3) Each family here today represents a son or daughter, a sister or brother, a mother or father, who was taken from you on that *terrible, terrible* day.

(Remarks by President Trump at the 9/11 Memorial Observance, September 11, 2017)[3]

In Donald Trump's Immigration Speech on August 31, 2016[4] the chances for reduplicated forms were as follows:

(4) a. many many: 4 occurrences/6860 words
     b. very very: 4 occurrences/6860 words
     c. horrible, horrible: 2 occurrences/6860 words

Two words sequence had a 0.0291 % chance of occurrence, while *very, very* with four occurrences had 0.116 % chance and *horrible, horrible* had two occurrences. In these usages, reduplication raises the scalar degree of degree words or adjectives. Assuming the contextually given degree d, following Kennedy (1997), degree d of a reduplicated degree word is higher than the degree d' of non-duplicated correspondence on the degree scale. If a degree adjective is a function from an individual to a scalar degree, the degree of the reduplicated forms is higher than the non-reduplicated forms on scale, as indicated by the ordering relation '$\prec$' in (5).

(5) sweet(x) = d
     sweet-sweet(x) = d'
     d $\prec$ d'

If we assume that the positive degree morpheme pos picks the contextual standard, the standard for the reduplicated *many, many* is higher than the single *many* when *many* is considered to be a degree adjective, in (6).

(6) a. pos = $\lambda g \in D_{<e,d>} \lambda t\lambda x : g(x)(t) \geq$ stnd(g)
b. pos (many) = $\lambda t\lambda x$:many$(x)(t) \geq$ stnd(many)
c. pos (many-many) = $\lambda t\lambda x$.many-many$(x)(t) \geq$ stnd(many-many)

3. Reduplication as Universal Quantifier and Indefinites

3.1 Nominal Reduplication in Tagalog

In Tagalog, reduplicated nouns represent universal quantification as discussed in Blake (1917).

(7) a. araw
day
'day'
b. araw araw
day day
'every day'

The concatenation of the noun phrases signifies "every," the universal quantifier.

(8) a. X → XX
b. araw: λx.day(x)
c. araw-araw: $\lambda P_{<t>} \forall t \subseteq$ day.P(x)(t)
d. Jabes gawa araw araw
James works day day
"James works daily."

Although the double NP construction is not productive, the data in Tagalog suggests that the semantic contribution of reduplication is universal quantification.

3.2 *Dog after Dog* Construction in English

English has a productive construction which Jackendoff (2008) termed *construction after construction* in the form NPN where two nouns (N) are identical and basically limited to singular count nouns. The prepositions (P) *by*, *for*, *to*, *after* and *upon* are productive. *N after N* and *N by N* have sequential meaning and quantificational force, with the latter signifying "each N," living *day by day*, or live one day each and get by every day in (9c).

(9) a. Niki is now reeling in car after car and...[5]
     b. Dog after dog came across.
     c. Marion and I are living day by day.[6]
     d. Every door to door salesman knows that.[7]
     e. The first census pairs them off man for man, leaving a surplus of 273
        who are redeemed by money.[8]

Matsuyama (2004), Oehrle (1998), Pi (1995), and Postma (1995) discussed that "N_i after N_i" has a quantificational force and can bind anaphora.

(10) Dog after dog$_i$ wagged its$_i$ tail.

Door to door does not mean traveling between two doors but between multiple doors.

(11) reduplication(N) = $\forall x.N(x)$

3.3 Reduplication in Japanese: Indefinites
3.3.1 Nominal Reduplication

There is quantificational force in reduplication in Japanese. Although nominal reduplication is not a productive construction, the reduplication contributes to universal quantification; e.g., *katagata* "people.HON," *hitobito* "people," *yamayama* "mountains," *kuniguni* "countries," *muramura* "villages," *hoshiboshi* "stars," *wareware* "1PL," *kamigami* "gods," *hoshiboshi* "stars," *hibi* "days," *hitoribitori* "individuals," and *kotaigotai* "taking turns."

In their discussion of the reduplication in Indonesian, Dalrymple (2012) analyzes that reduplication contributes to the meaning *relatively large*, specified either conventionally or contextually.

(12) meja-meja "tables"
λx.[table(x) $\wedge$ CL(x) = N($\wedge$N is relatively large)]
The pluralities constituted by tables which comprise N "portions" of table, where "table portions" (individual tables) are specified conventionally or, if no conventional specification is available, contextually by the generic classifier CL. Optionally, N is specified as a relatively large number in the given context.

(Dalrymple and Mofu (2012))

It is true that the set members of *ie-ie* "houses" compose a plural unit of the members as shown in (13).

(13) $[\![ieie$ "*houses*"$]\!]$ = *house = {a, b, c, a+b, b+c, a+b+c}
where *A is the closure of A under $\cup$

Moreover, *ieie* "houses" can refer to a subpart of houses, meaning ten houses out of six on the same street, and it does not simply refer to the maximum member:

(14) $[\![ieie$ "*houses*"$]\!]$ $\supseteq$ (σx.*house(x) = {a+b+c})

The reduplication is modifiable by both intersective and non-intersective modifiers. The referents of the reduplicated noun phrases are restricted in location in (15) while the size of the mountains and islands are depicted relative to the standard in (16).

(15) a. Kinjo-no   ieie
         neighborhood-GEN   house.RED

"houses in the neighborhood"

b. Kokyo-no   yamayama
hometown-GEN mountain.RED
"mountains in hometown"

c. Koen-no   kigi-ga   makka-ni   iroduit-ta.
park- GEN   tree.RED-NOM reddish-DAT   color-PAST
"The trees in the park turned real red."

(16) a. takai   yamayama
high   mountain.RED
"tall moutains"

b. chiisana   shimajima
small   island.RED
"small islands"

Carlson (1977) discusses both generic and existential uses of bare nouns in English:

(17)   a. Birds fly (in general). [generic statement]
$\forall x.bird(x) \rightarrow fly(x)$
b. (Some) birds flew in. [existential]
$\exists x.bird(x) \wedge fly\text{-}in(x)$

A generic statement has universal force that allows exceptions, for example, that sick birds may not fly. On the other hand, existential bare nouns parallel with other weak noun phrases and appear in existential sentences as in (18).

(18)   There were birds flying in.

The reduplication in Japanese seems to allow only existential readings.

(19)   a. {#Hitobito/√hito}-wa   honyurui-da. [generic statement]
person.RED/human-TOP mammal-COP
"People are mammals."
b. Shimajima-{#wa/√ga}   kieru. [generic statement/existential]

island.RED-TOP/NOM   disappear

"Islands disappear."

Therefore, reduplication is indefinite and similar to bare plurals—the plural noun phrases without a determiner, such as *houses*, *mountains*, and *trees*, which are universal but allow for exceptions. It is in harmony with Matsuyama (2006) who indicated the similarities between *dog after dog* construction and bare plurals.

3.2.2 Adverbial Quantification

There are reduplicated adverbs that depict certain degree of whiteness, earliness, blueness, roundness, frequency, coldness, or frequency of events which exceeds standard; e.g., *hayabayato* "quickly," *aoaoto* "greenly," *shirajirashita* "whitely," *hakihakito* "eloquently," *marumaruto* "roundly," *tokidoki* "at times," *sarasara* "dry," *samuzamu* "cold," *kaesugaesu* "in return," and *yoyoto* "in high spirits."

(20) Pan-o   tabetabe   kangae-ta.
       bread-ACC   eat.RED   think-PAST
       "I thought while eating bread"

These are the cases where reduplication contributes to universal quantification: *haya-baya* "quick-quick" does not depict twice as fast as *hayai* "quick," nor does *ao-ao* "blue-blue" mean two-times greener but rather being *very/really* quick or green. Similarly, event adverbs made of reduplicated verbs describe the frequency of events which exceed certain degrees, not the sequence of two events in (21-22).

(21) a. arukiaruki   kangaeta.
         walk-walk   think-PAST
         "(I) thought while walking."

      b. $\exists e''$.walk(e) $\wedge$ n $\geq$ stnd(walk)

(22) a. Ryo-wa   atama-o   kaki-kaki   shabet-ta.
      Ryo-TOP   head-ACC   scratch-scratch   speak-PAST
      "Ryo spoke while scratching his head."

   b. ∃e″.scratch(e) ∧ agent(e) = Ryo ∧ s≥tnd(scratch)

3.4 Partial Reduplication

There is also partial reduplication which is not compositional either. The following examples are of partial reduplication in Tagalog:

(23) a. súlat "write"
         susúlat "write"
      b. XY → XXY

In (23), what is supposed to be *súlatsúlat* becomes *susúlat*. The reason probably lies in the metrical structure in Tagalog where a strong-weak-strong-weak syllable sequence is less preferred to weak-strong-weak.

(24) a. su.   sú.   lat
         weak   strong   weak
         "write"
      b. sú.   lat   sú.   lat
         strong weak   strong   weak
         "write"

Then, partial reduplication is the phonological output of complete reduplication and *susúlat* is considered to be the reduplication of *súlat*.

3.5 Prototypicality Raiser

Another non-compositional reduplication is a prototypicality raiser. The books or students in the "NP*2" construction are typical books or students, and magazines or newspapers are excluded from *a book book*.

(25) a. a book book
       "the real book (not a magazine or newspaper)"
      b. a student student
       "a student-like student"

Similar examples are found in Japanese (Ono 2015)):

(26) Onna-no-ko   onna-no-ko   shita   asobi
      girl   girl   do   play
      "girlish play"

The reduplicated form sounds more girlish than the non-reduplicated form *onna-no-ko no asobi* "girl's play."

The prototypicality raiser-type reduplication is rather focus related phenomena. Non-prototypical alternatives *boyish* and the like are focus alternatives indexed with *f* which are excluded from the ordinary semantic value *o* (cf. Rooth (1985)).

(27) $[\![girlish - girlish]\!]^f$ = {girlish, boyish,?}
      $[\![girlish - girlish]\!]^o$ = girlish
      $[\![book - book]\!]^f$ = {magazine, journal, booklet, book}
      $[\![book]\!]^o$ = book

4. Compositional Reduplication

Reduplicated degree adjectives do not necessarily represent double degree of a single adjective. For example, a *wide, wide window* is not twice as wide as a *wide window*. If the reduplicated *many* does not represent double the amount of a single *many*, the Principle of Compositionality is violated with reduplication, and reduplicated forms are idioms in which the construction reduplication has a meaning. Reduplicated degree words do not simply represent double the amount and reduplication itself contributes to the meaning.

With birds' language, there is direct compositionality with reduplication. There is direct mapping between the number of times there is repetition of the sound and the size of the predator. Chicksaw birds' singing is compositional, in that three *bees* represent three times as far as a single *bee* (cf. Schlenker et al. (2014)).

(28) bee*3 = distance*3
$$X \rightarrow XXX \cdots$$
$$X \rightarrow X^n$$

Reduplication also depicts size compositionally among some birds. Among Chickadee birds in Africa, reduplication of the D key depicts size in birds' language (Templeton et al. (2005)). The number of repetition corresponds to the size of the coming predator birds. (29) shows the syntax and semantics of Chickadee bird language.

(29) Syntax: $D^n * X$
Semantics: $n*a$ = the size of the predator

Thus, direct compositionality is observed in birds' language and there is direct mapping between the number of repetition and spatial measurement.

5. Conclusion

Although there is compositional reduplication in non-human language, reduplicated forms are indefinites and contribute to universal quantification. It is true that there are also other uses of reduplication. For example, reduplication in vocatives draws attention of the hearer. In (30), the queen calls the mirror and draws its attention.

(30) Mirror, mirror, on the wall,

Who in this land is fairest of all?

(Jacob and Wilhelm Grimm, *Snow White*)

Such a vocative use of reduplication does not seem to contribute to quantification or focus semantics; instead, it is emphatic. Dogs seem to understand reduplicated forms more clearly and respond better. For example, *walk, walk* and *run, run* get a better response than the non-reduplicated single verbs and the effect of reduplication on dogs should be investigated more thoroughly.

* I thank Mariko Murayama for the discussion on Trump's speech and James Pauya for the data in Tagalog. The first incentive to write this paper was on hearing Ray Jackendoff's lecture at Stony Brook University some time between 2004 and 2007. Philippe Schlenker's lectures on Primate Linguistics at ESSLLI2015 gave me information on birds' language.

[1] https://www.latimes.com/politics/la-na-pol-presidential-transcript-20170120-htmlstory.html

[2] https://www.whitehouse.gov/briefings-statements/remarks-president-trump-2019-white-house-business-session-nations-governors/

[3] https://www.whitehouse.gov/briefings-statements/remarks-president-trump-9-11-memorial-observance/

[4] http://www.latimes.com/politics/la-na-pol-donald-trump-immigration-speech-transcript-20160831-snap-htmlstory.html

[5] Keith Botsford, *The champions of Formula 1 from Fangio to Piquet*, 1989, BNC web query result.

[6] *The Daily Mirror*, BNC query result.

[7] *Improve your people skills*, BNC query result.

[8] *The Lion concise Bible handbook*, BNC query result.

References

Blake, Frank R. (1917) "Reduplication in Tagalog," *The American Journal of Philology* 38, 425–431.

Carlson, Gregory (1977) "A Unified Analysis of the English Bare Plural," *Linguistics and Philosophy* 1, 413–458.

Dalrymple, Mary and Suriel Mofu (2012) "Plural Semantics, Reduplication, and Numeral Modification in Indonesian," *Journal of Semantics* 29, 229–260.

Jackendoff, Ray (2008) "Construction after Construction and Its Theoretical Challenges," *Language* 84, 8–28.

Kennedy, Christopher (1997) *Projecting the Adjective: The Syntax and Semantics of Gradability and Comparison*, Doctoral Dissertation, University of California, Santa Cruz.

Matsuyama, Tetsuya (2004) "The N after N construction: A Constructional Idiom," *English Linguistics* 21, 55–84.

Matsuyama, Tetsuya (2006) "A Note on the Two-Sided Behavior of N After N," *English Linguistics* 23, 446-453.

Oehrle, Richard (1998) "Noun After Noun," Annual Meeting of the Linguistic Society of America, New York City.

Ono, Naoyuki (2015) "Onna-no ko Onna-no ko shita Onna o Megutte," *Goi Imiron no Aratana Kanosei o Sagutte*, 463-490, Kaitakusha, Tokyo.

Pi, Chia-Yi Tony (1995) "The Structure of English Iteratives," *Proceedings of the 1995 Annual Conference of the Canadian Linguistic Association* (*Toronto Working Papers in Linguistics*), ed. by Päivi Koskinen.

Postma, Gertjian (1995) *Zero Semantics: The Syntactic Encoding of Quantificational Meaning*, John Benjamins, Amsterdam.

Rooth, Mats (1985) *Association with Focus*, Doctoral Dissertation, University of Massachusetts at Amherst.

Schlenker, Philippe, Emmanuel Chemla, Kate Arnold, Alban Lemasson, Karim Ouattara, Sumir Keenan, Claudia Stephan, Robin Ryder and Klaus Zuberbühler (2014) "Monkey Semantics: Two 'Dialects' of Campbell's Monkey Alarm Calls," *Linguistics and Philosophy* 37, 439–501.

Templeton, Christophe N. Greene Erick and Davis Kate (2005) "Allometry of Alarm Calls: Black-Capped Chikadees Encode Information About Predator Size," *Science* 308, 1934–1937.

The Missing Resultatives in Japanese: Why Can't the Shoes Be Run Threadbare in Japanese?*

Masashi Yamaguchi

Keyword: syntax, resultative constructions, Japanese

1. Introduction

This paper presents a theoretical explanation as to why a certain type of resultatives is missing in Japanese. It has been argued in the literature since Washio (1997) that resultative constructions can be divided into two types: weak resultatives and strong resultatives.

> (1)　a. *Weak resultatives*
> 　　　 John painted the wall red.
> 　　b. *Strong resultatives*
> 　　　 Mary ran her shoes threadbare.

They are classified depending on the meanings of the verbs employed; verbs of weak resultatives convey a result state, while those of strong resultatives do not.

> (2)　a. *paint*
> 　　　 to put a liquid on a surface, using a brush to make the surface a particular colour
> 　　b. *run*
> 　　　 to move quickly, by moving your legs more quickly than when you walk

The verb *paint* implies an endpoint in its meaning that is expressed by the phrase "*a particular colour*" in the infinitive clause in (2a). On the other hand, the verb *run* is not equipped with a result state in its meaning. This difference is the key to classifying resultative constructions.

English has both weak and strong resultatives, as shown in (1), but Japanese only has weak resultatives.

(3) a. Weak resultatives
>Taroo-ga   kabe-o   akaku   nut-ta.
>Taroo-Nom   wall-Acc   red   paint-Past
>'Taro painted the wall red.'
>
>b. Strong resultatives
>*Hanako-ga   kutu-o   boroboroni   hasit-ta.
>Hanako-Nom   shoes-Acc threadbare   run-Past
>'Hanako ran her shoes threadbare.'

It has been unclear why Japanese lacks strong resultatives. In this paper, I attempt to provide an explanation to this issue and argue that resultative constructions in English and Japanese do not share the identical structures, and that resultative predicates in Japanese are adjoined to VP. I contend that the property of resultative predicates as adjunct is the reason for the lack of strong resultatives in Japanese.

This paper is organized as follows. Section 2 shows some differences between English and Japanese resultatives. Section 3 introduces a major syntactic approach to resultative constructions in English, and demonstrates that it cannot be applied to the Japanese resultatives because of the difference in the categorical property. Section 4 presents a syntactic structure of resultative constructions in Japanese. Section 5 claims that the status of resultative predicates prevents strong resultatives from appearing in Japanese. Finally, Section 6 concludes this paper.

2. The Syntactic Properties of Resultatives in English and Japanese

In this section, we observe some of the syntactic differences between

English and Japanese resultative constructions. This section is particularly concerned with argumenthood of resultative predicates and the possibility of topicalization of the predicates.

2.1. Argumenthood
2.1.1. English

The difference in argumenthood serves as the first difference between English and Japanese resultative predicates. Evidence for this claim is found in the stringent restriction on the number of arguments, the violation of which results in ungrammaticality. On the other hand, the number of adverbs is generally not restricted.

(4) a. *John played soccer tennis.
     b. John played soccer [in the park] [yesterday].

If multiple resultative predicates in English are employed in one clause, we see the same result as arguments. Observe (5).

(5) a. John washed the clothes clean / white.
     b. *John washed the clothes clean white.   (Hasegawa (1991: 2))

From this perspective, it is reasonable to conclude that resultative predicates in English are arguments of verbs.

Another piece of evidence for argumenthood of resultative predicates in English is a long-distance extraction. Extracting arguments from a wh-island results in marginality, while adjuncts cannot undergo this extraction, as shown in (7). Based on this observation, Carrier and Randall (1992) argue that resultative predicates are arguments of verbs because they exhibit the same grammaticality as arguments when they undergo long-distance extraction.

(6) I wonder whether to punish these boys strictly.

(7) a. ?Which boys$_i$ do you wonder whether to punish t_i?
     b. *How$_i$ do you wonder whether to punish these boys t_i?
                                        (Carrier and Randall (1992: 185))
(8) a. ?What color$_i$ do you wonder which shirts to dye t_i?
     b. ?How threadbare$_i$ do you wonder whether they should run their
        sneakers t_i?
                                                              (ibid.)

The examples in (8) further show that resultative predicates in English are
arguments of verbs.

2.1.2. Japanese

The crucial difference between English and Japanese resultative predicates
is that resultative predicates in the latter have properties as adjuncts.

First, despite some semantic restrictions, more than one resultative
predicate can be used in one clause — that is, multiple resultative predicates
can be used in Japanese.

(9) a. Taroo-ga   pankizi-o   usuku   tairani   nobasita.
        Taroo-Nom   pancake-Acc   thin   flat   spread
        '(Lit.) Taro spread the pancake thin flat.'
     b. Hanako-ga   tetu-o   kireini pikapikani   migaita.
        Hanako-Nom   iron-Acc clean   shiny   polished
        '(Lit.) Hanako polished the iron clean shiny.'

The resultative predicates *usuku* 'thin' and *tairani* 'flat' in (9a) are both
allowed in one clause, contrary to the English resultative predicates in (5).
If *usuku* and *tairani* were arguments, resultative constructions in Japanese
would behave similarly to those in English, and the example of (9a) would
be ungrammatical. The status of Japanese resultative predicates as adjuncts
is supported by the grammaticality of this example. The same is true of the
example in (9b); *kireini* 'clean' and *pikapikani* 'shiny' appear in the same
clause. These examples indicate that resultative predicates in Japanese are

adjuncts.

Furthermore, extraction from negative islands serves one argument for adjuncthood of Japanese resultative predicates. In Japanese, arguments can be scrambled from negative islands, while adjuncts cannot. Take (10) and (11) for example.

(10) a. John-ga   [kessite yuka-o   *subayaku*   migaka-nakat-ta].
          John-Nom   never   floor-Acc   quickly   polish-Neg-Past
          'John never polished the floor quickly.'
     b. ??John-ga *subayaku*ᵢ [kessite yuka-o *t*ᵢ migaka-nakat-ta].
     c. ??*Subayaku*ᵢ John-ga [kessite yuka-o *t*ᵢ migaka-nakat-ta].
                                                              (Tanaka (2014))
(11) a. John-ga   [kessite   *hon-o*   yoma-nakat-ta].
        John-Nom   never   book-Acc   read-Neg-Past
        'John never read books.'
     b. John-ga *hon-o*ᵢ [kessite *t*ᵢ yoma-nakat-ta].
     c. Hon-oᵢ John-ga [kessite *t*ᵢ yoma-nakat-ta].   (ibid.)

The examples of (10b, c) demonstrate that the adjunct *subayaku* 'quickly' cannot be scrambled out of the bracketed negative island. Arguments, on the other hand, can successfully undergo scrambling from the island, as shown as (11). Let us examine the behavior of the resultative predicates in (12).

(12) a. John-ga   [kessite pankizi-o   *tairani* nobasa-nakat-ta].
          John-Nom   never   pancake-Acc flat   spread-Neg-Past
          'John never spread the pancake flat.'
     b. ??John-ga *tairani*ᵢ [kessite pankizi-o *t*ᵢ nobasa-nakat-ta].
     c. ??*Tairani*ᵢ John-ga [kessite pankizi-o *t*ᵢ nobasa-nakat-ta].

As in the case of adjuncts in (10), scrambling of resultative predicates out of the negative island results in malformation. These examples also indicate that resultative predicates in Japanese are adjuncts.

2.2. Topicalization

The second difference between English and Japanese resultative constructions lies in the possibility of topicalization. Resultative predicates of the former cannot undergo topicalization, while those of the latter can. Observe the following example in (13).[2]

    (13)   a. *Red$_i$ John painted the wall t_i.
           b. Akaku$_i$ Taro-ga kabe-o t_i nutta.

From these examples, it is reasonable to conclude that Japanese resultative constructions are different from those in English.

In the following section, we review a typical previous analysis of resultative constructions in English and observe that it cannot be applied to the Japanese resultative constructions.

3. A Syntactic Account for English Resultative Constructions

3.1. Hoekstra (1988): Small Clause Analysis

This section introduces a previous analysis of English resultative constructions, Hoekstra (1988), which is referred to here as a small clause analysis. Though resultative constructions in English have been analyzed in many ways (cf. Cormack and Smith (1999), Oba (2011)), this section reviews a small clause analysis. This is because it is a typical approach to the resultative constructions in English.[3]

Hoekstra (1988) is one of the most famed analyses of the resultative constructions in English. He proposes a small clause structure for the constructions.

    (14)   a. John painted the house red.
           b. John ran the pavement thin.

(15) a.

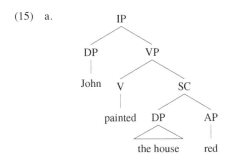

b.

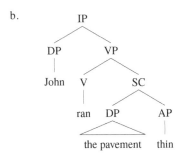

One of the motivations for a small clause structure is that unergative verbs are also available in resultative constructions. Take (16) for example.

(16) a. John laughed himself sick.   (Hoekstra (1988: 115))
     b. *John laughed sick.
     c. *John laughed himself.

The verb in (16) *laugh* does not usually take an object, but omitting the object *himself* yields an ungrammatical result, as in (16b). Moreover, the example of (16c) indicates that the resultative predicate *sick* cannot be excluded. Therefore, Hoekstra concludes that the object and the predicate form a constituent, indicating that they constitute a small clause structure.

    Hoekstra also claims that not only unergative verbs but also transitive verbs form small clause structures in resultative constructions. This claim is supported by the fact that transitive verbs take non-thematic objects.

(17) a. *He washed the soap.   (cf. (ibid.: 116))
      b. *The sopranos sang us.
(18) a. He washed the soap out of the eyes.
      b. The sopranos sang us sleepy.

The examples of (17) illustrate that the objects *the soap* and *us* are not available with the verbs *wash* and *sing*, but the resultative predicates enables them to function as objects, as in (18).

His proposal may account for the nature of resultative constructions in English, but the following section reveals that it is difficult to apply his analysis to Japanese resultative constructions.

3.2. An Application of a Small Clause Analysis to Japanese

Hoekstra's (1988) approach captures the syntactic properties of English resultatives, but as we have observed in Section 2, the syntactic properties of Japanese resultative constructions differ from English. Therefore, resultative constructions in Japanese should be treated differently from those in English.

Moreover, it is impossible for Japanese resultatives to form small clause structures. The Japanese language may indeed include small clauses as complements of some verbs such as *kanziru* 'feel'. Let us take (19) for example.

(19) Taroo-ga   Hanako-o   husawasiku   kanzi-ta.
      Taroo-Nom   Hanako-Acc   suitable   feel-Past
      'Taro felt felt that Hanako was suitable.'

As we have observed, Japanese resultative predicates are adjuncts. If we assume a small clause structure for Japanese resultative constructions, it is predicted that they will exhibit the same property as other instances of small clause structures such as (19). However, this prediction is not borne out. We have seen in (13b), repeated here as (20a), that Japanese resultative predicates may be topicalized. The predicates of small clauses, on the other hand, cannot.

(20)　a.　Akaku$_i$ Taroo-ga kabe-o t_i nut-ta.　　　　　(=(13b))
　　　b. ??Husawasiku$_i$ Taroo-ga Hanako-o t_i kanzi-ta.

From these examples, we can conclude that resultative constructions in Japanese have a different property from a small clause and do not form a small clause structure. Therefore, the analysis of Hoekstra (1988) cannot be applied to Japanese resultative constructions.

In the following section, I first demonstrate the position of the resultative predicates in Japanese, and present the structure of the construction.

4. The Structure of Resultative Constructions in Japanese

In this section, I argue that the resultative predicates are located in VP. The vP-fronting test reveals that the resultative predicates are at least in vP.

(21)　a.　[$_{vP}$ Kabe-o　　akaku　nuri　　sae]　　Taroo-ga　　si-ta.
　　　　　wall-Acc　　red　　paint even　　　　Taroo-Nom　do-Past
　　　　　'Even paint the wall red, Taro did.'
　　　b. *[$_{vP}$ Kabe-o　　nuri　　sae] Taroo-ga　　akaku　si-ta.
　　　　　wall-Acc paint　　　even Taroo-Nom　red　　　do-Past
　　　　　'Even paint the wall, Taro did red.'

As shown in (21), the resultative predicate *akaku* 'red' needs to be pied-piped with vP; otherwise, the example would be ungrammatical. Therefore, it is reasonable to assume that resultative predicates in Japanese are positioned within vP.

The following examples further disclose the position of the resultative predicates.

(22) a. Taroo-ga [$_{vP}$ [$_{VP}$ kabe-o *akaku*] [$_v$ nutta]]
  b. *Taroo-ga [$_{vP}$ [$_{VP}$ kabe-o] [$_v$ nutta] *akaku*]

As shown in (22), the resultative predicate *akaku* cannot precede the verb *nuru* 'paint'. This indicates that resultative predicates are located in a lower position than verbs. Assuming that verbs in Japanese are in *v* and do not move any further (Fukui and Sakai (2003)), resultative predicates must be in a lower position than *v* — namely, VP.

Following the observations so far, resultative constructions in Japanese should have the following structure.

(23)

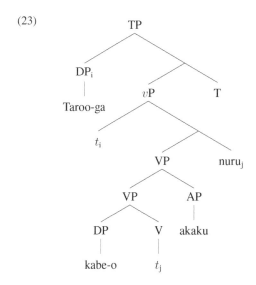

In the structure in (23), the resultative predicate *akaku* 'red' is adjoined to VP, and the predicate does not form a small clause with its semantic subject DP *kabe-o* 'the wall'. This status as adjuncts is crucial for the reason why the Japanese language lacks strong resultatives.

The following section finally delves into the primary issue of this paper — the lack of strong resultatives in Japanese.

5. The Missing Resultatives: Explanation

Adjuncthood of Japanese resultative predicates reveals the reason for the absence of strong resultatives in Japanese. We have observed that Japanese resultative constructions in Japanese do not carry small clauses in their structure. The relevant examples are (20), repeated here in (24).

(24)   a.   Akaku$_i$ Taroo-ga kabe-o t$_i$ nut-ta.   (= (13b))
       b. ??Husawasiku$_i$ Taroo-ga Hanako-o t$_i$ kanzi-ta.   (= (20b))

Moreover, the following examples in (25) demonstrate that predicates in Japanese small clauses have properties as arguments.

(25)   a.   Taroo-ga   kono   heya-o   kokotiyoku / tukaiyasuku kanzi-ta.
            Taroo-Nom   this   roomAcc comfortable useful   feel-Past
            'Taro felt this room comfortable / useful.'
       b. ??Taroo-ga kono heya-o kokotiyoku tukaiyasuku kanzi-ta.

The example in (25a) indicates that the predicates *kokotiyoku* 'comfortable' and *tukaiyasuku* 'useful' are available in a small clause but cannot be employed in the same clause, suggesting that predicates in Japanese small clauses have argumenthood.

The discussion above substantiates the claim that resultative predicates in Japanese cannot appear in the position of the predicates in small clauses because that is the position for arguments, but Japanese resultative predicates are adjuncts. This property of resultative predicates as adjuncts prohibits Japanese from carrying strong resultatives.

If strong resultatives were allowed in Japanese, it should be the case that Japanese allows nearly every adverb without any constraint on meaning because the resultative predicates of strong resultatives are not encoded in the meanings of verbs. This means that the predicates are not restricted by verbs with respect to meaning, and adverbs may be freely employed anywhere. However, Japanese is not such a language, and, in fact, Japanese resultative predicates are influenced by verbs, and are not free in terms of meaning.

(26) a. Taroo-ga   pankizi-o   usuku nobasita.
         Taroo-Nom   pancake-Acc thin spread
         'Taro spread the pancake thin.'
     b. ??Taroo-ga pankizi-o atuku nobasita.
         Taroo-Nom pancake-Acc thick spread
         'Taro spread the pancake thick.'

The example of (26b) sounds strange because the resultative predicate employed *atuku* 'thick' is cannot be implied by the verb *nobasu* 'spread'. This fact supports the claim that Japanese resultative predicates are not free in terms of meaning.

In English resultative constructions, on the other hand, small clauses may be formed and taken by a verb as its complement. What is crucial is that not a resultative predicate but 'result proposition' is directly selected by the verb. Therefore, the selectional restriction on the meaning of the predicate by the verb can be vague. This indirect selection allows non-thematic resultee objects in this constructions, and therefore, permits strong resultatives to appear in English.

6. Conclusion

This paper has conducted an analysis to reveal the reason why Japanese does not have strong resultatives. We have reviewed a typical previous study of English resultative constructions that cannot be applied to Japanese resultative constructions because resultative predicates in Japanese have properties as adjuncts, unlike those in English, which are arguments of a verb. Adjuncthood of resultative predicates prevents them from being rather freely selected as resultative predicates, leading to the lack of strong resultatives in

Japanese.

Notes

*This is a revised version of a part of my dissertation. I am grateful to my dissertation advisory committee members, Masaharu Kato, Takao Kamiyama, Sadayuki Okada, Eri Tanaka, and Yukio Oba, for their helpful comments. All the remaining errors are, of course, mine.

[1] The meanings in (2) is cited from Longman Dictionary of Contemporary English.
[2] Similar examples are presented by Matushansky et al. (2012: 3).
[3] This paper does not delve any further into the issue as to what it is that the structure of English resultative constructions is like because its goal is not to claim which analysis is the best to account for English resultatives, but to provide an explanation for the lack of strong resultatives in Japanese.

References

Carrier, Jill and Janet Randall (1992) "The Argument Structure and Syntactic Structure of Resultatives," *Linguistic Inquiry* 23, 173–234.

Cormack, Annabel and Neil Smith (1999) "Why Are Depictives Different from Resultatives?," *Working Papers in Linguistics*, 251–284, University College London, London.

Fukui, Naoki and Hiromu Sakai (2003) "The Visibility of Guideline for Functional Categories: Verb Raising in Japanese and Related Issues," *Lingua* 113, 321–375.

Hasegawa, Hiroshi (1991) "Secondary Predicates, VP-Internal Subjects, and Mutual C-Command," *English Linguistics* 8, 1–15.

Hoekstra, Teun (1988) "Small Clause Results," Lingua 74, 101–139.

Oba, Yukio (2011) *Eigo Kobun o Tankyusuru* (*Exploring Constructions in English*), Kaitakusha, Tokyo.

Matushansky, Ora Annemarie van Dooren and Lotte Hendriks (2012) "A Path to the Result(ative)," paper presented at Recontres d'Automme de Linguistique Formelle 2012.

Tanaka, Hideharu (2014) "The Distribution of Adjuncts in Japanese: Toward a Probe-Goal Theory of Scrambling," poster presented at 7th Meeting of Formal Approaches to Japanese Linguistics, National Institute for Japanese Language and Linguistics.

Masashi Yamaguchi

Washio, Ryuichi (1997) "Resultatives, Compositionality and Language Variation," Journal of East Asian Linguistics 6, 1–49.

Dictionary

Longman Dictionary of Contemporary English (5th edition), Pearson.

On the Connection Between Agreement and NP-Ellipsis: Evidence from Kikai (Ryukyuan)*

Yusuke Imanishi

Keywords : agreement, NP-ellipsis, genitive case, Kikai (Ryukyuan)

1. Introduction

The aim of the paper is to show, based on a set of novel data from Kikai (Ryukyuan), that NP-ellipsis such as the one shown in (1) is licensed by (strong) agreement, a hypothesis which has been proposed by Lobeck (1995, 2006) among others.

(1) I like Bill's wine, but Max's e is even better.   (Jackendoff (1971))

I will demonstrate that a comparative study of Kikai and Okinawan strengthens the connection between agreement and NP-ellipsis.

Lobeck (1995) proposes that NP-ellipsis is licensed by strong (spec-head) agreement. The elided element (= *wine*) or the empty category *e* (in Lobeck's analysis) in (1) is licensed by the agreement between *Max* and D: the former is in Spec-DP and the latter in D. Lobeck argues that her analysis can provide a unified account of NP-ellipsis and other types of ellipsis such as VP-ellipsis and sluicing. I will refer to this line of analysis as the *Agreement Hypothesis for Ellipsis* (AHE).

Adopting Lobeck's analysis, Hiraiwa (2016) demonstrates that Naha (/ Shuri) Okinawan (hereafter Okinawan), a Ryukyuan language, displays NP-ellipsis and argues that it involves deletion of an NP licensed by agreement. Unlike Japanese, Okinawan manifests overt DP-internal agreement, depending on the feature of a possessor. Hiraiwa shows that the presence or absence of DP-internal agreement correlates with the (un)availability of NP-ellipsis in Okinawan, thereby supporting the AHE.

As I will show, Kikai appears to serve as a counterexample to the AHE and Hiraiwa's analysis. Kikai seems to display DP-internal agreement just as Okinawan does, but does not allow NP-ellipsis. However, I will suggest that Kikai's genitive marker should not be treated as a case marker reflecting agreement, but is a linking element inserted according to a language-particular rule in the sense of Watanabe (2010). If the genitive marker of Kikai does not arise via agreement, the lack of NP-ellipsis does not pose a problem for the AHE but rather strengthens it.

The paper is organized as follows. Section 2 overviews an agreement-based approach to NP-ellipsis in several languages including Okinawan. Section 3 presents an analysis of the genitive marking and (the lack of) NP-ellipsis in Kikai. Section 4 concludes the paper.

2. NP-Ellipsis and Agreement

2.1. An Agreement-Based Approach

Among several approaches to NP-ellipsis is the agreement-based analysis advanced by Lobeck (1995) (see Lobeck 2006 and Lobeck and Sleeman 2017 for an overview of various analyses of the phenomenon). As briefly introduced in section 1, under the AHE, the licensing of NP-ellipsis calls for an agreement relation, particularly the one between Spec-DP and D. For Lobeck, the licensing head (e.g. D) or the element with which it agrees with must morphologically realize agreement features (= strong agreement) in order to allow elliptical elements. In the case of NP-ellipsis, D assigns genitive case to its specifier (= possessor), forming an agreement relation with it, and 's, which is affixed to a possessor, possibly realizes a genitive case feature. This agreement relation along with the overtly realized agreement then licenses the elliptical NP in the complement of the D head. The NP-ellipsis such as the one in (1) is licensed as below.

(2)

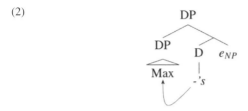

As Lobeck suggests, the agreement-based analysis can also explain the fact that adjectives in English do not allow NP-ellipsis as shown in (3). Since there is no agreement relation between the prenominal adjective and the modified noun in English, ellipsis is not licensed.

(3) *Susan wanted the Mexican beer, but Dennis chose the German *e*.

(Lobeck (1995))

In this respect, English contrasts with "rich-agreement" languages such as Spanish, which displays agreement in adjectives: the postnominal adjective agrees in gender and number with the noun. The noun can be ellipted in Spanish. The contrast between English and Spanish thus provides support for the AHE (see Lobeck and Sleeman 2017 for a summary of its problems and other competing analyses).[1]

2.2. Okinawan NP-Ellipsis

Hiraiwa (2016) proposes that Okinawan NP-ellipsis can be explained by the AHE. Hiraiwa shows that NP-ellipsis correlates with the presence of overt agreement in DPs, thereby supporting Lobeck's analysis. I will present an overview of Okinawan NP-ellipsis below.

Unlike Japanese, Okinawan displays overt agreement inside DPs. In Okinawan, the type of a case particle in DPs is sensitive to the features of a possessor.[2] When the possessor is first and second person, it does not carry a case particle as shown in (4).

(4) waa-ø   kuruma
    1Sg-ø   car
    'my car'   (Hiraiwa (2016))

On the other hand, when the possessor is a third person (singular) pronoun, nominative *ga* is attached to it.

(5) *'ari*-ga   kuruma
    3Sg.A-Nom   car
    'that person's car'   (ibid.)

By contrast, when the possessor is a third person inanimate pronoun (e.g. *'a* "that") or an ordinary noun (both animate and inanimate) like *Taraa* (= a male name) and *America*, the genitive case particle *nu* is attached to the possessor.

Hiraiwa demonstrates that NP-ellipsis is available only when the overt case particle appears on the possessor. Given the DP agreement paradigm shown above, NP-ellipsis is not allowed when the possessor is first and second person; the case particle is a zero form. NP-ellipsis is possible otherwise. This contrast is shown below.

(6) waa-ø   *(kuruma)
    1Sg-ø   car
    'my car'   (ibid.)
(7) *'ari*-ga/Taraa-*nu*   (shimuchi)
    that person-Nom/Tara-Gen   book
    'that person's/Tara's book'   (ibid.)

The light noun *mun* can also be used instead of the ellipted nominal. When it comes to a first or second person possessor, the light noun is the only strategy to replace the possessed noun.

Assuming that case reflects φ-agreement (George and Kornfilt 1981; Chomsky 2000), Hiraiwa argues that the presence of agreement inside DPs in

Okinawan licenses NP-ellipsis or NP-deletion. As for first and second person possessors, he suggests that no agreement takes place as there is no overt case particle as seen in (4). Hiraiwa thus takes the contrast between (6) and (7) as strong evidence for the AHE. Hiraiwa conjectures that the features involved in DP-internal agreement of Okinawan concern animacy, although he does not elaborate on its mechanism. Whatever its analysis may be, it is obvious that the DP-internal agreement in Okinawan displays a type of differential case marking in which case-marking is affected by the nominal features of a possessor such as person and animacy, a case-marking pattern similar to the one discussed by Silverstein (1976) and Dixon (1994) among others.

The way Lobeck and Hiraiwa implement their analyses suggests that DP-internal agreement is a necessary and sufficient condition for NP-ellipsis. Therefore, the lack of NP-ellipsis despite the presence of DP-internal overt agreement will pose a problem for the AHE. We will discuss whether Kikai, another Ryukyuan language, should be analyzed as such a counterexample.

3. NP-Ellipsis in Kikai

3.1. NP-Ellipsis and Genitive Marking in Kikai

In this section, I will show that Kikai appears to argue against the AHE at first blush because it lacks NP-ellipsis entirely although its genitive marking is sensitive to the nominal features of a possessor just as in Okinawan.

Kikai or the Kikai dialect of Amami (Ryukyuan) is spoken in Kikai Island of Kagoshima Prefecture in Japan (see Pellard (2015) for an overview of the linguistic classification of Ryukyuan languages). Alongside several other languages in Japan such as Okinawan and Ainu, Kikai is included in the 2009 UNESCO list of 2,500 endangered languages in the world: the eight languages spoken in Japan are included in the list. Kibe et al. (2011) provide a linguistic sketch of many dialects of Kikai, and Shirata (2016) is a detailed analysis of the Kamikatetsu dialect of Kikai (see also Matsumoto (1993), Honda and Imanishi (2015) and the references cited therein for other analyses of Kikai). I will discuss the Kamikatetsu dialect in what follows, and the data are drawn

from my field notes unless otherwise noted. I will adopt the orthography of
Kikai proposed by Shirata (2016).

In Kikai, first and second person possessors do not carry a particle just as in
Okinawan.

(8) a. waa-ø   kuruma
        1Sg-ø   car
        'my car'
     b. daa-ø   kuruma
        2Sg-ø   car
        'your car'

The particle -*nu* can be attached to first and second person subjects.[3] As noted
by Shirata (2016), first and second person pronouns (wan and da, respectively)
appear as different forms when they are possessors, as seen in (8). Kikai has
an inclusive vs. exclusive distinction for first person plural. Neither inclusive
nor exclusive possessors carry a particle.[4]

(9) a. wačaa-ø   kuruma
        1Pl.Incl-ø   car
        'our (inclusive) car'
     b. wannaa-ø   kuruma
        1Pl.Excl-ø   car
        'our (exclusive) car'

In contrast, third person possessors bear the particle -*nu*, whether they are
pronominal or non-pronominal.

(10) a. ari-*nu*   kuruma
         3Sg-Gen   car
         'his car'
      b. Taroo-*nu*   kuruma
         Taro-Gen   car
         'Taro's car'

Kikai displays a politeness distinction for second person pronouns just as in German (*du* vs. *Sie*) and Spanish (*tú* vs. *usted*). The distinction affects genitive marking in the language. While the regular possessive pronoun for second person singular (= *daa*) is a zero form as seen in (8b), its polite form (= *naami*) carries –*nu*, thereby patterning with third person possessors. The genitive marking in Kikai can be summarized as below.

Table1: Genitive marking in Kikai

	singular	plural
1st person	ø	ø(both inclusive and exclusive)
2nd person	ø	ø
3rd person, 2nd person (honorific)	-nu	-nu

The contrast between (8)/(9)(= first and second person) and (10)(= third person) might lead us to conclude that Kikai displays DP-internal agreement. One might then expect that NP-ellipsis is available with third person possessors if the presence of a particle is taken as suggesting that agreement takes place, as suggested by Hiraiwa (2016) for Okinawan.

However, NP-ellipsis is not possible with third person possessors or first/second person possessors, as shown in (11) and (12).

(11) waa-ø   kuruma   ari-*nu*   *(mun/kuruma)   kamu maisari.
     1Sg-ø   car   3Sg-Gen   (thing/car)   than big
     'My car is bigger than his.'

(12) Taroo-*nu*   kuruma   waa-ø   *(mun/kuruma)   kamu maisari.
     Taro-Gen   car   1Sg-ø   (thing/car)   than big
     'Taro's car is bigger than mine.'

The unavailability of NP-ellipsis in (12) is not unexpected if we assume with Hiraiwa that no agreement takes place in the case of first and second person possessors. This is consistent with what the AHE predicts. However, (11) appears to be a serious counterexample to the AHE. In addition, (11) contrasts sharply with its Okinawan counterpart such as the one in (7). If the particle *–nu* in (11) is an instance of agreement, the lack of NP-ellipsis poses a challenge for the correlation between DP-internal agreement and NP-ellipsis.

3.2. Linking Element

Despite the apparent counterexample of Kikai to the AHE, I will suggest that Kikai provides further support for it. As will be pointed out, the genitive of Kikai should be analyzed as a different element than that of Okinawan.

The genitive marker of Kikai does not display properties that can be taken as the result of agreement. Unlike in Okinawan, for example, the genitive marking in Kikai is not sensitive to the animacy feature of a possessor. As seen above, animate possessors are marked with *-nu*. Likewise, inanimate possessors carry the particle as shown in (13).

(13) a. yaa-*(nu)   yani
         house-(Gen)   roof
         'the roof of a house'
      b. ami-*(nu)   hi
         rain-(Gen)   day
         'a rainy day'

The particle *-nu* attaches to the possessor regardless of its animacy.

The possibility that person agreement (i.e., 1/2 person vs. 3 person) is at play for genitive marking can also be excluded by the following fact. There are certain cases in which the particle *-nu* can be attached to the first person possessor, as shown in (14).

(14) wan-*nu*   kuruma
      1Sg-Gen   car
      'my car'

While first and second person pronouns have special genitive forms with no genitive marker as mentioned above, it appears that the regular form of a first person pronoun (= *wan*) can be used as a possessor in the Kamikatetsu dialect of Kikai. In addition, as discussed by Shirata (2016), Kikai has a dual form for a first person plural inclusive pronoun (= *wattari*). This pronoun is marked with -*nu* when it appears in a possessor position (Shirata (2016: 53)). Setting aside a precise analysis of examples like (14) and the dual pronoun, it is obvious that the genitive marking in Kikai is not governed by the person feature of a possessor.

Given these facts, I suggest that the particle -*nu* found in a certain class of possessors of Kikai is not a case marker that arises via agreement but a linking element in the sense of Watanabe (2010) or a linker (Hiraiwa 2016). Watanabe (2010) proposes that the genitive marker -*no* in Japanese has two sources, based on the distribution of NP-ellipsis. One results from the assignment of genitive case, whereas the other is inserted as a linking element. The linking element is inserted according to a revised version of Kitagawa and Ross's (1982) *no* insertion rule as shown in (15).

(15) Mod-Insertion
[DP ... XP (-tense) N α] → [DP ... XP (-tense) Mod N α]
where the head noun is overtly realized and Mod = *no*
(Watanabe (2010))

The insertion of Mod (= *no*) is sensitive to morphological properties of a head noun. The genitive marker found in the numeral-classifier sequence such as *san-satsu-no* hon "three books" is a linking element under Watanabe's analysis.

As Watanabe claims, NP-ellipsis is allowed when a nominal is preceded by the genitive case marker. By contrast, NP-ellipsis is not possible when the genitive marker is a linking element. The nominal cannot be ellipted when it follows the numeral-classifier sequence (*san-satsu-no ~~hon~~). Hiraiwa (2016) points out that NP-ellipsis is not possible with the numeral-classifier sequence in Okinawan and suggests that the genitive marker found in such a context is a linker.

If *-nu* in Kikai can be analyzed as a linking element, it follows that NP-ellipsis is not possible even when *-nu* precedes a nominal, as independently proposed for Japanese (Watanabe (2010)) and Okinawan (Hiraiwa (2016)). I propose that the linking element in Kikai is inserted according to the insertion rule such that the genitive marker is inserted except when the possessor is a particular item such as a certain class of first and second person pronouns. Since this is a language-particular rule, it is reasonable to suggest that it does not belong to narrow syntax, as pointed out by Watanabe (2010) for (15): it may be part of the postsyntactic mechanism. This is consistent with our analysis that the presence of *-nu* does not reflect agreement, which arguably takes place in narrow syntax.

4. Conclusion

I have shown that the lack of NP-ellipsis in Kikai does not pose a challenge for the AHE since the genitive marker found with a certain class of possessors does not reflect agreement and thus should not be treated as a genitive case marker. I have proposed that the genitive marker is a linking element inserted according to a postsyntactic language-particular rule. This analysis is also supported by the correlation between the linking element and the absence of NP-ellipsis that has been argued to hold for Japanese and Okinawan. If this analysis is tenable, it can be taken as supporting evidence for the AHE. Another consequence of our analysis concerns the typology of genitive markers. According to Watanabe (2010) and Hiraiwa (2016), Japanese and Okinawan have two types of genitive markers: a case marker and a linking element (or a linker). By contrast, Kikai only has the latter type of a genitive marker under our analysis. While I leave it for further inquiry why this difference arises particularly for Kikai and Okinawan (both in a Ryukyuan subgroup), the interaction between the type of a genitive marker and the presence or absence of NP-ellipsis promises to be a useful testing ground for the identification of genitive markers across languages.

*I am indebted to Ms. Ikuko Hiro, Mr. Tsunenori Ikushima and Mr. Toshiaki Kohtoku, my Kikai consultants, for their patience and assistance with my fieldwork research. I would also like to thank Masaru Honda and Rihito Shirata for their helpful comments and discussions. All errors and inadequacies are my own. This research has been supported by the JSPS Grant-in-Aid for Young Scientists (18K12388). The following abbreviations will be used throughout the paper: A = animate; Excl = exclusive; Gen = genitive; IA = inanimate; Incl = inclusive; Nom = nominative; Pol = polite; Sg = singular.

[1] Saito and Murasugi (1990) and Saito et al. (2008) extend Lobeck's agreement-based analysis to Japanese. Saito and Murasugi (1990) argue that the NP-ellipsis in Japanese (or NP-deletion in their analysis) is licensed by a spec-head agreement just as in English and Spanish. In contrast, Hiraiwa (2016) proposes that Japanese NP-ellipsis is derived via pronominalization with the light noun *no*, which is deleted due to haplology.

[2] As in other languages such as Mayan languages (Imanishi 2019), possessive DPs in Okinawan and Kikai (to be discussed in section 3) neutralize various notional relations such as (in)animate possessors, kinship, body-parts among others. The word "possessor" will be used as a cover term for all these relations.

[3] In the Kamikatetsu dialect, nominative and genitive are homophonous: the particle *-nu* is used for both (all) subjects and possessors. In what follows, we will gloss its nominative and genitive uses as *Nom* and *Gen*, respectively.

[4] Following Shirata (2016), the symbol *č* represents the alveo-palatal affricate (= [tɕ]).

References

Chomsky, Noam (2000) "Minimalist Inquiries: The Framework," *Step by Step: Essays on Minimalist Syntax in Honor of Howard Lasnik*, ed. by Roger Martin, David Michaels, and Juan Uriagereka, 89–155, MIT Press, Cambridge, MA.

Dixon, R.M.W. (1994) *Ergativity*, Cambridge University Press, Cambridge.

George, Leland and Jaklin Kornfilt (1981) "Finiteness and Boundedness in Turkish," *Binding and Filtering*, ed. by Frank Heny, 105–127, MIT Press, Cambridge, MA.

Hiraiwa, Ken (2016) "NP-Ellipsis: A Comparative Syntax of Japanese and Okinawan," *Natural Language and Linguistic Theory* 34, 1345–1387.

Honda, Masaru and Yusuke Imanishi (2015) "The Syntax of Kikai: A Preliminary Study," *Journal of Policy Studies*, 61–68.

Imanishi, Yusuke (2019) "Parameterizing Split Ergativity in Mayan," *Natural Language and Linguistic Theory*. doi.org/10.1007/s11049–018–09440–9.

Jackendoff, Ray S. (1971) "Gapping and Related Rules," *Linguistic Inquiry* 2, 21–35.

Kibe, Nobuko, Haruo Kubozono, Kayoko Shimoji, Wayne Lawrence, Akiko Matsumori and Akiko Takeda, eds. (2011) *Kikaijima Hōgen Chōsa Hōkokusho* (A Research Report on the Kikaijima Dialects), National Institute for Japanese Language and Linguistics, Tokyo.

Kitagawa, Chisato and Claudia Ross (1982) "Prenominal Modification in Chinese and Japanese," *Linguistic Analysis* 9, 19–53.

Lobeck, Anne (1995) *Ellipsis: Functional Heads, Licensing, and Identification*, Oxford University Press, New York.

Lobeck, Anne (2006) "Ellipsis in DP," *The Blackwell Companion to Syntax*, ed. by Martin Everaert and Henk C. van Riemsdijk, volume 2, 145–173, Wiley-Blackwell, New York.

Lobeck, Anne, and Petra Sleeman (2017) "Ellipsis in Noun Phrases," *The Wiley Blackwell Companion to Syntax, second edition*, ed. by Martin Everaert and Henk C. van Riemsdijk, 1–35, Wiley-Blackwell, New York.

Matsumoto, Hirotake (1993) "Meishi-no ˈShutai = Kyakutaikakuˈ -no Yōhō to Mondaiten (The Usage and Problems of ˈSubject = Object caseˈ in Nouns)," *Nihongo-no Kaku-o Megutte* (Exploring Case in Japanese), ed. by Yoshio Nitta, 139–161, Kurosio, Tokyo.

Pellard, Thomas (2015) "The Linguistic Archaeology of the Ryukyu Islands," *Handbook of the Ryukyuan Languages: History, Structure, and Use*, ed. by Patrick Heinrich, Shinsho Miyara and Michinori Shimoji, 13–60, De Gruyter Mouton, Berlin/Boston/Munich.

Saito, Mamoru and Keiko Murasugi (1990) "N′-deletion in Japanese: A Preliminary Study," *Japanese/Korean Linguistics* 1, 258–301.

Saito, Mamoru, T.-H. Jonah Lin and Keiko Murasugi (2008) "N′ -ellipsis and the Structure of Noun Phrases in Chinese and Japanese," *Journal of East Asian Linguistics* 17, 247–271.

Shirata, Rihito (2016) *Ryūkyū Amami Kikaijima Kamikatetsu Hōgen-no Bumpō* (A Grammar of the Kikaijima-Kamikatetsu Dialect of Ryukyu Amami). Doctoral Dissertation, Kyoto University.

Silverstein, Michael (1976) "Hierarchies of Features and Ergativity," *Grammatical Categories in Australian Languages*, ed. by Dixon, R.M.W., 112–171, Humanities Press, New Jersey, NJ.

Watanabe, Akira (2010) "Notes on Nominal Ellipsis and the Nature of *no* and Classifiers in Japanese," *Journal of East Asian Linguistics* 19, 61–74.

空要素に対する日本語格助詞と英語前置詞の平行性 *

本田 隆裕

キーワード：統語論，格助詞，前置詞，関係節，*pro*

1. はじめに

　日本語では、(1a) のように名詞句の格が格助詞として顕在的に現れることが知られているが、一方で、(1a) と論理的に同じ意味を表すと考えられる (1b) のような文も文法的であることから、主格・対格については格助詞を省略する格助詞脱落が可能であると考えられている。

(1)　a. ジョンが リンゴを 食べた。
　　 b. ジョン Ø リンゴ Ø 食べた。　　　（「Ø」＝ 格助詞の脱落形）

　また、日本語は空の代名詞類である *pro* が生起可能な空主語言語の一つと考えられている。しかし、(1b) のように格助詞脱落は多くの場合随意的であり、(2a) が示すように格助詞は通常の名詞 (句) にも代名詞にも付けることが可能であるが、(2b) に示すように *pro* と格助詞は共起できない。

(2)　a. 彼 {が /Ø} 来た。
　　 b. *pro*{*が /Ø} 来た。

これは、*pro* も名詞の一種であると考えれば、不思議な現象である。[1]
　上記のような現象は、英語の関係節と前置詞の間にも見られる。関係代名詞が顕在的に現れない関係節において、関係代名詞は空演算子 Op となっていると仮定した場合、(3e) のように、前置詞と Op は共起できない。[2]

(3)　a.　the man [to whom I spoke]
　　　b.　*the man [to who I spoke]
　　　c.　the man [whom I spoke to]
　　　d.　the man [who I spoke to]
　　　e.　*the man [to Op (that) I spoke]
　　　f.　the man [Op (that) I spoke to]

(3c, d) と (3f) が示すように、Op は wh 関係詞と同じような振る舞いをすると考えられるが、(3e) は (3a) と異なり容認されない。

　本稿では、一見無関係に見える (2b) と (3e) の非文法性には、日本語の格助詞と英語の前置詞に共通する特徴が関係していることを示す。

2. 反ラベリング要素としての格助詞

　斎藤 (2013), Saito (2016) は、(4) のような例を挙げ、日本語においては DP だけでなく (φ 素性を欠く)PP も格助詞を伴うことから、日本語は英語のような φ 素性一致が見られない言語であると主張している。

(4)　[$_{PP}$ ここから]-が、富士山に登りやすい。　　　　　(斎藤 (2013: 5))

　斎藤 (2013) は、日本語において全ての範疇が「λ 素性」と呼ばれる素性を持っており、DP や PP の場合、この λ 素性は格助詞として具現され、述部においては屈折として具現すると主張している。また、斎藤によればこの λ 素性は反ラベリング素性として句を不可視的にする機能を持っており、これにより、日本語において多重主語の出現やかき混ぜが可能となっていると考えられる。例えば、(5) のような構造において、Chomsky (2013) のラベル付けアルゴリズム (labeling algorithm, LA) によれば、英語では α のみが <φ, φ> というラベルを付与され、β や γ はラベル付けが不可能である。

(5)　[$_γ$ DP-Nom [$_β$ DP-Nom [$_α$ DP-Nom [$_{TP}$ T …

このため、英語では多重主語は見られない。しかし、日本語の DP は λ 素性を持つため、これが格助詞として具現される一方で、反ラベリング素性として機能し、α，β，γ がすべて TP としてラベル付けされる。

　斎藤の分析は、日本語の様々な現象を的確に捉え、文法格の担う役割を明確にしているが、「反ラベリング」と言われる現象がどのようにして生じるのかは明らかにされていない。また、(1)–(2) に挙げた、格助詞脱落の場合はどのようにラベル付けが行われるのか説明されていない。

3. 英語関係節の主要部移動分析

　Donati and Cecchetto (2011) によれば、wh 関係詞は先行詞 N を補部に取る D であり、例えば、(3c) は (6) のように派生されると考えられる。

(6)　[$_{DP}$ the [$_{NP}$ man [[$_{DP}$ whom [$_N$ man]] [$_{CP}$ I spoke to [$_{DP}$ whom [$_N$ man]]]]]]

まず、D である whom と N である man が外的併合され、関係節内に現れる。次に、DP である [whom man] が関係節 CP の指定部へ内的併合し、さらにその位置から N である man のみが再び CP 指定部へ内的併合される。この段階で、構造全体は NP となり、D である the に補部として選択され得る。

　一方、Donati and Cecchetto は、(3f) のように wh 関係詞が現れない場合、(7) に示すように、先行詞 N は音形のない D の補部として基底生成し、N のみが関係節 CP へ移動すると主張している。

(7)　[$_{DP}$ the [$_{NP}$ man [$_{CP}$ (that) I spoke to [$_{DP}$ D [$_N$ man]]]]]

　以上を踏まえると、(3a) と (3e) の派生はそれぞれ (8)、(9) のようになる。

(8)　[$_{DP}$ the [$_{NP}$ man [[$_{PP}$ to [$_{DP}$ whom [$_N$ man]]] [$_{CP}$ I spoke [$_{PP}$ to [$_{DP}$ whom [$_N$ man]]]]]]]
(9)　[$_{DP}$ the [$_{NP}$ man [[$_{PP}$ to [$_{DP}$ D [$_N$ man]]] [$_{CP}$ (that) I spoke [$_{PP}$ to [$_{DP}$ D [$_N$ man]]]]]]]

(3a) は文法的であるが、(3e) は非文法的であることから、(8) の派生は可能であり、(9) のような派生は不可能であるということになる。しかし、(8) が可能である一方で、なぜ (9) のみが不可能なのであろうか。また、Donati and Cecchetto が仮定する音形のない D とは何かという問題も残る。

これに対して、Cecchetto and Donati (2015) では関係節に that が現れる場合について、(10a, b) のような派生を仮定している。

(10) the man that John saw
 a. [[_{DP} that man] John saw ~~that man~~]
 b. [_{DP} the [_{NP} man [_{CP} [_{DP→C} that ~~man~~] John saw ~~that man~~]]]
(Cecchetto and Donati (2015: 60))

(10) において、that は先行詞 N を補部に取る D として基底生成されるが、関係節の先頭へ移動し、DP の中から先行詞 N が取り出されることで、D であった that が補文標識 C となり、関係節 CP をラベル付けする役割を果たす。この分析では、that が現れる場合、(9) のような派生はそもそも不可能である。なぜなら、that が前置詞 to の補部に残ったままでは関係節 CP のラベル付けができないからである。また、that が省略される場合の派生については明らかにされていないが、音形のない C が that と同じ役割を果たすものと考えられる。この分析の利点は、(11) のように wh 関係詞と that が同時に現れることができないということを正しく予測できることである。

(11) *the boy who that left   (ibid.: 61)

しかし、以下の例はこの分析においてどのように説明されるのだろうか。

(12) the men {that/*those} I saw
(13) {*that/those} men

Cecchetto and Donati の主張のように、関係節における that が先行詞 N を補部に取る D として（that が指示詞として）現れるならば、N が複数名

詞の場合、(13) のように that は those となるはずであるが、(12) が示すように those は関係節に現れることができない。この点が課題として残ると考えられる。

4. 提案

4.1. 日本語の格助詞

上記のような先行研究の問題点を解決するために、本稿では、「音形を持つ名詞句は格を持たなければならない」とする格フィルター (Case filter, Chomsky (1981)) を逆の視点から捉えた (14) を仮定し、さらに、格助詞を伴う日本語名詞句の構造を (15) のように提案する。[3]

$$(14) \quad \text{音形を持たない D は、いかなる格素性も持たない。}$$
$$(15) \quad \{DP_{[-Case]}, K_{[+Case]/[-case]}\}$$

ここでは、Oba (1987) や Bittner and Hale (1996) に基づき、格助詞に該当する K を DP から独立した機能範疇の主要部として仮定する。ただし、本稿では、K は値を持った抽象格素性 [+Case] と値未付与の形態格素性 [-case] の両方を持っていると仮定する。後述のように、ここでの抽象格素性は日本語に限らず英語にも存在し、伝統的な分析における格素性に該当する。一方、形態格素性は少なくとも英語のような言語には存在せず、日本語のように顕在的格標示が見られる言語にのみ存在すると仮定しておく。さらに、K は英語の時制辞 T と同様に弱い主要部 (Chomsky (2015)) であり、ラベル付けのためには素性共有が必要であると仮定しておく。したがって、(16) のように、K と併合される XP が K と共有する素性を持たない場合、{XP, K} にはいかなるラベル付けも行われず解釈不可能となると考えられる。

$$(16) \quad *\{XP, K_{[+Case]/[-case]}\}$$

一方、(17) のように、DP と K が併合される場合は、K との一致により、DP の抽象格素性に値が与えられ、全体が <Case, Case> とラベル付けされ

る。

(17)　$[_{<\text{Case, Case}>} \text{DP}_{[-\text{Case}]} \rightarrow [+\text{Case}] \text{K}_{[+\text{Case}]/[-\text{case}]}]$

　　ここで、K の持つ形態格素性がどのようにして値付与されるのか考えてみたい。先に述べたように、(17) は日本語の名詞句の構造であるため、主語として TP の指定部に現れ得ると考えられる。Chomsky (2001) などで仮定されている格付与の仕組みでは、解釈可能な φ 素性と解釈不可能な格素性を持った DP が、(C から継承した) 解釈不可能な φ 素性を持った T と一致することにより、T の φ 素性に値が与えられ、この一致に伴う形で DP の格素性に値が与えられると考えられている。しかし、2 節で触れたように、日本語は φ 素性一致を欠く言語であり、また Chomsky の仮定する一致のメカニズムは値を与えるものと与えられるものが一対一の関係になることを前提としているが、(5) のような多重主語が日本語では可能であるため、この一致の仕組みを日本語の分析に用いることはできないと思われる。このような問題点を踏まえ、辻子 (2014) では、一致ではなく、併合による格付与が提案されており、名詞句の格の値は併合される要素の違いによって決まることになる。ここでは、辻子の分析を一部修正し、(18) を提案する。

(18)　K の [-case] は、
　　　a. TP と併合される時、主格の値が与えられる。
　　　b. VP と併合される時、対格の値が与えられる。
　　　c. DP と併合される時、属格の値が与えられる。

なお、(18) は形態格素性のみに適用されるものとし、抽象格素性については Chomsky が提案する一致による値付与が行われるものと仮定しておく。
　　この提案に基づき、(17) が TP と併合した (19) の構造を考えてみたい。

(19)　$[_{\alpha} [_{<\text{Case, Case}>} \text{DP}_{[-\text{Case}]} \rightarrow [+\text{Case}] \text{K}_{[+\text{Case}]/[-\text{case}]} \rightarrow [\text{主格}]] \text{TP}]$

まず、(19) の α はどのようにラベル付けされるのかという問題が生じる。

(17) のラベルは K ではなく <Case, Case> であるが、Chomsky (2013) で取り上げられているラベル付けのパターンは (20) に示す集合のみであり、(19) に示した {< 素性 , 素性 >, XP} という集合については検討されていない。

(20) a. {H, XP}   (主要部と句からなる集合)
　　　 b. {XP, YP}   (句と句からなる集合)
　　　 c. {H, H}   (主要部と主要部からなる集合)

本稿では、{< 素性 , 素性 >, XP} という集合のラベルは XP のラベルであると提案する。これは、ラベル付けが最小探索のための仕組みであるとするならば、句である XP がある集合においてラベルとなることができないのは XP よりも先に検出される (より埋め込みが浅い)H が存在する (20a) のような場合だけであることと、(20b) のような句同士の集合であっても、XP か YP のいずれかが移動すれば、残った方の句が (20b) のラベルとなることができることを考えれば、{< 素性 , 素性 >, XP} という集合において XP は潜在的にラベルになり得る要素であると考えられるためである。他方、< 素性 , 素性 > という集合が他の要素に対して何らかの優先性を持っているとは考えられないためである。これらの考え方に基づけば、(19) における α は TP とラベル付けされる。本稿では、これこそが斎藤 (2013), Saito (2016) が提案するところの「反ラベリング」に該当すると考える。

　(19) において、K は {DP, K} という集合のラベルではないがこの集合の主要部であることに注目されたい。したがって、K を主要部とする集合が TP と併合された (19) において、K の形態格素性は (18a) により主格の値を与えられる。これに基づけば、(5) は (21) のような構造により派生される。

(21) $[_{TP}$ $[_{<Case, Case>}$ $DP_{[-Case]} \rightarrow {}_{[+Case]}$ $K_{[+Case]/[-case]} \rightarrow {}_{[主 格]}]$ $[_{TP}$ $[_{<Case, Case>}$ $DP_{[-Case]} \rightarrow {}_{[+Case]}$ $K_{[+Case]/[-case]} \rightarrow {}_{[主格]}$ ... TP]

{DP, K} という <Case, Case> をラベルとする集合がいくつ TP と併合しよ

うとも、(21) に示すように全体のラベルは TP のままである。

　一方、英語には K が存在しないと仮定すると、主語名詞句と TP が併合した構造は常に (22a) となり、α のラベルは DP1 と T が一致し共有する φ 素性となるが、(22b) において、DP2 は T と一致せず、β にはいかなるラベルも付与されないため、英語では多重主語が許されないと考えられる。

(22)　a. $[_\alpha \text{ DP1}_{[+\phi]/[-\text{Case}]} \rightarrow [+\text{Case}] \text{ TP}_{[-\phi]} \rightarrow [+\phi]]$
　　　b. $[_\beta \text{ DP2}_{[+\phi]/[-\text{Case}]} [_\alpha \text{ DP1}_{[+\phi]/[-\text{Case}]} \rightarrow [+\text{Case}] \text{ TP}_{[-\phi]} \rightarrow [+\phi]]]$

　では、格助詞脱落についてはどのように説明されるだろうか。本稿では、日本語の格助詞脱落は K が派生に含まれず、DP が K を伴わずに派生に導入されることにより生じると提案する。ここで、K を伴わない DP が TP と併合した (23) のような構造について考えてみよう。

(23)　$[_\alpha \text{ DP}_{[-\text{Case}]} \text{ TP}]$

(23) は (22a) と同じように見えるが、日本語は φ 素性一致のない言語であるため、α のラベルは φ 素性とはならず、一致により値が与えられる DP の [-Case] は φ 素性一致により値が与えられることはない。では、(23) において DP への格付与と α のラベル付けはどのように行われるのであろうか。[4]

　Miyagawa (2010) によれば、φ 素性と話題 (topic) 素性はどちらも C が持っており、英語のような言語では φ 素性が T へ継承され、T と φ 素性一致を示す DP が TP 指定部に現れる。一方、日本語のような言語では話題素性が C から T へ継承され、この素性と一致する要素が TP 指定部へ移動する。

　Miyagawa の分析に基づけば、(23) において DP と T との間には話題素性の一致が起こっていると考えられ、話題素性が α のラベルとなっていると言える。また、英語の φ 素性一致に伴う格付与があるように、(23) の DP が持つ抽象格素性は話題素性の一致に伴い値が与えられる。これにより主格の格助詞脱落が生じると考えられる。さらに、(24) に示すように、主格の格助詞脱落は主節に限定されることから、(23) のような構造に

おいて DP と一致できる話題素性は主節の C のみに存在するものと考えられる。[5]

(24)　先生は [僕 {*Ø/ が} リンゴ {Ø/ を} 食べたと] 思っているよ。

(Narita (2018: 200))

　次に対格の格助詞脱落について考えてみよう。(1b) に加え、(24) の例から対格の格助詞脱落は主節でも埋め込み節でも可能であることが分かる。通常、対格を付与される目的語は内項として V の補部位置に現れるため、(1b) や (24) における「リンゴ」は (25) のような位置に生じていると考えられる。

(25)　$[_{VP} \, DP_{[-Case]} \, V_{[-\theta]}]$

Hornstein (1999) に基づけば、θ 役割は述語が担う素性であり、これが V にあるとすれば、(25) において DP と V が一致することにより、それぞれが持つ値未付与の [-Case] と [-θ] に値が与えられると考えられる。これにより対格の格助詞脱落が可能になっていると考えられる。また、内項が K を伴った場合であるが、(26) のように {DP, K} の集合が VP 指定部へ併合されることにより、K の [-case] に対格の値が与えられ、K が対格助詞として具現する。

(26)　… $[_{VP} \, [_{<Case, Case>} \, DP \, K_{[-case] \, \to \, [\, 対格 \,]}] \, [_{V'} \, [_{<Case, Case>} \, \text{DP K}_{[-case]}] \, V]]$

なお、θ 素性は述語のみが持ち、名詞句はそのような素性を持たないため、(27) のように外項が K を伴わずに現れた場合は、v*P 指定部の位置から TP 指定部へ外項が移動しなければ α のラベル付けが不可能となる。

(27)　$[_{\alpha} \, DP_{[-Case]} \, v\text{*}P_{[-\theta] \, \to \, [+\theta]}]$

結果的に、外項 DP は TP と併合されるので、K を伴わない場合、T と一

致し共有する素性 (つまり、話題素性) を持っていなければならない。[6]

　以上を踏まえて、*pro* がなぜ格助詞と共起できないのか考えてみよう。*pro* が格助詞を伴った場合、(28) のような集合が生成される。

(28)　　*{*pro*, K$_{[+Case]/[-case]}$}

pro は代名詞の一種であることから DP と考えられるが、(14) によれば格素性を持たない。よって、*pro* は K と共有する素性を持たず、(28) の集合には適切なラベルが与えられないため、*pro* は格助詞と共起できない。一方、*pro* は典型的談話要素であるため (Saito (2007))、話題素性を持っていると考えられるので、(29) の集合では話題素性がラベルとなると考えられる。

(29)　　{*pro*$_{[+Top]}$, TP$_{[-Top] \to [+Top]}$}

4.2. 英語の関係節

　提案 (14) により、(3) についても説明が可能となる。本稿では、英語前置詞は日本語格助詞と同様に解釈可能な抽象格素性を持った弱い主要部であり、(3a, e, f) はそれぞれ (30a, b, c) のような構造を持つと提案する。[7]

(30)　a.　[$_α$ [$_P$ to]$_{[+Case]}$ [$_{DP}$ [$_D$ whom]$_{[-Case]}$ m̶a̶n̶]]
　　　b.　*[$_α$ [$_P$ to]$_{[+Case]}$ [$_{DP}$ [$_D$ Op] m̶a̶n̶]]
　　　c.　[$_α$ [$_{DP}$ [$_D$ Op]$_{[+Pred]}$ m̶a̶n̶] [$_{CP}$ C$_{[-Pred]}$ I spoke to [̶$_{DP}$ [̶$_D$ O̶p̶]̶ m̶a̶n̶]̶]]

ここでは、Donati and Cecchetto (2011) に基づき、関係詞は D であるとしておく。まず、(30a) において、D である関係詞 whom と前置詞 to の格素性が一致する。これにより、α のラベルは格素性となる。who の格変化を (31) のように仮定した場合、(30a) の構造においては必ず斜格を与える前置詞と関係詞が一致するため、(3b) のように who は出現できないと考えられる。

(31)

	主格	対格	斜格
who の形態	who	who / whom	whom

また、本稿では音形のない関係詞として空演算子 Op が現れる分析を採用するが、Op は (14) より格素性を持たないため、(30b) において α のラベルは決定できない。このため、(3e) は容認されないと考えられる。一方、(3c, d) のような場合、前置詞は V と再分析されて一つの複合動詞となっていると考えられ、関係詞は V と一致して対格の値が与えられているため、who と whom の両方が出現可能となっている。(3f) の場合も、前置詞は V と再分析されている。(30c) において関係節主要部の C は述部 (predicative) 素性を持っており (Rizzi (1990))、これが Op と一致することにより wh 移動と同様の移動が引き起こされていると仮定すると、(30c) の α のラベルはこの述部素性と考えることができる。このため、(3f) は容認されると言える。

5. 結論

　本稿では、日本語格助詞と英語前置詞がともに格素性を持つ弱い主要部であると仮定することで、*pro* 及び空演算子が格助詞や前置詞と共起できない理由を検討した。(14) の提案により、これらの問題が説明できることから、格素性と音形の有無には何らかの関係性が認められると考えられる。

* 本稿は、The 43rd Annual Penn Linguistics Conference でのポスター発表 (2019 年 3 月 23 日、ペンシルベニア大学) の内容を修正・発展させたものである。また、本研究は JSPS 科研費 17K13479 の助成を受けている。

[1] Goto (2012) では、(iB) のように助詞のみが現れる例が指摘されているが、(iB) のような例は必ず (iA) のような先行文脈が必要であり、例えば、(ii) のような会話は自然であるが、(iii) の会話は不自然であると思われる。

　(i)　A: ジョンがどうしたの？
　　　 B: [e]-が /-は 会社を辞めた。

(ii) A: *pro* 来たよ。
   B: 誰が？
(iii) A: [e]-が /-は 来たよ。
   B: # 誰が？

本稿では、(iB) と (2b) は異なる現象により派生されていると仮定しておく。
[2] (3b) のような例が容認される場合もあるが、ここでは (3a) よりも容認されない傾向があるという事実に基づいて議論を進めることにする。
[3] 以下、「-」は値未付与の素性を指し、「+」は値が付与された素性を指す。
[4] 通常、DP の [-Case] への値付与は T との ϕ 素性一致に伴う操作であるため、T(あるいは V) そのものは格素性を持たないと考えられる。よって、格素性が (23) の a のラベルにはなることはない。
[5] DP と一致可能な話題素性がなぜ主節の C にのみ存在するのかという問題については今後の検討課題としたい。一つの可能性として、助詞の「は」には対比的なものと非対比的なものがあり、後者が主節にのみ現れることから、DP は非対比的な「は」と同じタイプの話題素性を持っており、主節の C のみがこの素性と一致できる素性を持つのかもしれない。なお、非対比的な「は」は主節だけでなく「言う」などの動詞の補文にも現れることがあるが、少なくとも関西方言では (i) のような格助詞脱落が可能と思われることから、主節の C 以外に、「言う」の補文の C もこの素性を持つと考えられる。

   (i) お前 {Ø/ が / は } [昨日、先生 (が) 来た] 言うたやん。

[6] 外項 DP の [-Case] への値付与が θ 素性一致に伴う操作によるものなのか、話題素性一致に伴う操作によるものなのかは今後の検討課題としたい。
[7] 英語前置詞の of や to そのものが、属格や与格を表すこともあることから、T や V と異なり、前置詞は解釈可能な格素性を持つと仮定する。

参考文献

Bittner, Maria and Ken Hale (1996) "The Structural Determination of Case and Agreement," *Linguistic Inquiry* 27, 1–68.

Cecchetto, Carlo and Caterina Donati (2015) *(Re)labeling*, MIT Press, Cambridge, MA.

Chomsky, Noam (1981) *Lectures on Government and Binding*, Foris, Dordrecht.

Chomsky, Noam (2001) "Derivation by Phase," *Ken Hale: A Life in Language*, ed. by Michael Kenstowicz, 1–52, MIT Press, Cambridge, MA.

Chomsky, Noam (2013) "Problems of Projection," *Lingua* 130, 33–49.

Chomsky, Noam (2015) "Problems of Projection: Extensions," *Structures, Strategies and Beyond: Studies in Honour of Adriana Belletti*, ed. by Elisa Di Domenico, Cornelia Hamann and Simona Matteini, 3–16, John Benjamins, Amsterdam.

Donati, Caterina and Carlo Cecchetto (2011) "Relabeling Heads: A Unified Account for Relativization Structures," *Linguistic Inquiry* 42, 519–560.

Goto, Nobu (2012) "A Note on Particle Stranding Ellipsis," paper presented at Seoul International Conference on Generative Grammar 14 (SICOGG 14), Dongguk University, Seoul, Korea, August 8.

Hornstein, Norbert (1999) "Movement and Control," *Linguistic Inquiry* 30, 69–96.

Miyagawa, Shigeru (2010) *Why Agree? Why Move? Unifying Agreement-Based and Discourse-Configurational Languages*, MIT Press, Cambridge, MA.

Narita, Hiroki (2018) "Cyclic Spell-Out as a Locus of Exocentric Linearization," *KLS* 38, 193–204.

Oba, Yukio (1987) "On γ-Assignment in LF," *English Linguistics* 4, 254–272.

Rizzi, Luigi (1990) *Relativized Minimality*, MIT Press, Cambridge, MA.

Saito, Mamoru (2007) "Notes on East Asian Argument Ellipsis," *Language Research* 43, 203–227.

斎藤衛 (2013)「日本語文法を特徴付けるパラメター再考」, 村杉恵子編『言語の普遍性及び多様性を司る生得的制約―日本語獲得に基づく実証的研究：成果報告書 II』1–30, 国立国語研究所／南山大学.

Saito, Mamoru (2016) "(A) Case for Labeling: Labeling in Languages without φ-Feature Agreement," *The Linguistic Review* 33, 129–175.

辻子美保子 (2014)「格と併合」, 藤田耕司・福井直樹・遊佐典昭・池内正幸編『言語の設計・発達・進化：生物言語学探求』66–96, 開拓社, 東京.

日英語における命令形の具現化
——視点移動の可能性 *

森 英樹

キーワード：命令形，過去命令文，視点，日英対照，する型・なる型

1. はじめに

　本論文の目的は、命令形の具現化が日本語では可能だが英語では不可能な用例に関して、両言語に見られる具現化の違いを視点移動の可能性から説明することである。議論の出発点は次の命令文である。3時の待ち合わせに遅刻し4時になって現れた相手に向かっての発話とする。

(1)　3時に来い（よ）！

同種の命令文を扱う Saito (2016) の "past imperatives" という名称に倣い、本論文では「過去命令文」としておく。Saito (2016) が指摘する通り、英語では、(1) と同じ文脈で (2a) の命令文は使えず、(1) の意味を表すには (2b) のように言う必要がある。

(2)　a. *Come at 3:00!
　　　b. You should have come at 3:00!

(2a) は命令形と過去の時刻の共起が不適切なだけでなく、事態が実現不可能となっている文脈では英語の命令形は生じない。

　本論文では、日英語における過去命令文の具現化の違いは視点移動の有無によるものと考える。こう考えることで、過去命令文はどのように典型から逸脱し、逸脱にもかかわらず命令形の具現化がなぜ可能なのかについて理解できるようになる。また、両言語で命令形が具現化する場合でも、具現化の基準となる視点の性質が日英語で異なることも明らかになる。

　本論文の構成は次の通りである。2 節では、過去命令文と関連表現の先行研究を概観する。3 節では命令文の典型性を提示し、日英語における命令形の具現化の相違を視点移動の観点から考察する。4 節では、本分析を日英語における視点の特徴と言語類型に基づいて再考する。5 節は本論文のまとめである。

2. 過去命令文と関連表現

　冒頭に挙げた過去命令文は、井上 (1993) において「タイミング非考慮／矛盾考慮」のタイプとして分類されている。(3) の命令形は、大学を 4 年で卒業できなかった息子に対する発話である。

　　　(3)　本当にもう。うちはお金がないんだから、ちゃんと 4 年で卒業しろよ。[1]

　　　　　　　　　　　　　　　　　　　　　　　　（井上 (1993: 337)）

井上 (1993) が言う「タイミング考慮／非考慮」は発話時において動作実行のタイミングにあるかどうか、「矛盾考慮／非考慮」は実行すべき内容とタイミングが現実世界の状況と矛盾するかどうかを意味する。(3) では、発話時点で動作実行のタイミングはすでに過ぎており、そのタイミングにない（「タイミング非考慮」）。また 4 年で卒業することは、それが達成できなかったという現実と矛盾する（「矛盾考慮」）。このように日本語の命令文では、話者の要求を発話時以降に実現させるという機能を欠く場合があり、過去命令文はその一例である。

　通時的研究の富岡 (2017) は、富岡 (2016) を踏まえ、「手遅れの希み」として中古和文の例を取り上げ、過去命令文のように実現不可能な事態を望む形式として「命令形＋かし」に着目している。

　　　(4)　〔三の君〕《(中納言ハ) しばし立ちどまりたまへかし。……》
　　　　　　　　　　　　　（富岡 (2016: 4); 落窪物語 , 巻之三 , 二六七・一）

(4) は、中納言が帰った後の三の君の心内文であり、中納言が立ちどまることがもはや実現されないことを前提とした三の君の望みを表している。

富岡 (2017) では、中古和文の「手遅れの希み」が事実に反した意向に注目する形式であるのに対し、現代日本語の過去命令文は意向に反した現状に注目する形式であるという一般化を試みている。

　続いて、過去を表す時間副詞との共起性の観点から日英語の例を見ておく。Saito (2016) は、オランダ語等の他言語における先行研究を踏まえながら、日本語の過去命令文の分析を行った。

(5)　昨日（は）学校に来いよ！[2]
　　　'You should have come to school yesterday!'

(Saito (2016: 1))

日本語の過去命令文は形態的に過去形を持たないが、過去のある時点での事態実現を要求するような過去解釈が得られる。Saito (2016) の主張では、時間副詞がこの解釈を導き、また時間副詞が顕在化されなくても "a covert temporal adverb *pro*" (Saito 2016: 7)が文脈に応じて過去解釈を導く。同じく過去の時間副詞との共起に関して、英語の命令形の分析が Davies (1986) や Takahashi (2012) に見られる。

(6)　A:　How was the party?
　　　B:　Turn up yesterday and you'd have had a real shock.
(Davies (1986: 165); Takahashi (2012: 72))

(6) は *and* が後続し条件節として機能する条件命令文で、過去命令文とは区別される。Takahashi (2012) によれば、話者の視点は *yesterday* の時点にあり、そこから事態が未来のことのように述べられている。この説明によって (6) の命令形でも、Takahashi (2012) や高橋 (2017) の主張する命令文の非過去性が裏づけられている。しかし意味的には、事態の内容が過去に言及しているというだけであって、過去の時点における事態実現や要求を特徴とする過去命令文とは本質的に異なる。[3] Davies (1986) や Takahashi (2012) は、(6) の命令形を本論文が注目する過去命令文として扱っているわけではない。

　命令形以外の関連表現として Van Olmen (2018) は、オランダ語やスペ

イン語等のヨーロッパ諸語における過去命令文相当の形式を取り上げる。

(7)　Had　　　　　toch　　gezwegen!
　　　have.PST.SG　　MP　　keep.quiet.PST.PTCP [4]
　　　'You should have kept quiet!'

(Van Olmen (2018: 122))

使用基盤の立場から、(7) は類推・慣習化・従属節の主節化のプロセスを通して、命令文・祈願文・条件文との相互作用によるものとして説明されている。英語訳から、(7) と日本語の過去命令文の意味的な共通性が示唆されるが、(7) は命令形 *zwijg* ではないという点で、日本語のように命令形が具現化した例ではない。

　通言語的な命令文研究の Aikhenvald (2010: 133) が言う通り、過去命令文は稀な用法である。英語等の他言語における関連表現は Takahashi (2012) や Van Olmen (2018) で扱われているが、意味的にも形式的にも日本語の過去命令文と同等というわけではない。日本語では、井上 (1993) や富岡 (2016, 2017)、Saito (2016) の共時的・通時的研究が示すように、過去命令文は古くから確立している用法と考えてよいだろう。命令文体系の中に過去命令文が組み込まれる言語もあればそうでない言語もあることを理解するためには、他言語との比較対照を視野に入れ、命令形の具現化の原理を解明する必要がある。そこで本論文では、日英語に焦点を絞り、井上 (1993) の矛盾考慮と Takahashi (2012) の視点の捉え方を敷衍することによって、命令形の具現化の違い、過去命令文と典型命令文の違い、他の非典型命令文との関連を包括的に扱えるような枠組みを提案する。

3. 過去命令文の日英対照分析

3.1. 命令文の典型性と命令形の具現化

　本論文では、命令文の典型性を考察する上で、「発話時」「要求実現時」「発話者視点」の 3 要素の関係が重要となることを主張する。発話時は命令文が発せられる発話の現在である。要求実現時は命令による要求が実現されると発話者が想定している基準時で、常に明示されるとは限らない。

(8) a. レポートを提出しろ！
 b. Submit the report!
(9) a. 正午にレポートを提出しろ！
 b. Submit the report at noon!
(10) a. レポートを提出するな！
 b. Don't submit the report!

レポート提出の実現の時点は、(8) では明示されていないが、(9) では正午として言語化されている。明示されない場合でも、発話者はある時点を実現の基準と想定して要求しているはずであり、非明示的な時点も含めて要求実現時として考える。また、(10) の忠告や禁止といった否定的な要求も同様に扱う。最後の発話者視点は、発話者がどういう時間的な位置に立って要求実現時を想定して発話するかを示す。

　以上を踏まえ、命令文の典型性と命令形の具現化を、それぞれ (11a) と (11b) のように一般化する。

(11) a. 発話時以降に要求実現時があり、発話者視点が発話時に置かれている。
 b. 相対的あるいは絶対的な発話者視点から見て、要求実現時が未来に
  位置する。

(11a) は命令文の典型性、(11b) は命令形の具現化に関わる。例えば、(9) では、発話したのは正午以前のはずで、発話時以降に要求実現時の正午が位置づけられ、発話者視点は発話時に置かれている。そしてこの発話者視点から見て要求実現時が未来に位置するため、命令形として具現化する。(11a) は、日英語に適用されるという点で典型命令文の理解に関して両言語に違いはない。違いが見られるのは、(11a) からの逸脱を視点移動によって是正するか、すなわち (11b) の視点が相対的か絶対的かという点である。

　典型からの逸脱を命令形の具現化と関連づけて考えるとき、次の区別が重要である。逸脱によって非典型命令文となるが命令形の具現化は可能な場合と、逸脱のために命令形の具現化が阻止される場合とがあるというこ

とである。日本語の過去命令文が、(11a) からどのように逸脱し、それでもなお命令形として具現化されるのはなぜか。そして、日本語で可能な具現化が英語では不可能なのはなぜか。これらの問いに対する答えを、発話者視点の移動を手掛かりに次節で探っていく。

3.2. 視点移動の有無

　視覚的に理解するため、発話時を「●」、要求実現時を「▼」、発話者視点を「↑」のように表記する。これらを時間軸上に位置づけ、次のような図を用いて命令文の典型性と逸脱を考察する。

(12)　--------- ● --------- ▼ --------->

これは (11a, b) を視覚的に表したものである。●以降に▼があり、↑が●に置かれ、↑から見て▼が未来に位置する。この図に適合するのが典型命令文で、命令形の具現化もこの配置が基本となる。

　日本語の過去命令文は非典型命令文であるため、(12) から逸脱した構造となるはずである。ただし命令形の具現化が可能である以上、(12) との関連づけもなければいけない。(1) の過去命令文は (13) のように表せる。

(13)　--------- ▼ --------- ● --------->

過去命令文は要求実現時を過ぎてからの発話であるから、発話時以降に要求実現時はない（井上 (1993) の言う「矛盾考慮」に対応）。また発話者視点が発話時から要求実現時以前に移動しているため、発話者視点は発話時に置かれていない（Takahashi (2012) の視点の捉え方に対応）。これらが命令文の典型からの逸脱を示す。重要なのは、逸脱が発話者視点の移動によって是正されていることである。過去命令文における発話時と要求実現時の時間軸上の位置関係は客観的で変わることはない。しかし発話者視点は発話者のもので、視点をどこに位置づけるかは発話者次第である。視点移動の結果、発話者にとって要求実現時は相対的に未来に位置するように

なるため命令形が具現化されるのである。ここから、日本語の場合、移動した相対的な発話者視点が (11b) の基準ということが分かる。

　命令形の具現化の可否が視点の移動によって決まることを支持する関連表現を 2 種類見ていく。最初の例は、実現したことに対して用いられる特殊な命令形表現である。

(14)　a. うそつけ！
　　　b. 馬鹿言え！

これらは相手の発言が信じられないときに使う否定応答表現である（命令形以外では「うそ（だ）！」「（そんな）馬鹿な！」等がある）。否定命令文とも言い換えられることから禁止の要求がなされていると言えるが、(14) では肯定表現による間接的（皮肉的）な要求である。(14) の非典型性と命令形の具現化は上で見た (13) の図から理解できる。図は過去命令文と同じだが、否定応答表現は、発話時に事態が実現しているという点で過去命令文と異なる。例えば、3 時に来るという (1) の事態は発話時の 4 時に実現していないが、うそをつくという (14a) の事態は発話時に実現している。こうした違いはあるが、過去命令文と同様、発話者視点が要求実現時点以前に移動して (11b) が満たされ、命令形として具現化されるようになる。[5]

　次に、発話者視点の移動によって命令形の具現化が不可能になる場合として、行動を促す場合等に用いられる「た」の命令用法を考える。

(15)　a. ちょっと待った！
　　　b. さあ、走った、走った！

命令形は使われていないが、命令文の機能を果たしていることは明らかで、実際、代わりに命令形を使っても問題はない。命令形が具現化しなくなる仕組みは次の図のように分析できる。[6]

(16)　

(16) では発話時以降に要求実現時があり、この点では典型命令文と共通し、実際、通常の命令文で言い換えることも可能である。しかし、発話者視点が発話時から要求実現時以降に移動しているため、命令形の具現化が阻止される。前述の通り、日本語では、(11b) の基準となるのが移動する相対的な発話者視点だとしたら、(16) の視点は命令形の具現化がないことを意味する。移動した発話者視点から見ると、要求実現時は、発話者にとって過去の時点に位置するようになり、「た形」が命令形に取って代わる。[7]

　ここで視点移動の動機を考える。過去命令文では、要求実現時が過ぎており事態実現は不可能だが、要求実現時以前に事態実現を要求する別の文脈（先行発話や規則等）がある。例えば、(1) では 3 時に来ることを求める何らかの発話や通知文等が要求実現時以前にあったはずである。この先行文脈が動機となり、その時点に遡るように視点が移動する。一方、否定応答表現は、事態が実現したことに対する応答である点が重要である。事態の内容はうそをついたり馬鹿げたことを言ったりすることに限られ（森 (2006)）、信憑性がない発言に対する非難として用いられる。つまり否定応答表現は、Grice (1975) の質の公理（根拠のないことや偽りを言わない）に違反したと話者が判断したときの表現である。この暗黙の質の公理が守られるはずの時点、すなわち相手の発言以前に遡って、公理に合う発言をするよう要求（偽りの発言を禁止）するもので、この意味で、相手の発言以前にあった質の公理が否定応答表現の視点移動の動機である。最後の命令用法の「た」では、差し迫った事態実現のために事態は実現済みのものとして述べられている。実現したものとして述べるためには、視点が要求実現時以降に位置づけられる必要があり、話者の意識として、意図的に実現後の状況に先回りしているのである。この「た」の用法では、緊急に事態実現を促そうとする意図が視点移動の動機となっている。

　発話者視点の移動が命令形の具現化に影響を及ぼすこととその動機を見てきた。この日本語の考察に基づき、英語との対照を行う。論文冒頭でも述べた通り、(1) の過去命令文は英語で命令形とならない。(14) の否定応答表現においても日本語の命令形は英語と直接対応しないという意味で英語では命令形の具現化がない。一方、(15) の「た」の命令用法に相当する

英語表現は命令形である。

(17)	a. *Lie!	(cf. (14a))
	b. *Talk nonsense!	(cf. (14b))
(18)	a. Wait a minute!	(cf. (15a))
	b. Run!	(cf. (15b))

英語の場合、過去命令文や否定応答表現に対応するのは (19)、「た」の命令用法に対応するのは (20) と考えられる。

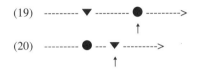

要求実現時は、過去命令文と否定応答表現では発話時以前に、「た」の命令用法では発話時以降に位置する。命令形の具現化が (19) では不可能、(20) では可能であることを踏まえると、英語における (11b) の基準は、移動しない絶対的な発話者視点ということになる。

　興味深いのは、日本語と違って、英語では発話者視点の位置が変わらず、命令形の具現化に決定的ではないということである。[8] 英語の発話者視点は発話時に固定していて移動しないとも考えられる。これは、英語では命令形の具現化が過去・現在・未来という絶対的な時間の流れ（時制）を基盤としていることを示唆する。発話者視点が、英語では絶対的、日本語では相対的とも言え、日英語の違いが浮き彫りとなる。次節では、視点が日本語では移動するが英語では移動しないことについて考察を深める。

4. 日英語における視点の特徴と言語類型

　本節では、これまで見てきた発話者視点の移動の考え方が日本語の持つ特性と合致することを確認する。視点の特徴として、森田 (1998: 174) の言う鳥類型・爬虫類型がある（金谷 (2004) の神の視点・虫の視点もこれ

に対応する）。前者の視点は状況を高みから俯瞰するもので固定しており、後者の視点は状況の中にあって自由に移動する。日本語は後者の特徴を持つとして、時制と「た」の使用が視点移動の観点から分析されている（板坂 (1971)、牧野 (1978)、森田 (1998) 等）。さらに日英語の視点の取り方の違いから、牧野 (1978) や池上 (2017) は、日本語では過去の事態でも視点をその時点に移して現在形を用いる頻度が英語に比べて高いという指摘をしている。視点移動が日本語の特徴であることを踏まえれば、命令形の具現化に関わる発話者視点の移動も日本語（話者）にとって不自然な現象ではない。その結果、日本語では過去命令文が他の命令文とともに古くから確立していたと考えられる。

　ここで英語との違いについて理解を深めるため、日本語の視点移動の特徴と池上 (1981) のする型・なる型の言語類型を考え合わせる。命令文のスキーマは、Takahashi (2012) や高橋 (2017) が示したように、肯定であれ否定であれ、話者が聴者に行為遂行を求めることである。する型・なる型の類型を延長して考えれば、典型命令文は「しろ型」である。しかし要求実現時を過ぎた発話では、事態実現は要求の対象ではなく、聴者の行為遂行より話者の願望的要素が色濃くなる。つまり、「なれ（なってほしい）型」である。池上 (1981) に従えば、英語はする型で日本語はなる型であるから、なれ型の過去命令文や否定応答表現は日本語の類型に適う。視点移動と相まって、日本語のなる的な傾向によって、英語で不可能な命令形も日本語では具現化されるのである。一方、英語で視点が発話時に固定しているのは、英語のする的な傾向と鳥類型の視点による状況把握から理解できる。仮に英語で発話者視点が移動して命令形が具現化すると、なれ型の命令文が生成され、する的な英語の特徴とそぐわなくなる。英語の発話者視点が絶対的で移動せず、過去命令文や否定応答表現が命令形にならないことの背景として、英語における視点の特徴と言語類型の影響も無視できない。

5. おわりに

　本論文では、日本語の過去命令文を英語と対照させ、両言語の命令形の具現化の違いを中心に考察した。発話時、要求実現時、発話者視点を定め

た上で、過去命令文の非典型性と命令形の具現化の仕組みを明らかにした。発話時が要求実現時以降にある点で典型命令文から逸脱するが、日本語では発話者視点が要求実現時以前に移動して命令形の具現化が可能となるという分析を行った。さらに、否定応答表現や「た」の命令用法における命令形の具現化の有無にも本分析が適用できることを示した。命令形の具現化に関して、日本語の発話者視点は要求実現時に対して相対的に移動するが、英語の発話者視点は発話時に固定された絶対的な視点であることを踏まえ、具現化の基準が日英語で異なることも指摘した。最後に、日英語の視点の特徴と言語類型に基づき、両言語の視点移動の有無を説明づけた。

* 本稿の作成にあたり、編集委員、査読者の先生方から有益な助言の他、今後につながる重要な示唆を頂いた。この場を借りて御礼申し上げる。

¹ 井上 (1993) の例文では、上昇調で発音される「よ H」と下降調の「よ L」、「ね」の間で容認性に差があることも明示されている (「よ L」のみ自然)。

² Saito (2016) の例文はローマ字で表記され、グロスが付されている。

³ (6) の条件命令文を日本語にしたとき、(1) の過去命令文との統語的な違いが現れる。条件の標識「てみる」が (6) では必須だが、(1) と共起しない。

 (i) a. 昨日 ¦* 来い／来てみろ¦、本当にショックだっただろう。
    b. 3 時に ¦来い／* 来てみろ¦ ！

⁴ グロスの略号は次の通りである。IMP (imperative)、MP (modal particle)、PST (past)、PTCP (participle)、SG (singular)。

⁵ 図で過去命令文と否定応答表現を区別しないのは、命令形の具現化における両者の共通性に注目しているためである。さらに、相手への非難も共通する意味で、これは要求実現時が発話時以前に位置することに基づく。発話時に事態が実現していない過去命令文では「しなかったこと」への非難、事態が実現している否定応答表現では「したこと」への非難となる。

⁶ 仁田 (1990: 238) によれば、命令用法の「た」の事態は発話直後に実現されるべき差し迫ったものである (したがって「来週」等と共起しない)。この緊急性は図の●と▼の間隔の狭さに反映されている。なお命令用法以外の「た」の分析では、視点移動を含む同様の図示が牧野 (1978) にある。

⁷ 命令用法の「た」の扱いは、「た」の先行研究と関連づけて考察すべきであるが、紙幅の都合により、今後の課題とする。

⁸ Takahashi (2012) に従うと、(6) の条件命令文では視点が移動していることになる。

本文で述べた通り、(6) は過去命令文のような要求の意味合いを欠き、本分析の設定する要求実現時がないため、別の分析が必要である。

参考文献

Aikhenvald, Alexandra Y. (2010) *Imperatives and Commands*, Oxford University Press, Oxford.

Davies, Eirlys (1986) *The English Imperative*, Croom Helm, London.

Grice, Paul (1975) "Logic and Conversation," *Syntax and Semantics 3: Speech Acts*, ed. by Peter Cole and Jerry L. Morgan, 41-58, Academic Press, New York.

池上嘉彦 (1981)『「する」と「なる」の言語学——言語と文化のタイポロジーへの試論』大修館書店, 東京.

池上嘉彦 (2017)『日本語と日本語論』筑摩書房, 東京.

井上優 (1993)「発話における『タイミング考慮』と『矛盾考慮』——命令文・依頼文を例に——」,『国立国語研究所報告 研究報告集』第 105 巻第 14 号, 333-360, 国立国語研究所.

板坂元 (1971)『日本人の論理構造』講談社, 東京.

金谷武洋 (2004)『英語にも主語はなかった——日本語文法から言語千年史へ』講談社, 東京.

牧野成一 (1978)『ことばと空間』東海大学出版会, 東京.

森英樹 (2006)「3 つの命令文：日英語の命令文と潜在型／既存型スケール」『言語研究』第 129 号, 135-160.

森田良行 (1998)『日本人の発想、日本語の表現——「私」の立場がことばを決める』中央公論社, 東京.

仁田義雄 (1990)『日本語のモダリティと人称』ひつじ書房, 東京.

Saito, Hiroaki (2016) "Past Imperatives in Japanese," paper presented at Theoretical Linguistics at Keio 2016 (handout), Keio University, Tokyo.

Takahashi, Hidemitsu (2012) *A Cognitive Linguistic Analysis of the English Imperative: With Special Reference to Japanese Imperatives*, John Benjamins, Amsterdam.

高橋英光 (2017)『英語の命令文——神話と現実』くろしお出版, 東京.

富岡宏太 (2016)「中古和文の『命令形カシ』」『國學院雑誌』第 117 巻第 8 号, 1-14.

富岡宏太 (2017)「中古和文の命令形——助詞が必須となる場合——」『日本語学会 2017 年度春季大会予稿集』, 33-40.

Van Olmen, Daniël (2018) "Reproachatives and Imperatives," *Linguistics* 56, 115-162.

間主観性の類型とグラウンディング
——いわゆる項の省略現象を中心に *

町田 章

キーワード：認知文法 , 間主観性 , グラウンディング , 省略

1. はじめに

人間は宿命的にそれぞれの個人的な立ち位置からしか世界を見ることができないうえ、自らの姿を直接見ることもできない。つまり、人間は基本的にそれぞれの主観世界の中で生きているのである。もちろん、だからと言って、人間は永遠に閉ざされた主観の中でそれぞれ孤独に生活しているわけでもない。実際、私たちは日常生活の中で他者と経験を共有しつついっしょに生きているという実感をもって生きている。また、人間は"直接的に"自らの姿を見ることはできないものの、鏡などの道具の助けを借りることにより"間接的に"ならば自らを見ることはできる。つまり、自らを客体視する術も持っているのである[1]。このような人間の認識の問題を手がかりに、本研究では、いわゆる省略と呼ばれるいくつかの言語現象の背後に存在する認知プロセスを明らかにしたい。

2. 二つの間主観性

他者との経験の共有のあり方を検討するためには、日常的な会話における話し手と聞き手の認知的なスタンスを例にとってみるのがよい。そこで、ここでは、デートにおける恋人同士の相互認識について考えてみよう。デートの際の相手の認識のあり方には少なくとも対峙型と同化型の2つがある[2]。典型的には、話し手が聞き手と向かい合って座る場合が対峙型であり、この場合、話し手は相手を意識すると同時に相手から自分がどのように見えているかを意識することになる。一方、同化型は映画館のように話し手と聞き手が並んで座る場合であり、この場合、話し手は相手も

自分と同じようにスクリーンを見ているはずだという認識のもとに、相手の意識に注意を払わなくなる。つまり、相手がまるで隣に座っていないかのように、相手の存在自体が話し手の意識から消えてしまうのである。そして、このような状況で起こっているのは、話し手と聞き手の体験の共有であり、その意味で話し手と聞き手のある種の同化であるともいえる。

　以上の考察をもとに、本研究では以下の 2 つの間主観性 (intersubjectivity) を提案したい。Zlatev et al. (2008:1) によると、間主観性とは、広義には複数の主体の間で体験（感情、知覚、思考、ことばの意味、など）が共有されることであるが、本研究はその下位区分を提案するものである。

対峙型間主観性：話し手が他者の視点（意識）をシミュレーションする (simulate) ことによって成立する間主観。

同化型間主観性：話し手が他者の視点を自己に同化 (assimilate) させることによって成立する間主観。

2.1 対峙型間主観

　Langacker (2015) は間主観の成立について (1) のように説明している。この説明によれば、私たちは、私たちが他者を客体として捉えるのと同じように私たちを客体として捉える他者が存在することを認識することができる。そして、私たちは、このような他者の体験をシミュレーションすることを通して、間主観的な認識に到達するのである。

(1) Being social creatures, we recognize the existence of other conceptualizers, who engage us as objects just as we engage them. And through our further capacity for simulating another subject's experience, we achieve the intersubjective awareness crucial for cognitive development, language acquisition, and linguistic interaction. (Langacker (2015: 122))

これを図示すると図 1 のようになる。図 1(a) は認知主体 S が客体 O に対して関与 (engage) している状況を描いている。図 1(b) は 2 つの認知主体 S_1 と S_2 が相互に客体として認識し合っている状況を描いている。この 2 つの認知主体が相互に相手の体験をシミュレーションすることにより図

1(c) に示す間主観性が成立する。最後に、図 1(d) に示すように、このように間主観を成立させた対話者が客体としての言語表現 E に関与することになる。

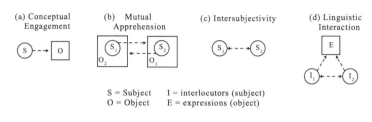

図 1 (Langacker (2015: 122))

　上記の説明は、子供は他者である大人の視点をモニターすることによって、自らを外側から見るようになるという Tomasello (1999: 99-100) の考察と基本的に同じことを述べており、対峙型の間主観性は自己の客体視と不可分の関係にあることがわかる。つまり、対峙型間主観性が成立する過程において話し手が他者の視点をシミュレーションすると、話し手は客体としての自己の存在を意識せざるをえなくなるのである。

2.2 同化型間主観

　一方、同化型間主観は、本多 (2005: 204) が言う「この人は自分と同じような人であり、自分と同じものを同じところから同じように見ているので、見たものに関して自分と同じような経験をしているだろう」という感覚に基づいている。同様に、Langacker も (2a) のような事例を (2b) のように説明している。つまり、(2a) のような表現は聞き手が話し手と同じ視座から状況を把握するように誘導するというのである。

(2) a. Don't trust him.
　　 b. Expressions like these correlate with lesser formality, as they invite the hearer to construe the situation from the speaker's own vantage point.

　　　　　　　　　　　　　　　　　　　　　　(Langacker (2008: 468-9))

　ただし、ここで本研究の主張として注意しておかなければならないのは、このような他者との「見えの共有」（本多 2005: 202）により、話し手は他者の存在自体を忘れてしまう、または他者が存在しないかのようにふるまってしまうことである。そしてこの点が対峙型の間主観性と決定的に異なる点である。つまり、対峙型の間主観は他者を意識することによって成立するのに対し、同化型の間主観は他者を意識しないことによって成立するのである。

2.3 間主観性の認知図式

　それでは、このような 2 つの間主観性の違いはどのように図式化されるであろうか。まず、(3) の事態把握に見られる差異を図式化した Langacker (2008) の分析から見てみよう。

　(3a) は、図 2(a) に示されるように、オンステージ OS に相当する直接スコープ IS 内でトラジェクター tr とランドマーク lm がプロファイルされている。この tr はグラウンド G 内にある話し手 S と同一指示されており、これは話し手 S が自己を客体として捉えていることを示している。一方、主語が明示されていない (3b) は、図 2(b) のような図式で捉えられる。ここでは、話し手 S が主体的な把握を受けているためプロファイルを受けておらず、そのため言語化されていないと考えられ、図式では IS(=OS) の外に位置づけられている[3]。

(3)　　a. I don't trust him.
　　　　b. Don't trust him.

(Langacker (2008: 468))

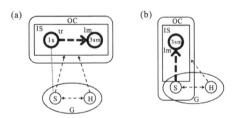

図 2 (Langacker (2008:468))

　ただし、この図2(b)には問題もある。この図式ではSとHが離れて描かれているため、(2b)の引用でLangackerが指摘しているような「聞き手が話し手の視座から事態を把握する」という特徴が正しく図示できていない。そこで本研究では図2を図3のように修正して用いることにする[4]。図3(a)は(3a)に対応し、対峙型間主観に基づいた事態把握を表しており、G内のSとHの間の双方向破線矢印で対峙関係を表している。一方、図3(b)は(3b)に対応し、同化型間主観に基づいた事態把握を表しており、G内のS/Hで両者が同化していることを表している[5]。

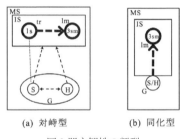

(a) 対峙型　　　　(b) 同化型

図3 間主観性の類型

3.いわゆる項の省略

　前節の間主観性に関する提案に基づいていわゆる項の省略と呼ばれる現象を見てみよう。例えば、車の助手席に座っている場面を想像してみてほしい。そのような状況で前の車に追突しそうになった場合、日本語では(4)のように言うのは全く自然である。

　　(4)　わあっ、ぶつかる！

　このように日本語では主語や目的語などの述語の項と呼ばれる名詞句を"省略"することができる。ただし、よく見てみるとこの場合の主語の省略と目的語の省略は全く同じ現象というわけではない。実際、町田(2016)では一見同じに見える(5)のような主語の省略でも実際には異なった事態把握のメカニズムが働いていることが提案されている。

(5)　a. わぁ、広いなぁ。
　　　b. あぁ、眠いなぁ。

　両者の違いは、言語化されていない要素の復元可能性にある。(5a) は、「わぁ、この部屋は広いなぁ」などのように主語を復元することが可能であるが、(5b) の場合は、主語を補い「? あぁ、俺は眠いなぁ」のようにすると特殊な文脈を考えない限り容認性が落ちてしまう。前者はゼロ代名詞と呼ばれる現象で、図 4(a) に示されるように、tr は OS 内でプロファイルを受けている。この tr は、英語のような省略を許さない言語では it などの代名詞に相当することからゼロ代名詞などと呼ばれている。概念上はプロファイルを受けている tr が言語上明示化されていないのである。一方、後者は主体的な把握を受けた例で、図 4(b) に示すように、主語は OS の外側にありプロファイルを受けていないため言語化されていない。

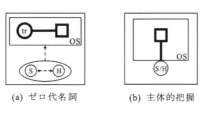

(a) ゼロ代名詞　　　(b) 主体的把握

図 4 いわゆる項の "省略"

　このような観点から先ほどの (4) を見るといわゆる "省略" とされている主語は実は主体的把握を受けており、目的語はゼロ代名詞であることがわかる。また、(6) のように (4) における非明示的な要素を明示した場合、自然な日本語とは言えなくなる。

(6)　# わあっ、僕たち（の車）が前の車にぶつかる！

　これは、追突事故を起こしそうな緊迫した場面では傍らにいる他者の存在を忘れるのが普通であるため、(4) のような同化型間主観（図 5(a)）をとるからである。一方、(6) のように自己を客体視する対峙型間主観（図

5(b)）はこのような緊迫した状況に合わないため、非常に不自然な感じがする。自己を客体視するとどこか他人事のような感じがしてしまうのである。

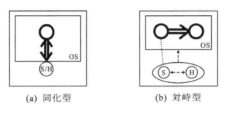

図5

　ところが、興味深いことに、同じように追突事故を起こしそうな車の助手席にいても、英語の場合は、(7) に示すように、いわゆる主語や目的語の省略は許されない。つまり、英語の場合、対峙型間主観性に基づいて事態把握を行うのである。次節では、このような日英語の差異を捉えるため、間主観性の類型とグラウンディングシステムの関係を見ていくことにする。

　(7)　a.　Whoa! We are gonna hit'em!
　　　b. *Whoa! Are gonna hit!

4. グラウンディングシステムの類型

　Langacker は冠詞や指示詞のようなグラウンディング要素が持つ機能を (8) のように述べ、話し手はグラウンディング要素を用いて聞き手の注意を意図した指示対象に向けさせる、としている。

　(8)　Through nominal grounding (e.g. *the*, *this* ......) the speaker directs the hearer's attention to the intended discourse referent, ...

(Langacker (2008:259))

このようなグラウンディングの説明から明らかなことは、従来の認知文法におけるグラウンディングは (9) に示すような間主観性（引用では「共同主観」）を前提としているということである。

> (9) まず、共同主観の成立はシナリオ的に捉えられる。まずは Traugott の意味で「話者が聴者の意識に注意を向け」たりする形で始まり、更に Verhagen が述べる「聴者の意識や理解を調整・修正する」という段階を経て、自己と他者との間で体験が共有された結果「共同主観」が成立する、というシナリオである。
>
> (早瀬 (2016: 221))

上記のようなグラウンディングや間主観性の説明に共通しているのは、話し手が聞き手に対して働きかけるということであり、このことは聞き手の存在を忘れてしまう同化型の間主観性には当てはまらないことである。そしてこの事実は、これまでのグラウンディングに関する研究は聞き手の存在を前提とする対峙型間主観に基づいて行われてきたということを示唆している。

それでは、本研究で主張している同化型の間主観性はグラウンディングには関与しないのであろうか。もちろん、同化型間主観性もグラウンディングに関わっている。ただし、グラウンディングの仕方が対峙型とは異なっているのである。実際、Langacker (2008: 264) は、グラウンディングは普遍的な言語の機能であるが、その実施に当たっては言語ごとにやり方が異なっていると述べており、明示的な手段によるグラウンディング (Overt Grounding) と非明示的な手段による (Covert Grounding) が存在するとしている（cf. Langacker (2008: 496-499)）。つまり、英語のようにグラウンディング要素が明示的に名詞表現に現れる言語とは異なり、日本語のように明示的文法要素が存在しない言語もあるのである。

では、このような非明示的グラウンディングに同化型の間主観性が関わっていると考えられないであろうか。そこで本研究ではグラウンディングの類型に関して次のような仮説を提案したい。

明示型グラウンディング：対峙型間主観に基づき話し手と聞き手の主観を調節する。聞き手の意識や理解を調整・修正す

るために明示的なグラウンディング要素（冠詞
など）が必要。

非明示型グラウンディング：話し手の主観＝聞き手の主観となる**同化型間
主観に基づくため両者の主観を調節する必要
性がない。そのため、明示的なグラウンディ
ング要素は不要。

　実は、Langacker (2008: 496) も指摘しているように、実際に行われている談話の中では、話し手が何を指示しているのかは聞き手にとってほとんど自明である場合が多いため、グラウンディング機能は実際には余剰的な場合が多い。それでも、話し手が聞き手を別の人格として認めている対峙型のコミュニケーションにおいては、話し手が丁寧に聞き手の注意を誘導することになる。一方、話し手が聞き手の存在自体を意識しないような同化型のコミュニケーションにおいては、話し手の意図している指示物が聞き手に理解されないことは原理的にありえないことになる。そのため、明示的なグラウンディング要素で聞き手の注意を誘導する必要がないのである。

　ただし、同化型間主観では、聞き手はことあるごとに「相づち」や「うなずき」などによって話し手と同化していることを示さなければならならず、同時に、話し手は「ね」や「よ」などの終助詞によって同化型間主観が成立していることを聞き手に確認しなければならい。その意味では「相づち」や「うなずき」、終助詞がグラウンディング要素に相当すると考えることもできる[6]。

　上述のグラウンディングの類型を受けて、本研究では、Langacker (2017) の枠組みを用いた名詞表現のグラウンディングの図式を提案する。(10a) の *the man* は明示的グラウンディングを図示した図 6(a) に対応し、(10b) の「男」は非明示的グラウンディングを図示した図 6(b) に対応する。

(10)　a. The man ran away.
　　　b. 男が逃走しました。

図 6 における DT は記述対象 (descriptive target) を表しており、談話にお
いて話題となっている対話者たちの心内世界 (mental universe) を表してい
る。また、w はこの DT 内における注意の窓 (window) を表し、脳内の認
知プロセスにおいて結合 (connections) やグループ化 (groupings) が行われ
る注意の枠のようなものである。

　DT を導入することの意義は、概念レベルと言語レベルを分けることで
あり、これにより記述の対象となっている概念レベルの事物と OS 上の言
語レベルの表現とを区別して図式化することができる[7]。そのように考え
ると、グラウンディングとは、DT 内の事物と OS 内の言語表現が同一で
あることを保証することであると言い換えることができる。つまり、(10a)
の the は OS 上で表現された人物が DT の w 内の人物を指していることを
話し手から聞き手に伝えるための要素だということである[8]。

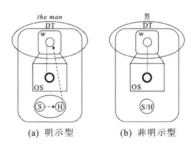

図 6 いわゆる項の "省略"

　このように、英語は、基本的に対峙型の間主観性に基づいているため、
明示的にグラウンディングをする必要がある。一方、同化型間主観性に基
づいている日本語の場合には、明示的な手段で聞き手の注意を DT 内の要
素に向けさせる必要がない。なぜなら、同化型では、聞き手は完全に話し
手に同化されているため、「男」が DT 内でどの人物を指すかは話し手だ
けでなく聞き手にとっても自明であるからである。つまり、同化型におい
ては、聞き手の注意を誘導するという意味でのグランディングは不要なの
である。同化型間主観においては、すでにグラウンディングは成立済みと
言ってもいい。

　もちろん、話し手と聞き手が同化するのか、対峙するのかという問題は

町田 章

二者択一ではなく程度の問題である。言い換えると、話し手が他者を意識する程度にはスケールがあるということになる。例えば、(11) の表現が同じ状況を表しているとした場合、下へ進むにしたがって他者を意識する程度が大きくなる。これを図示したものが図 7 である。

(11)　a. 痛い！
　　　b. 足が痛い！
　　　c. 俺は足が痛い！

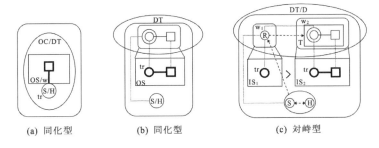

(a) 同化型　　　　(b) 同化型　　　　　　(c) 対峙型

図 7 同化—対峙のスケール

図 7(a) は (11a) に対応する[9]。これは、同化型間主観が成立した状況において話し手・聞き手 S/H が経験主または動作主として事態の成立に関与する場合であり、OC と DT、OS と w が一致している場合である。w 内では「痛い」という感覚だけがプロファイルされており、それが OS 内で言語化されている。この際、概念レベルの tr は OS の外にあるため言語化されない。次に、図 7(b) は (11b) に対応する。tr である「足」が主語として言語化されているという点では自己の客体化が生じている。しかし、この際の客体化は、他者の視点をシミュレーションした結果ではなく、Langacker (1990) からの引用 (12) が示すように、話し手が自身の体験を内省することによって生じる客体化である。

(12)　　　... suppose I experience an emotion, such as fear, desire, or elation. If I merely undergo that experience nonreflectively, both the emotion and my own role in feeling it are subjectively construed. But to the extent that I reflect on the emotional experience — by analyzing it, by comparing it to other such experiences, or simply by noting that I am undergoing it — the emotion and my role therein receive a more objective construal. (Langacker (1990:317-8))

つまり、自己の客体化には、(12) のように自己の内なる視点によって生じるものと、(1) に示したような他者の視点をシミュレーションすることによって生じるものの 2 種類があるのである[10]。

　このように考えた場合、認知主体の客体化は常に対峙型間主観を前提としているわけではないことがわかる。内なる視点によって認知主体（の身体の一部）が客体化される場合には同化型を維持することができるのである。ただし、(11b) の場合、同化型間主観を維持しつつも、ガ格によって痛みの発生場所を聞き手に示している点では (11a) よりも聞き手の存在を意識していることになる。最後に、(11c) は対峙型間主観の例となる。「僕」という一人称は、「私」「俺」などのいくつかの可能性の中から聞き手の存在を考慮に入れた上で選ばれているという点で対峙型の間主観に基づいた自己の客体化である（cf. 本多 (2005: 31)）。また、聞き手の注意を誘導する参照点構造を喚起する「ハ」が用いられていることからも、(11c) が聞き手の存在を意識した対峙型間主観の例であることがわかる。

5. まとめ

　本研究では、対峙型と同化型の間主観性の違いが日英語に見られるグラウンディングの明示性の違いを生み出すとし、話し手主語のゼロ化（主体的把握）、冠詞の有無などの現象も間主観性の観点から統一的に説明されると主張した。ただし、この間主観性の差異は絶対的なものではない。本研究で提案したいのは、同化型－対峙型という間主観性のスケール上で、日本語は同化型を出発点とし、英語は対峙型を出発点としてそれぞれの言語体系が構築されているという可能性の追求である。したがって、当然、日本語でも対峙型間主観が成立することはあり、英語でも同化型間主観を前提とした表現は可能である。そのため、実際の言語現象では有標性の違いしか見られない場合もある。また、間主観は、言語使用の現場 (usage event) で生じるため、語彙や構文自体にその類型が慣習的に組み込まれている場合もあれば、場面ごとに視点構図の差異として現れる場合もある。そのため、例えば、文を構成する要素に対峙型が用いられているのにもかかわらず、文全体としては同化型の間主観を表すようなケース、またはその逆のケースも頻繁に生じるものと予想される。

* 本研究は、JSPS 科研費 17K02682 の助成を受け、日本英語学会第 36 回大会（町田 (2019)）において発表された内容の一部を発展させたものである。

[1] このような自己の認識のあり方と言語の関係を認知言語学の観点からいち早く詳細に検討したものに本多 (2005) がある。

[2] 大薗 (2018:34) は浜田 (1995) の考察を受け、話し手と聞き手の関係として相補的スタンスと同型的スタンスを挙げているが、この分類は本研究と軌を一にするものである。

[3] 図 2 に描かれている客体的内容 OC とは、記述の客体となる内容 (Langacker (2008: 462)) を指している。

[4] 客体的内容 OC に関しては、客体的状況 (OS: objective scene) とどこか異なるのかなどの不明確な点があるだけでなく、本章 4 節で新しく導入される記述対象 DT という概念でカバーすることができる可能性があるため、本研究では用いないことにする。

[5] 対峙型の図 3(a) と同化型の図 3(b) は、Langacker (1985) の optimal viewing arrangement と egocentric viewing arrangement に、また町田 (2016) の事態外視点と事態内視点にそれぞれ対応している。

[6] 「相づち」や「うなずき」がグラウンディングに関与しているという指摘は本多 (2005: 209) にある。

[7] 概念レベルと言語レベルを分けて考える必要性は、主語・目的語と節レベルの tr/lm を同一してはいけないという文脈で以前から指摘されてきた（cf. 山梨 (2004: 162)、Langacker (2008: 521)）。

[8] もちろん、the は当該の w よりも前に生じた CDS 内の要素を参照せよという定冠詞の機能を持っているが、ここでは図式を単純化するためにこの機能に関しての記述は省略した。詳しくは Langacker (2007) 参照。

[9] 図 7(a) のような事態把握の様式は町田 (2016) などが事態内視点と呼んできたものに相当する。

[10] 内なる視点による自己の客体化と他者の視点による自己の客体化は、Langacker (1985) の言う displacement と cross-world identification にほぼ相当すると考えられる。また、この区別は、廣瀬・長谷川 (2010) の私的自己・公的自己の区別にも対

応している可能性がある。

参考文献

浜田寿美男 (1995)『意味から言葉へ』ミネルヴァ書房 , 京都 .

早瀬尚子 (2016)「懸垂分詞構文から見た (inter) subjectivity と (inter) subjectification」, 中村芳久・上原聡 (編)『ラネカーの（間）主観性とその展開』, 207-229, 開拓社 , 東京 .

廣瀬幸生・長谷川葉子 (2010)『日本語から見た日本人』開拓社 , 東京 .

本多啓 (2005)『アフォーダンスの認知意味論』東京大学出版会 , 東京 .

Langacker, Ronald W. (1985) "Observations and Speculations on Subjectivity," *Iconicity in Syntax*, ed. by John Haiman, 109-150, John Benjamins, Amsterdam.

Langacker, Ronald W. (1990) *Concept, Image and Symbol,* Mouton de Gruyter, Berlin.

Langacker, Ronald W. (2007) "Constructing the Meanings of Personal Pronouns," *Aspects of Meaning Construction*, eds. by Günter Radden, Klaus-Michael Köpcke and Thomas Berg Peter Siemund, 172-187, John Benjamins, Amsterdam.

Langacker, Ronald W. (2008) *Cognitive Grammar: A Basic Introduction*, Oxford University Press, Oxford.

Langacker, Ronald W. (2015) "Construal," *Handbook of Cognitive Linguistics*, eds. by Ewa Dabrowska and Dagmar Divjak, 120-143, De Gruyter Mouton, Berlin.

Langacker, Ronald W. (2017) "Cognitive Grammar," *The Handbook of Cognitive Linguistics*, ed. by Barbara Dancygier, 262-283, Cambridge University Press, Cambridge.

町田章 (2016)「認知図式と日本語認知文法−主観性・主体性の問題を通して−」, 山梨正明他 (編)『認知言語学論考』No.13, 35-70, ひつじ書房 , 東京 .

町田章 (2019)「事態把握様式における他者−認知文法から見た 2 つの間主観性−」 *JELS* 36（日本英語学会）, 58-64.

大薗正彦 (2018)「ドイツ語の事態把握をめぐって−日独英対照の観点から−」, 堀田優子他 (編)『ことばのパースペクティヴ』, 28-40, 開拓社 , 東京 .

Tomasello, Michael (1999) *The Cultural Origins of Human Cognition*, Harvard University Press, Cambridge, MA.

Zlatev, Jordan, Timothy P. Racine, Chris Sinha and Esa Itkonen (2008) "Intersubjectivity: What Makes Us Human," *The Shared Mind*, eds. by Jordan Zlatev et al., 1-14, John Benjamins, Amsterdam.

索　引

※

執筆者紹介 (論文掲載順)

前川　貴史（まえかわ たかふみ）
龍谷大学社会学部准教授
神戸市外国語大学外国語学部卒業，大阪大学大学院文学研究科博士後期課程単位取得退学，PhD in Linguistics, University of Essex, UK
- "An HPSG Analysis of 'A Beautiful Two Weeks'" (*Linguistic Research* 30-3, pp. 407–433, 2013)
- "Seminumerals, Determiners and Nouns in English" (*Proceedings of the Joint 2016 Conference on Head-Driven Phrase Structure Grammar and Lexical Functional Grammar* (Doug Arnold, Miriam Butt, Berthold Crysmann, Tracy Holloway King and Stefan Müller (eds.)), CSLI Publications, pp. 422–441, 2016)
- "English Prepositional Numeral Constructions" (*Proceedings of the 24th International Conference on Head-Driven Phrase Structure Grammar* (Stefan Müller (ed.)), CSLI Publications, pp. 233–247, 2017)

田中　英理（たなか えり）
編著者欄に記載

山口　麻衣子（やまぐち まいこ）
追手門学院大学・神戸女子大学非常勤講師
ノートルダム清心女子大学文学部卒業，大阪大学大学院文学研究科博士後期課程単位取得退学
- "A Study of Head Movement in the Complement Clause of the C-Head *Kes* in Korean" (*Osaka University Papers in English Linguistics* 19, to appear)
- "A Note on Dialectal Variation in the Embedded Main Clause Phenomena in English" (*Osaka University Papers in English Linguistics* 18, pp. 67–82, 2017)
- "Head Movement and Its Consequences in the Right Periphery" (*JELS* 34, pp. 292–298, 2017)

執筆者紹介

岩橋　一樹（いわはし かずき）

京都先端科学大学教育開発センター嘱託講師

神戸市外国語大学外国語学部卒業，大阪大学大学院文学研究科博士後期課程単位取得退学，修士（文学）

・「英語における具体名詞の中核的意味とメタファー表現」（『言葉のしんそう (深層・真相）―大庭幸男教授退職記念論文集―』（大庭幸男教授退職記念論文集刊行会（編），英宝社，pp. 549–560, 2015)

・「英語における形容詞の意味変化の双方向性をめぐって」（*JELS* 33, pp. 38–44, 2016)

・"On Core Function of English Sensory Adjectives"（*Osaka University Papers in English Linguistics* 18, pp. 127–146, 2017)

黒川　尚彦（くろかわ なおひこ）

大阪工業大学情報科学部専任講師

大阪教育大学教育学部卒業，大阪大学大学院文学研究科博士後期課程修了，博士（文学）

・*Oppositeness and Relevance*（大阪大学大学院文学研究科博士学位論文，2013)

・"A Descriptive Study of *the other way (a)round*"（*Memoirs of Osaka Institute of Technology* 63-2, pp. 21–35, 2019)

水谷　謙太（みずたに けんた）

大阪大学大学院文学研究科博士後期課程

大阪大学大学院文学研究科博士前期課程修了

・"On Japanese Adverbial Quantifiers and their Interaction with Proper Nouns"（*KLS Selected Papers* 1, pp. 85–98, 2019)

・"New Arguments for the Situation-based Analysis of Adverbial Quantifiers"（*JELS* 34, pp. 105–111, 2017)

・"Decomposing Individual-level Gradable Adjectives"（*KLS* 37: *the Proceedings of the 41st Meeting of Kansai Linguistic Society*, pp. 205–216, 2017)

南　佑亮（みなみ ゆうすけ）

編著者欄に記載

米倉　よう子（よねくら ようこ）

奈良教育大学教育学部准教授

大阪大学大学院文学研究科博士後期課程単位取得退学

・『認知歴史言語学』（認知日本語学講座 7，共著，くろしお出版 , 2013）

・ "(Inter)subjectification and (Inter)subjective Uses of the Modal *Can*" (*Studies in Modern English: The Thirtieth Anniversary Publication of the Modern English Association*, Eihosha, Tokyo, pp. 339–354, 2014)

・ "Accounting for Lexical Variation in the Acceptance of the Recipient Passive in Late Modern English: A Semantic-Cognitive Approach" (*Studies in Modern Englis*h 34, pp. 1–26, 2018)

岡田　禎之（おかだ さだゆき）

大阪大学大学院文学研究科教授

大阪大学文学部卒業，大阪大学大学院博士後期課程中途退学，博士（文学）

・ "On the Function and Distribution of the Modifiers *Respective* and *Respectively*" (*Linguistics* 37-5, pp. 871–903, 1999)

・『現代英語の等位構造』（大阪大学出版会 , 2002）

・ "Comparative Standards and the Feasibility of Conceptual Expansion" (*Cognitive Linguistics* 20-2, pp. 395–423. 2009)

吉本　圭佑（よしもと けいすけ）

龍谷大学政策学部准教授

PhD in Linguistics, University of Essex, UK

・ "The Syntax of Japanese *Tokoro*-Clauses: Against Control Analyses" (*Lingua* 127, pp. 39–71, 2013)

・ "Dissociating Japanese Scrambling from Controller Movement" (*Iberia: An International Journal of Theoretical Linguistics* 4-2, pp. 170–200, 2012)

・ "The Left Periphery of CP Phases in Japanese" (*Acta Linguistica Hungarica* 59-3, pp. 339–384, 2012)

平山　裕人（ひらやま ゆうと）

大阪大学大学院文学研究科博士後期課程 / 日本学術振興会特別研究員

大阪大学文学部卒業，大阪大学大学院文学研究科博士前期課程修了，修士（文学）

・ "The Temporal Anteriority/Posteriority Parameter in Inferentials" (*Penn Working Papers in Linguistics* 26-1 (*Proceedings of PLC* 43), to appear)

・ "A Temporal Restriction in the Semantics of Evidence" (*Japanese/Korean Linguistics* 26, to appear)

・ "Epistemic Adverbs That Can/Cannot Be Embedded under Imperatives" (*Proceedings of Linguistics Society of America* 4-20, pp. 1–15, 2019)

嶋村　貢志（しまむら こうじ）

立命館大学講師

同志社大学経済学部卒業，同志社大学文学部卒業，大阪大学文学研究科博士前期課程修了，コネチカット大学言語学科博士課程修了，Ph.D. (Linguistics)

・ "The Hidden Syntax of Clausal Complementation in Japanese" (*Proceeding of GLOW in Asia XII & SICOGG* 21, pp. 369–388, 2019)

・ "The Features of the Voice Domain: Actives, Passives, and Restructuring" (with Susi Wurmbrand) (*The Verbal Domain* (Roberta D' Alessandro, Irene Franco and Ángel J. Gallego (eds.)), Oxford University Press, Oxford, pp. 179–204, 2017)

・ "A Non-conversion Approach to Dative-Nominative Conversion in Germanic" (*Proceedings of the Poster Session of the 33rd WCCFL*, pp. 121–130, 2014)

田中　秀治（たなか ひではる）

三重大学教養教育院特任講師

岡山大学文学部卒業，大阪大学大学院文学研究科博士後期課程修了，博士（文学）

・ "The Derivation of *Soo-su*: Some Implications for the Architecture of Japanese VP" (*Japanese/Korean Linguistics* 23, pp. 265–279, CSLI Publications, 2016)

・ "Exhaustiveness in Japanese Compound Verbs: A Mereological Approach" (*Japanese/Korean Linguistics* 24, pp. 157–171, CSLI Publications, 2017)

・ "Pseudogapping in Japanese" (with Shintaro Hayashi) (*Japanese/Korean Linguistics* 25, online, CSLI Publications, 2018)

西口　純代（にしぐち すみよ）
小樽商科大学言語センター准教授
大阪大学文学部卒業，大阪大学大学院文学研究科博士後期課程中途退学，大阪大学大学院言語文化研究科博士後期課程修了，博士（言語文化学）

- "Context-shift in Indirect Reports in Dhaasanac" (*Indirect Reports and Pragmatics in the World Languages* (Alessandro Capone, Manuel García-Carpintero, Alessandra Falzone (eds.)) , Springer, Cham, Switzerland, pp. 345–354, 2019)
- "Bipolar Items" (*Topics in Linguistics* 17-2, pp. 1–11, 2016)
- "Fake Past and Covert Emotive Modality" (*Cahiers Chronos 23: In the Mood for Mood*, pp. 159–174, Rodopi, Amsterdam, 2011)

山口　真史（やまぐち まさし）
関西外国語大学外国語学部助教
立命館大学文学部卒業，大阪大学大学院文学研究科博士後期課程修了，博士（文学）

- *The Directionality of Agreement and the Nature of Secondary Predicate Constructions*（大阪大学大学院文学研究科博士学位取得論文 , 2019）
- "Deriving Direct Object Restriction" (*English Linguistics* 35-1, pp. 151–172, 2018)
- "On Nominal Depictive Predicates: A View from Agreement" (*JELS* 33, pp. 195–201, 2016)

今西　祐介（いまにし ゆうすけ）
関西学院大学総合政策学部准教授
マサチューセッツ工科大学言語・哲学科博士課程修了，Ph.D. (Linguistics)

- "Parameterizing Split Ergativity in Mayan" (*Natural Language and Linguistic Theory*, doi.org/10.1007/s11049–018–09440–9, 2019)
- "The Clause-Mate Condition on Resumption: Evidence from Kaqchikel" (*Studia Linguistica* 73-2, pp. 398–441, 2019)
- "Pseudo Noun Incorporation and Its Kin" (*A Pesky Set: Papers for David Pesetsky* (Claire Halpert, Hadas Kotek and Coppe van Urk (eds.)), MITWPL, pp. 427–436, 2017)

本田　隆裕（ほんだ たかひろ）
編著者欄に記載

執筆者紹介

森　英樹（もり ひでき）
福井県立大学学術教養センター准教授
大阪大学文学部卒業, 大阪大学大学院文学研究科博士後期課程修了, 博士（文学）
・「「くれる」の求心性動詞化：give との対照研究」（『福井県立大学論集』44,
　pp. 25–39, 2015）
・「日英語の動詞表現が表す試行性：『坊っちゃん』の場合」（『福井県立大学論集』
　47, pp. 1–17, 2016）
・「修飾節に生じる発話の認知言語学的分析」（『福井県立大学論集』50, pp.
　1–14, 2018）

町田　章（まちだ あきら）
広島大学大学院総合科学研究科准教授
青山学院大学文学部卒業, 大阪大学大学院文学研究科博士後期課程単位取得退学
・「事態把握様式における他者－認知文法から見た 2 つの間主観性」（*JELS* 36,
　pp. 58–64, 2019）
・「日本語間接受身文の被害性はどこから来るのか？－英語バイアスからの脱却
　を目指して－」（『日本認知言語学会論文集』17, pp. 540–555, 2017）
・「認知図式と日本語認知文法－主観性・主体性の問題を通して－」（『認知言語
　学論考』13, ひつじ書房, pp. 35–70, 2016）

編著者紹介

南　佑亮（みなみ ゆうすけ）
神戸女子大学文学部准教授
大阪大学文学部卒業, 大阪大学大学院文学研究科博士後期課程修了, 博士（文学）
- 「形容詞属性叙述文にみられる属性判断の階層性について」（『日本認知言語学会論文集』6, pp. 106–116, 2006）
- "*Mary is pretty to look at* vs. *Mary looks pretty*: Property Cognition through Visual Information" (*Papers from the 11th National Conference of the Japanese Cognitive Linguistics Association*, pp. 92–102, 2011)
- 「受益二重目的語構文における間接目的語の意味について」（『神戸女子大学文学部紀要』48, pp. 19–30, 2015）

本田　隆裕（ほんだ たかひろ）
神戸女子大学文学部准教授
大阪大学文学部卒業, 大阪大学大学院文学研究科博士後期課程修了, 博士（文学）
- "A Split Phi-Features Hypothesis and the Origin of the Expletive *There*" (*English Linguistics* 37-1, to appear)
- "Effects of a Morphological Approach to Raising Learners' Awareness of Sentences with *Be*"（『英語教育研究』39, pp. 17–36, 2016）
- "Accusative Case in the Passive" (*English Linguistics* 26-1, pp. 33–66, 2009)

田中　英理（たなか えり）
大阪大学大学院文学研究科准教授
大阪大学文学部卒業, 大阪大学大学院文学研究科博士後期課程修了, 博士（文学）
- "Scalar Particles in Comparatives: A QUD Approach." (*New Frontiers in Artificial Intelligence: JSAI-isAI 2018 Workshops, LNAI 11717* (K. Kojima et al. (eds.)), pp. 357–371, 2019)
- 「英語の裸複数形の総称的用法の習得に向けて」（『最新言語理論を英語教育に応用する』（藤田耕司・松本マスミ・児玉一宏・谷口一美（編）), 開拓社, 東京, pp. 108–118, 2012）
- "The Notion of Path in Aspectual Composition: Evidence from Japanese" (*Event Structures in Linguistic Form and Interpretation* (J. Dolling and T. Heyde-Zybatow (eds.)), Mouton de Gruyter, Berlin, pp. 199–222, 2008)

英語学の深まり・英語学からの広がり

──新・阪大英文学会叢書 2──

2020 年 3 月 15 日　印　刷　　　　　　2020 年 3 月 30 日　発　行

編　著　者ⓒ　　南　　佑　亮
　　　　　　　　本　田　隆　裕
　　　　　　　　田　中　英　理

発　行　者　　佐　々　木　　元

発　行　所　株式会社　英　　宝　　社

〒101-0032 東京都千代田区岩本町 2-7-7
TEL 03 (5833) 5870-1 FAX 03 (5833) 5872

ISBN 978-4-269-77057-7 C1082　［製版：伊谷企画／印刷・製本：日本ハイコム株式会社］

阪大英文学会叢書

1 玉井　暲／仙葉　豊　共編　　A5判／356頁／本体3,800円／2004年5月刊

病いと身体の英米文学

[執筆者] 服部典之／武内正美／米本弘一／片渕悦久／渡辺克昭／三浦誉史加／仙葉　豊／小口一郎／小川公代／太田素子／西村美保／春木孝子／白川計子／垣内由香／山田雄三

2 成田義光／長谷川存古　共編　　A5判／264頁／本体2,600円／2005年10月刊

英語のテンス・アスペクト・モダリティ

[執筆者] 毛利可信／沖田知子／堀田知子／梅原大輔／田村幸誠／坂口真理／西川盛雄／長谷川存古／家木康宏／濱本秀樹／甲斐雅之／竹鼻圭子／松本マスミ／柏本吉章／稲木昭子／田岡育恵

3 玉井　暲／新野　緑　共編　　A5判／404頁／本体4,200円／2006年11月刊

〈異界〉を創造する　──英米文学におけるジャンルの変奏──

[執筆者] 宮川清司／村井美代子／吉田泰彦／上山　泰／村田幸範／石川玲子／仲渡一美／松阪仁伺／安達賀代子／新野　緑／桐山恵子／西川盛雄／橋本雅子／服部慶子／市橋孝道／中井麻記子／鴨川啓信／平井智子

4 河上誓作／谷口一美　共編　　A5判／224頁／本体2,400円／2007年11月刊

ことばと視点

[執筆者] 大森文子／岩崎一樹／森川文弘／岡田禎之／谷口一美／早瀬尚子／南　佑亮／町田　章／轟　里香／米倉よう子／吉村あき子／西口純代／西川盛雄／竹鼻圭子

5 森岡裕一／堀　恵子　共編　　A5判／248頁／本体2,600円／2008年8月刊

「依存」する英米文学

[執筆者] 西村美保／吉田泰彦／田邊久美子／吉野成美／森本道孝／岩橋裕幸／堀　恵子／森岡裕一／片渕悦久／馬渕恵里／小久保潤子／藤江啓子

6 大庭幸男／岡田禎之　共編　　A5判／320頁／本体3,200円／2011年4月刊

意味と形式のはざま

[執筆者] 谷口一美／北爪佐知子／千田　愛／西川盛雄／田中英理／西口純代／濱本秀樹／田岡育恵／白谷敦彦／岡田禎之／米倉よう子／竹鼻圭子／町田　章／森　貞／堀田優子／森　英樹／南　佑亮／坂口真理／大庭幸男／春木茂宏／大森文子

7 石田　久／服部典之　共編　　A5判／312頁／本体3,200円／2013年12月刊

移動する英米文学

[執筆者] 田邊久美子／服部典之／中村仁紀／村井美代子／麻畠徳子／片山美穂／市橋孝道／馬渕恵里／伊藤佳子／乙黒麻記子／鈴木元子／小久保潤子／関　良子／高橋信隆／仲渡一美／阪口瑞穂／森本道孝

8 沖田知子／米本弘一　共編　　A5判／264頁／本体2,800円／2015年10月刊

英語のデザインを読む

[執筆者] 米本弘一／長谷川存古／馬渕恵里／田岡育恵／服部慶子／堀田知子／山田雄三／関　良子／大森文子／森　道子／金崎八重／田邊久美子／仲渡一美／河上誓作／柏本吉章／竹鼻圭子／小口一郎／森本道孝／稲木昭子・沖田知子